# AMERICAN GOVERNMENT & POLITICS

## A CRITICAL INTRODUCTION

# AMERICAN GOVERNMENT & POLITICS
## A CRITICAL INTRODUCTION

BLANCHE D. BLANK

PROFESSOR OF POLITICAL SCIENCE/HUNTER COLLEGE OF THE CITY UNIVERSITY OF NEW YORK

ALDINE PUBLISHING COMPANY/CHICAGO

**ABOUT THE AUTHOR**

Blanche Davis Blank received her B.A. from Hunter College, her M.A. from Syracuse University and her Ph.D. from Columbia University. She has taught at City College, The New School for Social Research, Sarah Lawrence College, and is now Dean of the Division of Social Sciences at Hunter College of the City University of New York. She has been Research Associate for the Tax Foundation and Executive Director of the Mayor's Task Force on City Personnel.

320.473
B642a

*Robert A. Hirschfield*
*Consulting Editor*

First published 1973 by
Aldine Publishing Company
529 South Wabash Avenue
Chicago, Illinois 60605

ISBN 0–202–24135–1, cloth; 202–24136–X, paper
Library of Congress Catalog Number 72–92838

Designed by DesignMarks Corporation
Printed in the United States of America

*For my remarkable husband, Bud,*
*and daughters, Laura, Barbara, and Alice.*

# CONTENTS

This book weaves together two threads. One is basic information about American political institutions; the other is an argument about the style of thinking most fruitful for analyzing these structures. The argument claims that there are too many unexamined premises in our political thinking, too many unnoticed ambiguities, too many unresolved ambivalences. As a result there has been a locking of gears in the political machinery. We have had too many recurrent problems and too many habitual rather than rational ways of thinking about them. This is the first decade in which large numbers of Americans have seen the political system as failing from within rather than threatened from without.

This book is therefore dedicated to putting political matters into a focus that will permit a greater degree of rationality than is usual today. I try to press the point that what we think and do (or do not do) counts. The more we understand about ourselves and our public machinery, therefore, the better. We cannot expect to achieve Utopia (indeed, the very name suggests as much); but the hope throughout this volume is that we can at least reduce persistent myopia. By "heightening our consciousness" about our own ambivalences and about the ambiguities inherent in a complex polity, by sorting out the conflicts and determining which are creative and which perhaps destructive, by stacking the cards in favor of rationality, we may improve that elusive but nonetheless real conglomerate, the quality of life.

There are arguments here about the need for priorities among our principles, about the assignment of public functions to various government units, about the merits of cost-benefit analysis as a tool for decision-making, and about dozens of political conflicts that beset us as a nation.

The first chapter describes the discipline and its own internal controversies in order to make clear the biases of political science at the outset. The second chapter goes into the ambiguities and tensions that surround our most basic myths. The third and fourth deal with contradictory values embodied in the American Constitution.

Chapters 5 through 9 are organized around the policy-making institutions of our government: the judiciary, legislature, executive, the public bureaucracy, and our system of pressure groups and political parties. In each case, the institution in question is analyzed in the light of what I believe to be its basic conflicts, the tensions that make it what it is. In some instances I recommend relieving the conflict by making up our minds about certain issues. In other instances I believe we might best leave matters in the realm of what I call "creative conflict."

Chapter 10 deals with the problem of allocating public functions among the various levels of government; that is, coping with federalism. Here I also take up the variety of American political styles. Chapter 11 gives a very brief bird's-eye view of the distribution of basic privileges and resources. I try to analyze why it is important to keep an eye on the resource distribution patterns in our nation. The final chapter offers some concluding observations about procedural changes that I believe might be profitable—an attempt to harness democratic majoritarianism to administrative rationality.

In sum, this book is about conflicts in the American value system and conflicts in the political system. I bow to the salutary aspects of conflict but also point out the occasional junctures where we need consensus. My major argument is in favor of a certain style of thinking and analysis, and therefore my major purpose in writing the book is to stimulate further argument. If, in consequence of this thrust, there appears to be undue emphasis on the problems and negative aspects of American politics, it is only a reflection of my deep commitment to the many virtues of this system and my ardent hope that we may preserve and enhance these strengths for future generations.

My gratitude extends to Professor Ruth G. Weintraub who first stimulated my academic interests, to hundreds of students and dozens of colleagues who sustain it, to Professor Robert S. Hirschfield who stimulated this particular book, and to my graduate assistant, Joseph Viteritti, who helped me sweep up some loose ends. I must also thank the manuscript editor, Barbara Salazar, and my typist, Charlotte Pecelli.

**ACKNOWL-
EDGMENTS**

# AMERICAN GOVERNMENT & POLITICS

## A CRITICAL INTRODUCTION

# CHAPTER 1

# INTRODUCTION

In all societies, but especially in America, there is a fundamental need to understand politics. Politics alone, among our
conscious areas of study, is nonelective. Our understanding of
political processes (or our failure to understand them) profoundly influences the world in which we live. A person's
understanding or ignorance of the planetary system has little
influence on that system's functioning, but each citizen's understanding of the political system has an inevitable and very
strong influence on *its* workings. Everyone is born into some
political system and consciously or unconsciously he affects it.
There is no escape. Political systems in no way function automatically. The way one views politics shapes the role one
plays, and the chosen role rests on one's political socialization.
This in turn is daily shaped by family, school, and media; perhaps a role of apathy, perhaps a role of violence. Whatever
the role, it inevitably rocks the political boat we all share. In
our nation, the political science profession, both directly and
indirectly, plays a large part in this socialization process, and
in consequence has some influence on the large arena of
politics as well. It seems useful, therefore, to begin our study
with the origin and substance of the discipline, and with a
brief explanation of its intramural controversies.

Political science does not exist in the world of events. It
exists in the world of people's minds, in universities, and in
books. Governments exist as world realities, and political science is the study of the processes, behavior, and phenomena
connected with governments. It is similar, let us say, to the
relationship between plants, which abound in the physical
world, and botany, which exists in the laboratory. Botany
describes, examines, catalogs, classifies, and perhaps makes
recommendations. So too with political science and government. Indeed, the study of political phenomena manages to
occur whenever and wherever people have lived together and
kept records. Even before such famous Greek discourses as
Plato's *Republic* or Aristotle's *Politics,* the Egyptians, Meso-
potamians, and Hebrews speculated on political matters. But
whereas in previous eras concern was limited to a few phi-

**POLITICAL
SCIENCE:
The Discipline
and the
Profession**

losophers who speculated about the "good life" or the "education of the ruler," it is only in our century and in our nation
that the study has become widespread, professionalized, and
specialized. The self-conscious arrangement of political writings, the orderly collection of data, the advent of new methodologies, and the training of specialists have taken place only
since the end of the nineteenth century and primarily in the
United States. It is at this time and in this nation that one
begins to find separate university departments devoted to the
study of politics, special journals on politics, and systematic
research into political phenomena. Perhaps this association of
political science with the United States is not completely accidental, since this nation has from its inception been concerned
with political questions and optimistic about the fruits of
politics. To some degree, it has also been dedicated to the
proposition that politics is the concern of the general citizenry,
not just of a special elite.

While there are many disputes about nuances in the definition of politics, most of the profession views it as the process
by which men assign and distribute power (that is, values and
resources), a process that large groups or societies accept and
defend as ultimate. In other words, the political system is that
power spectrum which has a monopoly on the legitimate use of
physical force, even to the point of taking human life. There
are minor squabbles over certain gray areas, but in general
the focus of professional concern is power and its arrangement. One of the United States' most renowned political scientists defines politics cogently and more succinctly: "Who
gets what, when, and how?"[1] It is a pithy way to encapsulate
the phenomenon, yet few basic texts try to address themselves
to precisely these questions. This short study of American
government intends to do just that. Indeed, it ambitiously
wishes to add one more question to the classic quartet: Why?

**Who Gets What
—and Why?**

To accomplish this task even in cursory fashion requires that
we dip into all the social sciences (and beyond them) for
possible answers and modes of inquiry. Indeed, certain social
sciences seem singularly connected with each of the particular
questions in this series. The "who" in "who gets what, when,
and how," for example, is very much in the domain of sociologists. In their works we find both descriptive and theoretical
constructs about group life and intergroup relations and be-
haviors. We can learn about "status" and "roles" in terms of
income, occupation, ethnicity, and other demographic factors.[2]
Similarly, we can learn about "what" from economists, who
are in the best position to provide data and theories on resource
aggregation, development, and distribution.[3] "When" and
"how" are the traditional preserves of political scientists them-

selves, and it is they who dissect the tools and timing of power.[4] And finally, "why" might best be pursued by philosophers and psychologists.[5]

Of course, many other disciplines must also come into play: anthropology and history to provide the case studies and longitudinal analyses to test the accuracy of the propositions that emerge from the other disciplines; mathematics to lend us tools for model-building, statistical studies, game theories, and other forms of logical analysis; biology, other branches of life science, and psychology to provide insight on motivation, behavior patterns, and the ultimate possibilities inherent in human behavior. And the list is still not complete.

Since this is a book written by a political scientist, it will deal primarily with the "how" and "what" questions of politics: the structures, processes, and results of power in American government. There is also a thesis about power offered here: that America is currently suffering a power failure. Despite an elaborate apparatus of government, and despite the resounding rhetoric of power which assails us all in the media (black power, student power, woman power, great power, power elite), there is less here than meets the eye. There is too often a systematic stalemate in the American polity. Today's problems were with us yesterday and may well be here tomorrow. Most change, in other words, is likely to be merely incremental. Why? My explanation leans heavily on two concepts: ambiguity and ambivalence.

Ambiguity refers to intellectual uncertainty. It applies to a situation in which there is conflicting evidence or incomplete evidence. Thus it is highly applicable to most of the complexities that beset our political system. But ambiguity makes people uncomfortable. They prefer simplicity and certainty. They would like to ignore ambiguity whenever possible. And they do. There are certain kinds of slogans, certain kinds of rigid reactions, certain kinds of pseudosolutions that give aid and comfort to those who wish to overlook ambiguities. Our political system is fraught with opportunities to do just this. Party labels substitute for party policies. Public personalities substitute for public plans. Facing up to ambiguity may require tolerating loose ends, at least for a while. But at a minimum, facing up to ambiguity is preferable to forcing it down. Absorbing uncertainty is not the same as accepting it. To absorb it is to risk not knowing that one does not know. Acceptance of ambiguity leads to caution, perhaps to compromise, but at least to some degree of rational calculation. To my mind it is a preferable style of thinking—but it is not in vogue. The American polity gives ambiguity short shrift. I

**THE AMERICAN POLITICAL STRUCTURE: Ambivalence and Ambiguity**

think it needs a renaissance. We should make a far greater effort than we do now to understand the ambiguities involved in many political conflicts and to develop a tolerance for those ambiguities. Specific examples of the ways in which ambiguity fogs our political system will be given throughout the book.

**Ambivalence**     Ambivalence, on the other hand, refers to contradictory emotional attitudes and reactions. It is a psychological term. It describes the simultaneous struggle of love with hate, disgust with attraction, dependence with independence, and so on. These too are painful situations from which people almost always seek to escape. Psychologists have built a number of theories to describe both ambivalence and the devices that individuals use to avoid or reduce it. Much of Freudian theory is devoted, for example, to the love-hate theme and the various ways in which this form of ambivalence is disguised and sublimated.[6] Leon Festinger, to take another example even more relevant to political life, built his "dissonance theory" to explain the ways in which people handle the pain of ambivalence.[7] But whatever the usual ways of escaping, they invariably involve some sort of rationalization and perceptual peregrination, and these devices invariably distort matters. Such distortions are frequently harmful in private affairs; in public affairs they are even more dangerous. They rarely serve the purpose of a rational polity. Failure even to recognize the existence of ambivalence in certain situations makes the case against social sanity even stronger. For example, ambivalence about the role of the police (that is, mixed and often contradictory feelings of admiration, fear, and hatred of policemen) often replaces ambiguities about the role of the police (that is, the actual evidence, often inconclusive, of police ineffectiveness). If we were in the habit of recognizing the existence of the first, however, we might more easily be able to deal with the latter. Heightened consciousness on both levels would unquestionably help us toward more rational solutions of police problems. But once again, the American political system provides its own rather special devices to handle mass ambivalence, and these devices are as dysfunctional to the public health as many of the personal devices are to an individual's health. The complexities of our procedures, the circular activities that provide motion without direction, the interstices among the many units of government which allow issues to disappear—all of these provide an effective smoke screen behind which ambivalence may lie unrecognized, and therefore need not be resolved. And while resolution may often be impossible (or even undesirable), frank recognition of any problem helps in its ultimate solution.

Nor should confusion over ambivalence and ambiguity be

permitted to masquerade as flexibility. Flexibility connotes a rational decision and an order of priorities. Flexibility permits room for individual tailoring of a program when the basic commitment is established. It is not aimless self-contradiction. Flexibility provides for healthful, explicit, and conscious experimentation. Genuine competition among various programs in fields where uncertainty is high because of ambiguous evidence is a reasonable way to proceed. But all too often our current way of conducting the public business substitutes camouflage for competition. It encourages inappropriate ambivalence, and discourages what I call creative conflict. It thus stacks the cards against rational problem-solving.

Creative conflicts are not disguises for unending and self-defeating compromise. They are not masks for either unresolved ambivalence or unrecognized ambiguity. On the contrary, they are conscious efforts at tentative resolutions, when "final solutions" appear premature or dangerous. Clearly I agree here with Bertram Gross:

**Creative Conflicts**

> Internal conflicts are inescapable even in the "normal" personality. They are created by the multiplicity of competing or even contradictory human interest, social roles and group attachments. Similar conflicts develop between and within the subsystems of all systems. The common interests and goals that keep a system together are always embedded in a network of divergent and competing interests and goals. Conflict usually becomes more dramatic in the intersystem relations of rivalry, competitions and combat. Extreme forms of conflict, of course, may readily undermine or destroy a system. On the other hand, *some degree of conflict*—both internal and external —is an *essential stimulus* to system adaptability and creativity.[8]

Thus some conflicts are certainly necessary and even productive, but not all.

The difference between healthful and destructive conflict is, of course, difficult to define. Yet I feel some such diagnosis must be made for society by scholars, just as it is made for individuals by psychotherapists. The line between unavoidable and understandable ambivalence and the dissolution of a personality may be hard to discern, but a line nevertheless exists; and so too with a profession or a society. It is my contention, however, that many of our conflict areas, both within the profession and within the polity, have been so deeply buried that they have never received public attention, much less public resolution. It is up to political scientists, therefore, to provide this attention. We should be trying to put things together in such a way as to allow some portions of emotional ambivalence to be replaced by the intellectual exercises congruent with ambiguities, and in the remainder of instances to allow the ambivalence at least to be frankly faced.

Since the role of the political scientist is delicately and inextricably entwined with the workings of the polity itself, it is important to understand a few basic cleavages within the ivy-covered walls of the profession before examining the conflicts, ambiguities, and ambivalence in the political system at large.

**CLEAVAGES IN THE POLITICAL SCIENCE PROFESSION**

The internal struggles of the profession have become more pronounced, it seems to me, as our role in the world has become enlarged. As more and more professors leave the lectern and find their way into the political arena, the significance of their squabbles has been heightened. It becomes increasingly clear that the profession has an impact on more than university programs, research methodologies, and the philosophic outlook of a handful of undergraduates. The biases that used to be largely confined to somewhat obscure professional journals are now bouncing directly into presidential ears. So we do have to pay attention to the bickerings of these academicians.

The fundamental controversy in the profession can be billed as a fight between behaviorists and traditionalists. At least, these have been the terms used over past generations. Traditionalists deal with political institutions as such—legislatures, courts, cabinets—and often discuss them chronologically, legalistically, and ideologically. Personal experiences, historical anecdotes, legal reasoning, and shrewd insights characterize these analyses. The courses of these scholars often emphasize individual nations or regions, and comparisons are made on a fairly macro level. Opposed to them are the behaviorists, who eschew moral judgments and yield only to the empirical findings of statistics, mathematics, psychology, and other sciences. They borrow the most sophisticated tools available among companion disciplines and use them to observe, measure, aggregate, and record human behavior as directly as possible. Their courses tend to emphasize particular processes in the political domain, such as voting and decision-making. This long-standing argument, however, might by now have faded away were it not for the reinforcement supplied by some more recent and overlapping developments.

First there is the division between the "logical positivists" and the "value-committed" political scientists. These are two sets of scholars who fit somewhat, but not exactly, into the camps of the behaviorists and the traditionalists. The logical positivists are firmly dedicated to separating fact from value. They insist that fact alone belongs to the realm of political science; value questions belong to moral philosophy. Moreover, they feel keenly that the confusion of fact-value questions leads to grave errors. It makes objectivity impossible and thus reduces political science to mere conjecture. If, for example, war is studied, as it rather ubiquitously is, in terms of its morality—whether to wage it or avoid it—then it becomes a hopelessly muddled question in their view. Even posing the war question in these terms makes vast cultural assumptions that they feel are inappropriate to the pure and neutral study of the phenomenon.

Yet to many other political scientists this separation of fact and value is not only impossible, but irresponsible. The newest converts to the antibehavioral, antipositivist view are in general the younger members of the profession. They call themselves "The Caucus for a New Political Science" and they have openly challenged the "establishment" by running rump sessions at recent annual meetings of the august American Political Science Association and by offering their own slate of nominees for positions in that body. There is some irony as well as great confusion in the alignment of troops in this latest battle. On certain questions of ideology, such as commitment to the need for asking moral questions, the youngest and most radical members are aligned with some of the oldest and most conservative among the traditionalists. Yet the traditionalists would hardly call themselves part of the Caucus. Without trying to straighten out the allies here, we might better point to the significant issues. The Caucus is primarily worried lest the overweening concern with "objectivity" and "methodology" expressed by behaviorists, logical positivists, and others becomes a red herring that diverts political scientists from meaningful pursuits.

They claim, at the outset, that objectivity is a delusion. Political scientists, unlike astronomers, have stakes in the system they study. Whether or not we seriously recognize it, political outcomes affect us all. As soon as we are born, we are in a political system and are thus continuously socialized to accept it and its myths without examination. Little of what we commonly call "fact" is therefore indeed fact. Most facts are values so conventionally accepted that they remain unquestioned. We speak, for instance, of "warm climates" and "cold climates," taking these terms as objective realities, whereas warm and cold are simply individual judgments, as can readily be seen in any office where the eternal controversy over opening or shutting the windows rages. We speak of old and young, tall and short in the same way. They are used as fixed objective categories instead of personal and relative judgments. The more complex the problem, the more difficult it is to thread our way out of cultural assumptions. The Caucus people want us to face these difficulties squarely and deal with basic value problems head on.

The significance in these conflicts lies, as I have indicated, not only in the fact that a departmental or individual bias in

"Objectivity"
and
"Methodology":
Radicals
versus
Traditionalists

**Objectivity
versus Activism**

either direction can shape a university's curriculum offerings; it can also shape future research activities and public policies. Thus professional conflict finally infiltrates the political system itself. The questions that are raised are the ones that will be answered. A commitment to objectivity moves the profession away from activism; the reverse moves us toward it. The Caucus people are dedicated activists. They want political science to produce policy results and they want colleagues to face up to the charge that the pursuit of the Holy Grail of "objectivity" and "scientism" leads not only to sterile and puerile research, but also to hypocrisy, since value-freedom cannot be achieved. Their opponents fear that precisely such involvement will impair their usefulness as scientists and as teachers.

I believe these intramural conflicts can be left without final resolution. They are creative conflicts inasmuch as they draw attention to professional biases and thus raise certain fundamental questions that have hitherto remained "nonissues." The nonissues that are now enjoying some heightened consciousness as a result of political science infighting range from culturally encrusted fundamental myths to specific policy alternatives that were previously overlooked. The remainder of this book will be an attempt to help heighten consciousness about some of these conflicts in the political arena itself. The reader will be expected to judge for himself (despite the rather frequent opinions) the degree to which these conflicts involve genuine ambiguities, the degree to which they involve recognized ambivalence, and the degree to which the conflicts are, in sum, creative.

# CHAPTER 2

# THE BASIC MYTHS
# OF AMERICA

All nations, like individuals, have myths, and these myths are both necessary and inevitable. "Myths," as I shall use the term, are deeply held convictions that are often illusory. They are part of our unconscious ideology. Indeed, one prominent sociologist says they are "collective representations which tell us about the kind of people we wish to be and why we should hope to be that kind of people. They *account for our regularized way of doing things, our institutions.*"[1] And because they do account for so much and are so likely to be shrouded in ambivalence, I believe we must examine them. I choose to confine the term "myth," however, to those ideas so well accepted and so thoroughly socialized into our belief system that they do not generally merit much public or even professional review. Other basic beliefs that have been made more explicit (raised, for instance, to the level of constitutional expression) I choose to call "values," and I reserve them for the following chapter.

Just as the protagonists of Eugene O'Neill's cycle of dramas could not live without their individual myths, so too peoples like the Japanese, Chinese, Germans, and Americans cannot live without their national myths. Indeed, nations might well be measured and judged by the quality of their myths. Some myths may prove to be more functional and salutary than others. Not all myths are universally and automatically healthful. Myths of exclusivity and superiority (like the Superman myth) may perhaps be ultimately destructive. The contention here is merely that a heightened consciousness about these national myths might improve their quality and their usefulness. Distinguishing areas of ambiguity from areas of ambivalence may help here.

Among the myths of the United States, there are two that I believe merit particular attention. One is our blind belief in scarcity and the other our blind belief in enemies. Together these two myths profoundly influence "who gets what, when, and how." Heightening our awareness of these two ideas, even if we cannot reduce our ambivalence about them, should at a minimum improve our understanding of the American political

"Myths"

system. The two myths are actually reverse sides of the same coin. The notion of unexamined scarcity makes enemies rationally possible, perhaps inevitable; and the notion of unexamined enemies makes scarcity possible and even acceptable. Perhaps the two notions woven together into the fabric of American politics contribute to making ours a politics of stalemate. Let us therefore examine these twin stars that seem so fixed in our firmament.

**SCARCITY** Take first, scarcity. To begin with, let me define the term. It means "insufficiency in number in *proportion to needs and demands.*" This is its primary dictionary meaning as well as its most commonly accepted usage. Note that it does not mean merely a limited or fixed amount. It depends on a relationship. Most people use words without being fully aware of nuances in meanings, and these common usages and their undertones influence behavior. With this said, I wish to argue that we have far too readily accepted scarcity as a profound general and inflexible fact, and we base our political decisions upon this presumed fact. We start with the assumption that there is not enough of anything we want to go around, and we move on from there. Scarcity thus narrows the range of political choices. It spawns the further assumption that poverty cannot be abolished. But must this mean that malnutrition cannot be abolished? Indeed, is existing hunger a result of any genuine scarcity of food? Does infant mortality rest on a scarcity of doctors? Is there any inevitable scarcity of adequate housing? Is self-esteem scarce? Is love scarce? Or do we *choose* some scarcities, or do we at least blindly accept them?

When a society becomes convinced that basic and important resources are irrevocably and inevitably scarce, will it not be induced to behave in barbaric ways? Have you ever observed, for example, the eating habits of a habitually ill-fed person facing a temporary abundance of food? Compare his gluttony with the behavior of someone who is secure in the knowledge that another good meal will follow. I am suggesting that there is a type of scarcity behavior. It is short-term, greedy, and self-defeating. This pattern was very much in evidence in the United States in the early 1940s, the period of food and gasoline rationing, when many families hoarded foodstuffs that often spoiled before they could be consumed. Behavior based on abundance (whether of a material thing or a nonmaterial quality like security or love) is, I believe, more adaptable to longer-term and more intelligent discretion. Indeed, there is even a scholarly study that suggests as much.[2] This study shows that there are certain classes of voters who are more disposed than others to rest their political choices on some concept of the "public interest" or the "welfare of the community." The conclusion here is that upper income groups, along with certain ethnic groups, vote *against* any narrowly conceived self-interest. In other words, generosity and range of view may be influenced by (among other things) a full belly.

What I am pleading for, at the outset, is a more careful analysis of the unrefined assumption of inflexible scarcity. I believe we have unconsciously (and improperly) grafted an *economist's* concept of scarcity onto a political world without benefit of sufficient pruning. We have not examined this myth. Almost the entire economics profession, certainly its most influential members, quite properly accept scarcity as an axiom. But with far less propriety, so too have political scientists. An axiom does not require proof. Yet even an axiom, when it shifts domain, should merit at least careful explanation. I do not choose to quarrel with the usefulness of the idea of scarcity in classical economic theory. I quarrel only with its undiluted and unexamined acceptance as part of our *political* equations. In the political arena scarcity must be more explicitly defined and measured. Its implications must be reviewed.

Consider, for example, Professor Paul A. Samuelson's statement of the scarcity axiom in his basic college economics text (a book that influences hundreds of thousands of citizens directly and indirectly): "Economics must still contend with scarcity as a *basic fact of life*."[3] He claims this is true both here and abroad. To illustrate just how scarce things are, he points out that "even if our national income were divided up equally between every man, woman, and child, there would be only $75 per week to go around." Now when an idea like this is merged into the political realm unexpurgated (which I am sure Samuelson did not intend), it is easily converted into a bias against policies that might try to eliminate or at least mitigate this scarcity. After all, you can't do much about a "fact of life." And if scarcity is accepted in terms of Samuelson's arithmetic, it certainly does seem utopian to try to cope with it. This economist, along with most others, does not mention the *relative* nature of scarcity. That is unnecessary for his enterprise. Yet $75 per week per person amounts to more than $17,000 per year per family. (A typical American family is generally considered to consist of 4.4 persons.) But is this a *politically* defensible description of scarcity? An income of over $17,000 is well above the income of even an above-average urban eastern householder, and it is light-years away from the official poverty level of approximately $3,350 per year. This is therefore not an illustration of a scarcity life scale by any stretch of fact or fancy, even in the United States. Certainly it is not scarcity in terms of any meaningful political "fact of life."

Indeed, politically speaking, scarcity not only need not be assumed, it could be expunged. We can make scarcity virtually disappear as far as basic public choice (or politics) is concerned by (1) recognizing the element of political choice in the so-called scarcities of our public way of life; (2) recognizing the public *restraints* that now operate against productivity; (3) recognizing the degree to which our public choices are clouded by waste and mismanagement; (4) recognizing the degree to which public choice is constrained by failure to restrain and conserve existing resources; (5) recognizing the degree to which public choice is hampered by failure and irresponsibility in making rational estimates of "needs" and fulfillments.

**Public Choice in Scarcity**

At a minimum, close examination of existing scarcity in the public domain suggests that there is always a political choice available in selecting these scarcities. Only certain things are scarce at certain times. It is here that the high drama of rationally reordering priorities should be played out. Among the various estimates of our war expenditures, for example, there is one made by the War Tax Resistance group.[4] It is based on the U.S. Government Printing Office Publication *Budget in Brief*. It puts U.S. military spending at $1 trillion since 1946. One-tenth of this has been spent on the Vietnam war alone ($100 billion). Thus 64.8 percent of our budget goes into what some people believe to be a counterproductive, even a destructive enterprise. This same group dramatizes the choices that could have been made. Take just a few of their examples: $809 million for military-family housing, but only $575 million for the Model Cities program; $39 million for Department of Defense public relations, but only $5 million for Department of Justice civil rights enforcement. These figures indicate that some items may indeed be scarce in the United States, but if so, it is the product of our choice. Or, as a *New York Times* editorial said:

> The typical urban taxpayer, the father of two making $10,000 a year, paid $19 for space exploration last year but only $1.00 for mass transportation. This same taxpayer paid $26 for more federal highways to accommodate more automobiles and only $4.00 to fight pollution of both the air and the water.[5]

Most of us certainly go around feeling that mass transportation is scarce and so too is good air and water. But, again, these are choices that must be made; and some of the choices, were they clearly understood, would in fact never be made. This is the sort of arithmetic that must be done before we conclude that scarcity is a politically usable "basic fact of life."

**Restraints on Productivity**

The potential for technological increases in our productivity should also count heavily in our consideration of scarcity.

Assess here the carefully documented opinion of Professor Seymour Melman.[6] He has analyzed the effects of military expenditures, which figure importantly in our gross national product, and concludes that they are actually corrosive in terms of genuine "national productivity." He views *productive* growth as including goods and services that form part of the level of living or can be used for further production." In these terms, a large portion of our public budget has been going to economically parasitic growth, and this accounts for some of the anomalies and apparent scarcities in our society. Professor Melman argues that we are neglecting some of our machine tool stock and are employing 50 percent of the nation's technical researchers in work that can have *no productive results.* Here, Melman believes, is the explanation for big-city power failures, transportation breakdowns, housing shortages, and a declining ratio of physicians to population; in other words, our so-called scarcities.

We must also recall here that most material scarcities as they now appear to exist in the United States are *induced* scarcities. That is, we pay farmers not to produce (our agricultural farm parity programs), pay workers not to work (our unemployment insurance plans, our welfare programs, our unreasonably long and delaying educational programs), and often reward our investors for not investing (our occasional tight-money and balance-of-payments policies). We are also a society that has not yet chosen to tighten our controls over resource conservation and population growth. All of these policies are man-made and could be undone or redone. We could unlock far greater supplies of food, shelter, clothes, and other necessities than we do now. Scarcities thus are not inevitable, they are selected.

It is also ironic to note that there is much unexamined waste included in the conventional portrayal of scarcity. Dr. Carl Kaysen, director of the Institute for Advanced Study at Princeton and former special assistant to President Kennedy for national security, made this clear in an important message to a subcommittee of the Senate Foreign Relations Committee. He explained that the defense budget for nonnuclear forces could be reduced by $10 billion in the next year or so simply by more appropriate management within the area of defense spending itself.[7] This would have reduced many budgetary "scarcities." Moreover, virtually every management survey ever made in this country finds vast chunks of fat and acres of deadwood. Health, Education, and Welfare Secretary Eliot Richardson, for example, spoke recently of our "excess hospitals and excess hospital beds," which he claimed cost us $3.6 billion to maintain in 1970 (and which have long been part of the hospital trend) in spite of supposed shortages.[8]

**Waste and Mismanagement**

**Failure to
Restrain and
Conserve**

Scarcity is always relative to the ratio of population to resources. Population is also a matter for political choice. The
Malthusian proposition has long since been demonstrated false.
Population does not *have* to overtake food supply. A single
farmer today feeds one hundred times the number he did at
the turn of the century. Moreover, we have at hand simple and
cheap ways to control population growth itself. That we do
not offer inducements for the use of birth control methods is,
again, a matter of political choice, not economic necessity.

Similar, too, are our uneconomic methods of soil, fish, and
forest conservation. We are not yet essentially committed to
long-run and future-oriented environmental conservation. And
this too produces illusions of scarcity.

**Needs and
Fulfillment**

Finally, scarcity has several internal dimensions that require
analysis before we can pronounce it politically dead. Scarcity
implies needs and fulfillment. We could exorcise part of the
myth of scarcity if we rationally defined the elements and made
them manageable for public choice. What, after all, are human
needs? Perhaps we could adopt a hierarchy suggested in part
by psychologist Abraham Maslow.[9] He posits (a) physiological needs (food, shelter); (b) safety needs (reasonable assurance of continued fulfillment of basic physiological needs
plus continuation of life free from bodily harm); (c) social
needs (affection, human companionship, and exchanges);
(d) ego needs (status and self-respect); and (e) self-actualiz-
ing needs (intellectual fulfillments, artistic creativity, and so
forth). While this hierarchy cannot be so neatly arranged in
life as on paper, it does provide a quite widely agreed-upon
classification. For certain relatively rare individuals, the order
can be different, and certain steps in the hierarchy might even
be eliminated. In the main, however, it appears that all human
beings have these five cravings and have them in roughly the
order suggested. That is, persons will probably not seek intellectual self-fulfillment until after extreme hunger and the rest
are satisfied. The basic *needs* of mankind are thus known and
ordered, and therefore their limits and degrees of their fulfillment are perhaps susceptible to quantification.

There are, of course, many practical problems in establishing
the dividing line between wants and needs in a particular
society. The difficulties are well illustrated by the following
observation made in 1770 by the famous scholar-adventurer
Edward Banks, on the society he found in New Guinea when
he visited it with Captain Cook.

> Thus live these I had almost said happy people, content
> with little nay almost nothing, far enough removed from the
> anxieties attending riches, or even the possession of what we
> Europeans call common necessaries. . . . From them appear

how small are the real wants of human nature, which we
Europeans have increased to an excess which would certainly
appear incredible to these people could they be told it. Nor
shall we cease to increase them so long as Luxuries can be
invented and riches found for the purchase of them; and how
soon these Luxuries degenerate into necessaries may be
sufficiently evinced by the universal use of liquors, tobacco,
tea, etc. etc.[10]

This division between necessary and unnecessary (or even between healthful and unhealthful) is the very problem to which
our social and physical scientists should be devoting themselves. If our scientists were to explain more fully the implications of technological innovations and social engineering policies (indeed, if they themselves were more fully aware of their
long-range implications), the public just might utilize this information in ordering the particular items of our hierarchy of
collective needs. We might, in other words, determine the line
between necessity and luxury, between sense and nonsense.
Ralph Nader's exposé of the automotive industry did awaken
the public to the wisdom of valuing cars equipped with safety
equipment over cars with chromium trim. This type of assessment is an important step in the business of allocating the
costs and benefits of "public" goods as well as private ones.
Consider, for a further example, Lewis Mumford's suggestion
that we reassess the transportation problem. He asks:

What is the function of transportation? What place does loco-
motion occupy in the whole spectrum of human needs? . . .
If we took human needs in recasting the whole transportation
system, we should begin with the human body and make the
fullest use of pedestrian movement not only for health but
for efficiency.[11]

**Measures
of Need
Fulfillment**

We can only hope that education and a more responsible
attitude on the part of the mass media may soon combine to
introduce this kind of sanity into our thinking on reasonable
needs and reasonable fulfillments. Moreover, even though it is
still true that what assuages one man's hunger whets another's
appetite, societies nonetheless can and do, even now, establish
rough measures of need fulfillment for at least the first two
levels of the Maslow hierarchy by using national norms (average situations and average expectations). We can and do know
what middle America believes fulfills its needs. We know what
is our "average income" and we know what is our "average
dream." (I discuss this more fully in Chapter 10.) And with
such norms in mind for the United States, I believe we can
flatly state that there are no politically relevant material
scarcities in the United States.

I also believe that once physical and safety wants were thus
fulfilled, we would probably find the spirit and creativity

needed to reach the more subtle requisites of the higher levels of need. It *is* possible to bring down to human scale such enterprises as education, art, health services, and even manufacturing, so that the human need for self-respect and person-to-person association can be made abundant instead of scarce. In this connection, I have in mind the work of such men as Elton Mayo and his associates, Alvin Gouldner, Warren Bennis, and Chris Argyris, all of whom have done considerable research demonstrating the efficiency of participatory administration, circular communications, and similar administrative reforms.[12] Current movements toward decentralization, consultation, sensitivity programs, and the reduction of hierarchal categories in both public and private bureaucracies are ongoing attempts to make possible increased feelings of self-respect, self-efficacy, self-fulfillment, group cohesiveness, and other ingredients in the higher echelons of Maslow's need structure.

**ENEMIES**

The irrationality of our unexamined scarcity myth is dwarfed only by its twin: our commitment to the idea of an enemy. The two are inextricably connected in a number of ways. Our domestic policy is inextricably intertwined with our foreign policy; that is, our foreign policy is dictated by what we perceive to be our domestic needs and our domestic budget is what is left over after we have taken care of foreign policy. Our foreign policy is based in large part on the need for aggressive preparedness against "the enemy." And enemies, indeed, appear to abound. They are made all the more plausible in a world of ordained "scarcity." If one believes in the inevitable scarcity of basic needs, I suppose one can more easily believe in the inevitability of fights for fulfillment of those needs. But in truth scarcities are an unexamined assumption, and so too, I claim, are enemies.

Enemies require the same careful reexamination as scarcity. Again, let us define the term. An enemy is an individual or group that is hostile to one and manifests a desire to *harm or destroy* one. Thus the word, very properly, is closely associated with war. Ironically enough, while scarcity may have suffered from too much of the bias of economics, enemies suffer from an insufficiency of this bias. That is, enemies seem not to be made of the stuff of economics at all. Nor are they the stuff of biology or ethnology, though such is often alleged to be the case. Unfortunately, enemies reside primarily in the domain of psychology. Enemies seem to me to be compounded of mistrust, misunderstandings, and miscalculations. The idea of the enemy is fed by failure to recognize either the ambiguity or the ambivalence involved. We should reconsider the traditional arguments about national interest and the inevitability of enemies and their concomitant wars. We need to review the implications of psychological and ethnological findings, of self-fulfilling prophecies, and of miscalculation in the present era.

The conventional view of national interest equates this some-what mystical concept with national security. In turn, national security is commonly married to a defensive, or better yet offensive, set of policies and potentials vis-à-vis enemies. These policies enlist the State Department, the Defense Department, the President, and often many others in vast and expensive undertakings to promote or protect "American interests abroad." It is more than usual for these interests to be defined for us by either practicing politicians or military pundits. Typical is the statement of Admiral Arleigh A. Burke, retired Chief of Naval Operations. He sees our interests as "requiring a very large and modern Navy capable of 'showing the flag' and conducting the necessary supporting military operations in all areas of the world." He further sees clearly that it is against the national interest to be relegated to the "status of second-rate power"—although that is nowhere clearly defined. So too retired General Mark W. Clark, who equates our national interest with national security, and this in turn requires us to "let the enemy know that we will use strength as necessary to maintain the security of the United States."[13]

In their world view Russia and China and others are enemies and must be contained, confronted, and if necessary fought. Yet the question "Why?" is never put into clear focus. Is it that they wish to take our land? Do they want our people as slaves? Do they need war machines to enlist their own labor forces and keep their economies going? Or do *we* have any of these needs and motives? Are enemies the outgrowth of economics, psychology, biology, or what? It is here that we urgently need to use the tools of economic analysis. While economists deal with "competitors," I know of none who require "enemies" for their analyses and outcomes. What is more, all of the modern economic analyses that I have read seem to interpret our heavy "national security" expenditures as unnecessary. This seems to me to point to the idea that enemies are indeed not economically defined. There are economists such as those mentioned earlier, for example, who can point out our systematic *over-expenditure* for various missile systems and other defense materials in terms of inappropriate and costly results, obsolescence, and sheer waste. There is also the line of economic reasoning that calls defense expenditures into question because so many of them are at once "both the cause and effect of international disunity."[14] More often defense measures are indeed the cause. The economists also point out that "selfish economic interests often wrap themselves in the flag and try to justify uneconomic projects in terms of national defense."[15] Here we might well be reminded of President Dwight D. Eisenhower's warnings against letting the "military-industrial complex" take over our key decision-making apparatus. Furthermore, alternative non-"defense" spending might have not only equally desirable internal economic consequences, but better ones. Here, for example, is what Paul A. Samuelson says: "America's potential and actual growth rate, far from depending on war preparations, would be markedly *increased* by an end to the cold war. Is the story fully as optimistic as this? Yes."[16] In sum, military-style conventional thinking about the "national interest" should be replaced by other views.

**The Profitability of Friendship**

When economics does take over, there are countless examples of the ease with which enemies become friends. People appear capable of understanding the profitability of friendship. Consider, for example, the remark of an Australian veteran of World War II as he watched Prince Mikasa, brother of the Japanese emperor, placing a wreath on a soldier's grave in Canberra: "Twenty-five years ago you wouldn't have believed that anything like this could ever happen." Nor could anyone have then conceived of an Australian tour director conducting Japanese citizens through the New Guinea allied war memorial cemeteries so that suitable offerings and prayers might be said. The explanation for this new cordiality, like that between Americans and Germans or between Americans and Japanese or between Yugoslavs and Italians, is simple indeed. It is the by-product of a burgeoning and mutually profitable economic situation. Today Japan is Australia's best customer for raw materials while Australia provides a market for about $539.5 million worth of Japanese manufactured goods. Yet much of the geopolitics of the area has remained the same. Boundary lines, population figures, life styles have not changed that much in their *relative* proportions. There has simply been a mutual discovery of mutual profit. This is very understandable.

What is less understandable, because it must be explained in terms of a mystique of one sort or another, is why any two nations are so ready to kill so many hundreds of thousands of each other's people. Here the social psychologists take over. There are any number of analyses that help explain the existence of enemies. But the unfortunate truth of the matter is that these analyses do no more than offer explanations for the dark underbelly of irrationality of which human beings are capable. Neither individually nor collectively do they add up to an inevitable truth. They set forth pathological findings that should help us to understand a disease we wish to cure. I am in no way casting these findings aside; on the contrary, I am suggesting that they be dealt with as explicitly as possible. In this way we may be able to raise a few submerged areas of ambivalence to at least a more conscious and treatable level. We can try, in other words, to treat the evidence here in terms of the intellectual ambiguities they reveal, as well as the ambivalences.

Ralph K. White, a social psychologist, explicitly analyzes war in terms of certain images. Among these are what he calls "the diabolical enemy image": certain persons or groups are relegated to inhuman or subhuman or other categories that evoke conditioned responses.[17] Here I would call attention to such subcategories as "traitors," "aliens," and "agitators." Clearly this sort of name-calling is not a thinking process at all. It is a form of brainwashing. It rejects ambiguity and substitutes irrational outlets for humanity's deepest love-hate ambivalences. Then there is the "moral self-image," which glorifies our own motivations beyond fact or reason and is another style of nonthinking made possible by such psychological devices as selective perception and selective attention. Most important, there is a persistent inability to empathize.

There are further nuances that can be added here from the findings of those psychologists who have probed our unconscious with batteries of opinion items and have emerged with an "authoritarian personality" syndrome.[18] They hold that this factor influences attitudes on a large number of items and is highly correlated with such other factors as "ethnocentrism." Whether such factors actually influence behavior, however, is not clear, and to this day research continues and findings appear to move in equal and opposite directions.

All such image factors are exacerbated by what the social psychologists can tell us about such forces as "conformity" (which provides momentum and staying power for images based on the foregoing items)[19] and "distortion."[20] Comformity studies merely confirm the common-sense impression that people prefer to go along with their friends and peers. Studies on rumors and distortions, however, illustrate that this pathology is far from random. Distortion usually moves to support unconscious emotional needs like hostility, fear, and a desire to relieve ambivalence. The devices of distortion, moreover, move across all levels from information giving to information receiving, transmission, and interpretation. This cycles us back to our understanding of selective attention, perception, and retention. The device of distortion also involves overt techniques ranging from information classification to outright suppression. We have been witnesses to the whole sordid story of public distortion in the exposure of both the atrocities at Mylai

*Nonthinking*

and the uncertainty absorption at the Pentagon (that is, the manner in which speculation takes on the patina of fact). These stories are also illustrative of the way we "rationalize" and "project"—two more psychological explanations for some of our less than rational behavior patterns.

Most people harbor stereotypes, and many of these exist on a conscious national level vis-à-vis other nations. Interviews with Australians and Japanese reveal, for example, that each retains a marvelously similar stereotype of the other. "You never know what is behind that toothy Japanese smile," says an Australian industrialist. "When you deal with the Australians you can never really tell what they are thinking," says a Japanese businessman. What is hopeful here is the psychological finding that stereotypy can be reduced by exposure and contact. There are some early studies in point here, as well as more recent ones that show how black-white school integration has reduced false images.[21] In 1971 a *New York Times* poll conducted in seven European towns indicated that hatred against the Germans was greatly reduced. Among the chief reasons cited for the relaxation of hostility were "new ties of tourism, trade; and school and labor-union exchanges." These have "softened the image of Germany." A Dutchman going on holiday to Germany and doing business with Germans "cannot always live in a divided way. So when the Dutchman is obliged to be friendly to make a *profit*, he goes home and thinks, 'That is a nice German.'"[22] Once again contact and profit seem to drive out the basic coin of fear and hostility.

There is, in sum, no persuasive evidence that our darker psychological drives *must* be projected onto the screen of "national interest" once we are taught to recognize these factors for what they truly are, and once we are stimulated to substitute for ethnocentrism, stereotypy, and other false images, a well-sharpened and realistic ability to *empathize;* that is, to project the states of mind, motivations, feelings, and information of others onto our own cognitive map. This will take learning and practice, but again, like the practice of economic-style thinking, it is a tool that will help restore sanity to our understanding of "national interest."

**On the Inevitability of Enemies: Views from Ethology**

There are many who rest their belief in the inevitability of enemies on the supposed findings of ethologists. But like the world of Adlerian drives and other psychological explanations, findings in the field of animal behavior are more in the nature of tentative probes than prophetic pronouncements. Just as there may well be innate wellsprings of human brutishness, envy, aggression, greed, and so forth based on death wishes and other paraphernalia of psychiatric insights, there also may be animal instincts of aggression. But most of the data here are being misread, I believe. There is far too much room for slippage in any analogy between nonreasoning animals that cannot have a sense of history, express conceptual ideas, or act with self-consciousness and reasoning animals who can and routinely do have the capacity to do these things.

Moreover, the findings of ethologists such as Konrad Lorenz[23] lead as easily to positive views of aggression as to negative ones. That is, it seems to me that animal aggression stems essentially from behavior oriented more to the idea of competitors than to the idea of enemies. Note that predatory animal behavior stems primarily from food or territorial needs. This suggests a type of competition that in the human world ought to yield to the previously described methods of reducing scarcities. That is, aggression offers political choices other than war. Territory and food have indeed been less and less even *perceived* as requiring war (and thus enemies). Note further that the remainder of aggressive animal behavior is satisfied by ritualistic games and nondeadly forms of simple competition. All of this suggests that human beings can benefit from the positive aspects of aggressive "instincts" revealed by ethological research: creativity, social order, selective adaptation. Moreover, we can control (indeed we do control) some of the nastier behavioral possibilities through diversionary tactics. In those nations organized according to what are often described as democratic principles, internal aggression is diverted into sectional competition, economic competition, party politics, pressure-group tactics, and the like. For those polities that are organized along more authoritarian lines, aggression is usually channeled to meet the needs of forced industrialization, to combat the destructiveness of natural phenomena, and to perpetuate the institutionalized pecking order. In either case, aggression finds acceptable outlets. It does not seem to require acknowledged enemies within the national gates. Texans may feel mildly hostile to or superior to New Yorkers and vice versa, but neither of them would be likely to use the term "enemy" or use the tactics and weapons associated with enemies. So too with Uzhbeks and Byelorussians. When groups do degenerate into enemies, the forces of unmitigated and frequently unrecognized irrationality are usually at work.

**On Self-fulfilling Prophecies**

If enemies are economically unprofitable, ideologically unnecessary, and psychologically assailable, why then do they persist? Here we get to the crux of the matter—to an idea that is the core of both the phenomenon and its cure: the concept of the self-fulfilling prophecy. Although our civil servants take oaths to support the government against its enemies, and our youngsters are barely out of first grade before they have learned to recognize the enemy, and the very warp and woof of our life includes a belief in enemies, those of us who have lived an entire lifetime in a state of war cannot escape noticing that the enemy is vague, always changing, always dependent on a mirror image in adjacent nations for its very existence; and we have begun to suspect that the enemy is only a self-fulfilling prophecy.

The point is well made by an international relations scholar, Professor John G. Stoessinger, who noted in 1971 that "For an entire generation, Chinese and Americans have perceived each other through dark screens that often produced caricatures out of realities. They have fashioned images of one another that were based on their deepest fear and terrors."[24] It is Professor Stoessinger's view that "if a nation *believes that another is its implacable enemy* and reiterates this often, making it the guideline of its national policy, it will eventually be right."[25]

Indeed, almost all political scientists are willing to concede *this* proposition the mantle of truth. The self-fulfilling prophesy posits that many of the things one believes to be true become so because of nothing more than that belief itself. If, for example, your mother warns you not to be clumsy every time you are about to pour wine into a glass, her warnings will in all probability so unnerve you so that you will spill the wine. This then produces proof that you *are* clumsy—and so the cycle continues. Since unquestionably such cycles can exist (and they are usually cycles of negativism and despair), why not initiate cycles of hope and charity? If we view people as kind and generous, perhaps they will indeed become so. The large and widely recognized area of plasticity in our nature makes this not at all impossible.

**Miscalculation**  Finally we must face one last factor that weighs heavily against the automatic acceptance of the idea of enemies: the idea of miscalculation. Take, for example, our continuing penchant for zero-sum games in determining State Department and Defense Department policies. I believe this is a miscalculation and a costly one. As things run now, our analyses seem married to the idea that one side's gain must be the other's loss. Rarely do calculations proceed from the notion of positive games—that is, situations in which two or more competitors stand to gain or lose commensurately. Positive gamesmen say, "We're both in the same boat. If it floats we both gain." Zero-sum games stem from enemy-oriented thinking. They are calculated to produce not only self-fulfilling prophecies, but miscalculated ones at that.

The enemy idea adds to miscalculation in another way. It patently affects the very process of decision-making by forcing our decision-makers to work largely in the dark. What I have in mind here is the well-documented tendency for Congress to approve Pentagon budgets with far greater ease and speed than any other budgets. The more a government official can lean on the idea of enemies and security needs, the more he can retreat into the world of classified documents and secrecy. It is in precisely this atmosphere that some of our largest policy commitments are made. The compounding of miscalculations made from such flimsy stuff was well illustrated by the famous incident of the Pentagon Papers, in which the unexpected publication of a set of classified documents revealed a sad story of the decision-making process of our Vietnam policy. Error was piled upon error, uncertainties were swept under the rug, and the basic unexamined premise of enemies blinded both the Congress and the people to the actualities of the situation. The miscalculations here are too dramatic to require comment.

Compounding
Miscalculations

The way initial miscalculations get permanently pressed into our policy apparatus can be illustrated by remarks with the flavor of *Alice in Wonderland,* but which are actually from the mouth of President Nixon's adviser on foreign policy, Henry Kissinger. During a CBS news analysis program he argued that if the administration were wrong in Indochina, it had to stick to its decisions. "All the tough decisions, the sort of decisions that come to the President, are very close and you make your decision on the basis of maybe a fifty-five–forty-five balance. . . . Once you've made the decision you are committed to it or you are stuck with it one hundred percent." Why? Is this the stuff of which rational decision-making is made? Or even rational enemies? But it certainly dramatizes the odds in favor of miscalculation in the first place and of continuing miscalculation thereafter.

For a summary opinion on this whole matter, let us turn to a man who is unlikely to be accused of any softheaded sentimentality. Herman Kahn, the Rand analyst, who in the recent past was quite willing to "think the unthinkable" and to plan nuclear strategies, has this to say about causes of wars:

> I would say that today most of the traditional causes of war among the major nations have pretty well disappeared. In Europe the territorial boundaries are firmly set and with some exceptions, they have been accepted by public opinion. Nations no longer go to war because they have been insulted and most of the prestige arguments had to fall by the wayside. The basic remaining causes of formal war would stem from consideration of defense: one nation *feeling threatened* by some crises which it could only resolve by force or because it feels threatened by the pre-emptive strike potential of its rival. But it is *highly unlikely* that any military request for nuclear weapons to be used to achieve positive gains would be condoned either by the United States or the U.S.S.R. For all these reasons it is very difficult to write credible scenarios for formal war in the nineteen-seventies or nineteen-eighties.

However, he goes on:

> One cannot rule out nuclear war by *accident* or *miscalculation*. Bluffing and intimidation may backfire, especially if this makes accident or miscalculation more likely.[26]

The whole complex picture of war is under investigation by J. David Singer and four of his associates at the University of Michigan. Underlying Singer's mathematical approach to the study of war is an obvious value bias. He quite evidently believes in the possibility of prevention, of a world perhaps without enemies. Indeed, this possibility motivated the investigation.

But such talk of replacing scarcity and enemies with abundance and friends is the talk of an ordinary citizen endowed with ordinary common sense. It therefore finds little place in the higher realms of policy-making. Yet data from polls, election returns, and congressional mail make it abundantly clear that there is increasing dissatisfaction with a political system that has allowed the problems of the nineteenth century to drift only mildly abated, if at all, into the twentieth. There is certainly no widespread desire to continue this drift into the twenty-first. We are a patently wealthy economy that is not feeding all the hungry; a great technological civilization that is not sufficiently protecting its environment; a great military power that is not even winning its wars; a great society, in short, with abundant resources to meet our crying needs but without the political thrust to forge the necessary connections between needs and fulfillment. It appears, therefore, that we require new visions, new myths, and perhaps some changes of procedure to set us on more productive paths. The needed thrust to legitimate a basic reordering of priorities does not appear to be emerging from our traditional political subsystems. Our policy-makers continue the old round of hot and cold wars and selective scarcities. Our negative images must somewhere begin to give way to a different perception if we are ever to break out of what is a historically documented cycle of suspicion and consequent aggression. We need, in other words, a capacity to empathize and a capacity to construct alternative strategies without enemies and without scarcities. There is need for a new style of thinking. It is eloquently summarized by Lewis Mumford:

**Reordering Priorities**

> The whole economy is becoming unworkable. What is in store is not merely a change of pace, or a reallocation of individual priorities, but a basic change of purpose and direction. This transformation will be directed toward shifting from an overheated economy based on war, waste, forced consumption and meretricious affluence to a temperate "steady state"

economy such as J. S. Mill theoretically described a century ago. That new economy will be based, not on power, productivity, and pecuniary enrichment, but on well *distributed plenitude* and the general enrichment of human culture.

No responsible mind will venture to write out in detail the prescription for such a deep seated ideological and social change. . . . We need time, not only to make a more thorough canvas of "unprofitable" human needs, but also to change our minds and to reformulate our purposes—an even slower process.[27]

Rethinking wants and needs (reordering our choices); reducing waste; revamping our productive resources, both human and technological; reevaluating both scarcity and enemies in terms of new policies and new myths if you will—these form the order of business for the United States. Perhaps a myth of abundance will serve us better than a myth of scarcity, a myth of innate friendliness better than one of enemies.

In forging our new myth we must be equally wary of treading on air and of barricading ourselves in the streets. The utopians offer only vague mystiques or new forms of totalitarianism; the "revolutionaries" offer only a blueprint for destruction. These are not the stuff of which genuine progress is made. While it is certainly possible that the proposals suggested here will also fall short of the announced goal, I am convinced that the basic style of thinking advanced is sound and profitable.

Although the propositions that have informed my reevaluation of basic myths are to some degree patently future-oriented, this should not discourage us. We should not underestimate the potential packed into the explosion of knowledge. So far we have failed to learn one necessary lesson of history: predictions based solely on the past are likely to be erroneous. Check the predictions of any statesman of the nineteenth century against the realities of the twentieth. The gap is fantastically large. This should convince us that we cannot even begin to imagine the possibilities of the future. In my own childhood there was an unquestioned adage used to describe the impossible. We used to say that any impossible dream was as likely as "flying to the moon." Need I say more?

**Past versus Future: Predictive Value**

# CHAPTER 3

## AMERICAN VALUES AND THE AMERICAN CONSTITUTIONAL SYSTEM: The Basic Controversies

**Constitution as Creed**

I use the term "values" to refer to explicit and conscious statements of fundamental principles. I shall confine this discussion to those principles so highly cherished in this nation that they have been elevated to constitutional status. Constitutions generally do reflect the fundamental values of any nation. But in the secular United States our national Constitution is not only the "supreme law of the land"; it is the closest thing we have to a national creed. In the United States few writings other than the Constitution pretend to encompass the national philosophy. And even those that do, such as the Declaration of Independence and the Gettysburg Address, cannot claim legal status. It is for these reasons that we must pay such close attention to the Constitution. Other societies have extralegal writings that are the sacrosanct source of their overall goals and values. Communist societies, for example, have the *Communist Manifesto,* Lenin's *State and Revolution, The Thoughts of Chairman Mao,* and other neo-Marxist writings. Mohammedan societies have the Koran. Papal encyclicals in Catholic nations may also have extremely important quasi-legal effects and certainly reflect values. But in the United States we have only the briefly stated fundamentals in the Constitution.

Our national Constitution grew from the minds and pens of a few dozen statesmen who met in Philadelphia in 1787 after six years of frustration and confusion under a compact called the Articles of Confederation. The Articles had not provided a sufficiently powerful national government to allow for the successful conduct of either the Revolutionary War or the postrevolutionary peace. The Philadelphia group, our Founding Fathers, therefore took it upon themselves to construct a new document, which was finally ratified, after much debate, by conventions in nine of the thirteen existing states. The story of the background of these men, of the debates, and of the compromises reached has been well explored in American historical literature. I shall not reiterate this history. As the document was finally accepted and as it is now amended and interpreted, the Constitution is, of course, the product of the necessities and dreams of each succeeding generation. Our state constitutions, which I shall discuss later in this chapter, also have long and varied histories.

Moreover, our Constitution must be understood as a central component in what many political scientists like to describe as a "feedback system." It is, on the one hand, a major factor among the imputs of the system, since it is a major symbol in the socialization of our citizenry as well as a formal statement of the rules of the game. It tells us what our values should be and how they must be achieved. On the other hand, the Constitution as it evolves is an output of the political system. When we change a constitution's value, as we often do, we are shifting an important resource. The Constitution thus influences our attitudes and ultimately our actual behavior.

Continuous reinterpretation of this document by our courts and government officers over subsequent generations has resulted, however, in what often appear to be mutually contradictory sets of principles. Although it is common to speak of America's "shared values," "common goals," and "consensus on basic principles," in truth there are fewer common values and goals than we often take for granted, and very little consensus is revealed by a contemporary review of the Constitution. One man's meat seems clearly to be another man's poison. The roots of our controversies over very basic values go deep because they *are* embedded in our national Constitution and are recapitulated in our state constitutions.

This notion of conflict among the very principles of our political system is crucial. Too great tension between any contradictory principles, or between a principle and reality, may produce great danger of national disintegration—a sort of societal schizophrenia. And since these value conflicts permeate all of the political institutions with which we shall be dealing, they inevitably contribute to the weakness and the ultimate stalemate with which I suggest we must do battle. In sum, our values are often so confused that they virtually mandate ineffective procedures.

**Principle versus Reality: Societal Schizophrenia**

The century and a half of what has been satisfactory "muddling through" is perhaps today a historical anachronism. While we should not forsake political machinery that has demonstrated value, or attempt the impossible and inappropriate task of resolving *all* conflicts, we might wish to resolve *certain* conflicts so as to allow our political machinery to operate more successfully in a high-speed society. Just as an uncertain, hesitant, slow driver is a hazard on a modern expressway, so too an overly uncertain, hesitant, gear-shifting polity may be a hazard in an increasingly swift-paced society.

At a minimum, our basic national values should be part of a heightened consciousness. All too often, fundamental beliefs remain undefined and unargued. Yet clear definition and study are always needed. It is toward this end that I have ventured to classify our constitutional values into two distinct categories, and to suggest a method for value reconciliation where it appears needed. Each category contains two or more pairs of contradictory or at least conflicting principles. The first category contains the conflicts that I believe require some degree of resolution through explicitly assigning priority status to one competing value or another. Without some rational ranking device, Americans will delude themselves into believing that they can achieve mutually contradictory benefits, and this delusion will ultimately permeate our political operations. This is, of course, a snare. And it is a particularly destructive snare since it critically impairs problem-solving in some of the most crucial clinches by creating sterile and repetitious deadlocks. These particular stalemates appear to me to be susceptible of resolution through the application of logic and evidence. It is thus unnecessary to "muddle through" in these few instances. This first category includes: (1) *vox populi* versus *vox nobili* (majority rule versus elitism); (2) liberty versus security; (3) liberty versus equality; (4) individualism versus class and caste; (5) proceduralism versus vigilantism.

My second category, to be discussed in Chapter 4, consists of conflicts that I am willing to see remain unresolved. Here priorities seem dependent on specific situations rather than broad sweeps of evidence or logic. These are the conflicts I call creative controversies. Ambivalence here may be inconvenient, but it is unlikely to be fatal. This is a class of conflict that seems fraught with ambiguity and therefore to require continued experimentation. This category includes: (1) flexibility versus stability; (2) pluralism versus centralism; (3) limited versus unlimited government.

The major purpose of this exercise is not so much to urge agreement with the specific propositions as to urge the reader to recognize that there *are* conflicts involved. We cannot have the world with a fence around it. Decisions of one sort or another must be made. Indeed, indecision is itself a decision. In essence I am arguing for a certain style of thinking rather than for the substance of any particular opinion.

**CONFLICTS IN NEED OF PRIORITY RESOLUTION**

My intention here is to present the constitutional evidence that supports each of five pairs of contradictory principles. In each case I believe we might be better off if we were to try to resolve the controversy by defining each principle rather closely and then assigning it, or certain portions of it, a rank order. That is, some parts of some principles will be urged as having priority over others. In any event, the materials presented should at least clarify the matter even if they do not convince.

I conclude, for example, that majority rule should be given undiluted preference over minority rule (which usually masquerades under the term "minority rights"). Similarly, I argue that liberty should be given ascendance over security when they cannot be reconciled, as so often happens. Individualism, similarly, is seen as having priority over class and caste. And proceduralism (or the rule of law) must have clear ascendance over any appeal to violence. Among the distinguishing characteristics of these controversies is the fact that failure to grant priority status to the particular principles in question will, in my judgment, leave our society indistinguishable from tyrannies and autocracies. And although arguments in favor of autocracy and tyranny clearly exist, they appear to me totally unconvincing. I think that these are the areas where the evidence is sufficiently in and the logic sufficiently persuasive.

The logical thread that runs through my priority ranking here is this: There is no existing proof for the ultimate rightness, wisdom, or superiority of any value. Clearly they must be left open to change. Not even our foremost scientists and scholars claim total knowledge. They do not claim undying certainty for even their own "scientific" principles. Indeed, the truths of one era often become the falsehoods of the next. We therefore must choose a system of governance that most closely accommodates itself to this ubiquitous uncertainty and the consequent need for change. This must surely mean, at a minimum, a government that never stops or stifles debate about change. There is no *a priori* way of knowing which side of a debate is right; but since governments require a practical operational method for getting things done, we must have a decision mechanism that allocates choice as equally as possible. The majority principle best approaches that necessary equality of opinion in the decision-making apparatus. However one views the argument, it is important to understand our constitutional treatment of majority versus minority rule.

**VOX POPULI VERSUS VOX NOBILI**

Whatever else it may connote, the idea of democracy, to which Americans generally claim total commitment, conjures up an image of the "voice of the people." It comes as a shock to most citizens to learn that the voice of the people is hardly a firm commitment of the United States Constitution. Indeed, the Constitution provides far more protection for a quite contrary principle, the voice of the elite. The Constitution hardly foresaw "the people" as a controlling factor in the American polity.

In the *Federalist* papers, for example, Hamilton, Madison,

and Jay are at great pains to explain how this constitution, with its elaborate mechanism for checks and balances, separation of powers, and division of power between state and nation, forestalls any possible "tyranny of the majority" or "majoritarian faction."[1] It was through such arguments that they expected to (and indeed did) persuade the electorate of that era to accept the Constitution. One of the methods for attenuating the possible ill effects of the voice of the people was the use of a two-house legislature. In itself the guarantee of two senators from each state, regardless of population, serving in a legislature where both houses have virtually equal power, is blatantly antimajoritarian. Moreover, the Senate in its original conception was to be elected indirectly by state legislators, thus removing it still further from any contamination by the grass roots.

Tying presidential elections to the electoral college system extended the same inequity into another arena. Electoral college votes are still allocated to states on the basis of their total congressional representation. Electors from small states thus have greater influence than electors from large states.

**Elitist Suffrage**

As for the suffrage itself, the Constitution explicitly leaves this matter to the laws of each state. This provision originally augured a very restricted, elitist suffrage. Although by now suffrage restrictions have been greatly eased, almost to the point of universal adult suffrage, this has come about only after long and costly delays. And cumbersome state registration requirements still impose many restraints on the voter.

The Constitution also requires a two-thirds vote in the legislature to override a presidential veto and to propose a constitutional amendment. And since the Constitution permits each house to adopt its own procedural rules, there are other occasions when a two-thirds vote is mandatory. Whenever a two-thirds vote is required, majority rule is subverted. Journalistic practice dubs these two-thirds votes "substantial majorities," but the phrase is a piece of subterfuge. Majority means one more than half, and anything that requires a larger vote simply insures minority rule. In essence, a requirement that two-thirds of the Senate concur in anything puts control in the hands of *one-third* plus one of that body. That is clearly not the voice of the people.

Any countervailing pull toward the principle of majoritarianism, on the other hand, finds far fainter echo in our Constitution. Universal suffrage awaited constitutional amendments that came after some seventy years, and the amendments in turn had to await judicial review before race, religion, previous condition of servitude, and sex were actually enjoined as grounds for denying people the vote. Full enfranchisement, indeed, is still being worked out through two voting rights acts passed as recently as 1965 and 1968.

Majority rule, quite naturally, is also a product of the way the votes are counted. Here too the Constitution was silent, and the moves toward "one man, one vote" did not even start until 1962. It was at that late date that the U.S. Supreme Court agreed to adjudicate a case involving malapportionment in a state legislature.[2] Today both state and federal apportionment systems are subject to judicial scrutiny, and equal protection must at least be approached, if not fully realized. Here too we are moving slowly toward majority rule, more or less in spite of the Constitution rather than because of it.

There is also an assault currently being mounted against the electoral college. If the movement is successful, this antimajoritarian device will be supplanted by one or another method of direct popular election.

But even with all these inroads against elitism, genuine and unqualified majority rule is unlikely to result. There is one unamendable obstacle, the United States Senate, whose membership cannot be changed by our regular amendment procedures since the Constitution specifies that the state in question would have to acquiesce before any change could be made in senatorial allotment. And there is another, far more profound obstacle to genuine majoritarianism: the mood of the people themselves. All too few are enthusiastic about popular rule. Among opinion leaders in particular there is continuing evidence of distrust of the people. The major works of innumerable political scientists disclose either an explicit or an implicit elitist bias. Robert Dahl, for example, is quite clear about how he feels: the system gets on *in spite* of the man in the street, not because of him.[3] Most voting studies are at pains to present the public as inconsistent, illogical, and uninformed. The popular press and the rest of the media have a generally disdainful attitude, and college students as a whole are extraordinarily fearful of "the people." Herbert Gans, to take just one example, wrote an influential *New York Times* article whose title contained its message: "We Won't Solve Our Urban Problems Until We End Majority Rule."[4] It received widespread and favorable comment. This attitude against majoritarian democracy exerts a powerful influence on all our political institutions.

Until there is a ground swell of opinion in favor of "the man in the street," we are likely to see elitism triumph over populism at every turn. It's odd, but it surely appears that most of the people do not trust most of the people. The principle of majority rule should be given clear priority in our system as the guiding commitment of Americans. This does not mean there is never room for decision-making by a single individual

**Obstacles to Majority Rule**

—the President, a judge, an engineer. It only means that when there is great doubt on broad value-laden policy matters, when the most *legitimate* apparatus for decision-making is needed, there is persuasive logic in turning to the voice of the people. Naturally, this implies the use of intelligent methods for making that voice clear and meaningful. The logic here was outlined earlier and some further thoughts will be reserved for the final chapter. In brief, it seems rational to count each preference equally when none can prove certain or superior. We should be at pains to distinguish those situations in which genuinely scientific findings are available as a basis for decision from those situations in which uncertainty has been absorbed and the people have merely become habituated to abandoning their birthright for a mess of pseudoscientific pretense.

**LIBERTY VERSUS SECURITY**

There are two important tensions that involve liberty: the controversy over liberty versus security and that between liberty and equality. The ambivalence we suffer over our need for security as against our quest for freedom was verified by a 1970 CBS poll that showed that 76 percent of a sample of 1,100 adults believed that even in the absence of any clear and immediate danger of violence, not all groups should be allowed to organize protests against the government. Forty-five percent felt that newspapers and other media should not enjoy an absolute right to publish stories that "would be harmful to the national interest," even in peacetime. Sixty percent believed that protection against double jeopardy need not be extended to an acquitted defendant if later incriminating evidence were to turn up.[5] Data of this sort make it clear that Americans are not totally committed to freedom; nor is the American Constitution. We can trace the ascendance and diminution of each of these contradictory themes by reviewing the Supreme Court's none too consistent interpretation over the years. Once again the Constitution and its judicial interpretation provide a basis for claiming community security as well as individual liberty as our fundamental value.

In general, the Constitution protects individual liberty through three types of clauses: (a) those specifying freedom of thought, speech, and movement; (b) those bestowing specific safeguards and privileges upon an accused person; and (c) those that guarantee privacy. But the protection of liberty is balanced—perhaps outweighed—by the commitment to security.

**The Protection of Individual Thought, Movement, and Dissent**

The guarantee of freedom of speech, press, and assembly is rooted in some of the clearest and strongest language in the Constitution. The First Amendment states unequivocally that "Congress shall make no law respecting an establishment of religion, or prohibiting the free exercise thereof; or abridging the freedom of speech, or of the press; or of the right of the people peaceably to assemble, and to petition the government for the redress of grievances."

Yet the preferred position implicit in this language and implicit in the logic I have presented earlier has never been the law of the land. Supreme Court decisions have threaded an uneven course around this language; and popular opinion, as nearly as can be judged from public opinion polls, has also wavered. Even those citizens willing to express a belief in the principle of free speech may show withdrawal symptoms when faced with specific cases involving, let us say, a Communist's right to harangue a crowd.[6] An absolute priority status for freedom to present and debate ideas has not yet been established.

Over the years the Supreme Court has alternately enlarged and circumscribed the scope of the First Amendment's protection. In 1925, for example, the Court held that "for present purposes we may and do assume that freedom of fundamental personal rights and liberties are protected by the due process clause of the Fourteenth Amendment from impairment by the states."[7] Thus the prohibition against *congressional* invasion of free speech, press, and assembly was here interpreted as embracing a restraint against *state* legislative curtailment as well. This interpretation was clearly an enhancement of liberty. In the 1940s the Supreme Court further enlarged the scope of this freedom by extending the meaning of free speech to encompass picketing,[8] and later motion pictures.[9] More recently the Court has acted vigorously to protect the rights of students to refrain from "pledging allegiance"[10] and the right to wear armbands and political buttons.[11]

Circumscription of this freedom, on the other hand, has come through another series of judicial interpretations, which have supported congressional or state laws that clearly abridge fundamental freedoms. For example, in 1918 (a war year) Congress passed a law that made it a crime to print, write, or publish disloyal or abusive language about the government of the United States. This action, when challenged, was upheld by the Supreme Court on the ground that there is a reasonable limit to freedom of speech, and that this limit (called the "clear and present danger" doctrine) is passed when words spoken or written can be considered of "such a nature as to create a clear and present danger that they will bring about substantive evils that Congress has a right to prevent."[12] In 1940 a peacetime Congress passed the Smith Act, which makes it a crime to advocate the overthrow of the government by force or to organize or help any group having such a purpose. This law was upheld by the Supreme Court on the grounds

**The First Amendment's Scope**

that the "gravity" of a possible occurrence could counterbalance its improbability.[13] In other words, the loose "clear and present danger" was now attenuated to an even looser "grave and possible danger," on the grounds of the special nature of the communist threat to our government. In 1957, however, the Court had second thoughts and modified this formula by noting that speech could be viewed as warranting conviction under the Smith Act only if such speech advocated direct and immediate *action* toward overthrowing our government, not merely revolutionary beliefs.[14]

Thus it is clear that some verbal assaults against our political system have been and continue to be permitted. When they are curtailed it is usually to promote the presumed national interest, or in some way to reconcile one form of individual freedom with another. For example, there is a delicate balance between a publisher's freedom to report a happening and a defendant's right to have a fair trial, since free and thus possibly irresponsible reportage can often prejudice jurors. Moreover, free reportage may also jeopardize the "national interest." This dilemma was rehearsed in the matter of the Pentagon Papers.[15] The *New York Times* and the *Washington Post* published excerpts from a classified Pentagon study on the way we became involved in Vietnam and the development of our various policies there. The government obtained a temporary injunction against further publication essentially on the grounds that this would injure "national interest." Shortly thereafter the U.S. Supreme Court ruled on the propriety of this action. The questions involved here were sufficiently knotty that there were five different opinions concurring with the majority position (in favor of permitting publication), and the dissenters also followed three different lines of reasoning. While the decision was a small specific victory for a free press, it was hardly an unequivocal promotion of this value into the special preferred status advocated here. It is still a game of ploy and counterploy. The deciding factor in this case was the failure of the government to prove that national security was truly involved. Nobody suggested that freedom of the press might stand above national security, or that freedom could in itself never jeopardize a proper understanding of national security.

The many decisions of the Supreme Court on questions of national, state, and local book and movie censorship reveal a similarly ambivalent position. The Court has, on the one hand, upheld freedom for particular publications or movies in a preponderance of the individual cases in which local censorship laws have been tested. Thus many controversial books and movies have been spared the censors' blacklists by the Court's generous and worldly interpretation of the meaning

**Reportage and the "National Interest"**

of such statutory words as "sacrilegious," "prurient," and "obscene,"[16] and also by a vigorous judicial assault on any statutes that were vague, improperly executed, or insufficiently supplied with procedural directions.[17]

But the Court has again fallen short of the ideal of individual liberty as a superordinate value in its failure to meet the censorship problem in *principle*. As recently as 1967 the Court again upheld in principle the right of a state to censor obscene publications and movies,[18] and in 1970 it upheld the right of a federal agency to deny mailing privileges to publishers of obscene materials.[19] The right to censor continues little diminished. The principle has never been revoked. Chief Justice Burger has stated his belief that the First Amendment grants state officials broad discretion to suppress obscene materials.[20]

National safeguards seem more stringent than state. An administrative censorship scheme created by the Postal Reorganization Act allowing the Postmaster General, after administrative hearings, to determine whether mailed matter is or is not obscene on mere showing of probable cause was held to violate the First Amendment since it lacked adequate judicial safeguards.[21]

Court decisions upholding any work against the restriction of a state law have not mitigated the serious problem involved in a large number of censorship episodes that never become court cases. I am alluding here to the fact that most state and local censorship goes unchallenged.

Perhaps an illustration will dramatize the insidiousness of this state of affairs. In the 1940s I was doing some licensing research that took me to Providence, Rhode Island. There I learned that control of licensing for motion picture theaters was in the hands of two elderly policemen whose chief concern was that the films shown in Providence should be in the "best interests" of the citizenry. Although this is not a small town, it had at that time only one central movie house, and every Friday those two policemen assiduously previewed the film that the theater owner intended to show the following week. They and they alone were the arbiters of the best interests of Providence. While the motivation of the two censors was above attack, their taste, intelligence, and educational attainment were highly individualistic. Their notions of appropriate film fare never departed from the least-common-denominator musical comedy of that era. Moreover, their particular tastes dominated more than the moral content of those offerings. They also concerned themselves with matters of high foreign policy, like the Neutrality Act of 1940. Thus the people of Providence, right up to our declaration of war against Japan and Germany in December 1941, were spared the inappropriate shock of German atrocities. Now whether this careful insulation was in anybody's best interests is, at the very least, a debatable proposition. Most damaging of all, however, was the fact that this situation obtained without the slightest degree of controversy. In fact, almost nobody in Providence was aware of the censorship. Everybody went to the one available movie house when in the mood for movies, and saw what was shown without knowledge of its rather special selection. The owner, who *did* know what was going on, chose to follow the path of least resistance. He was in business for profit, not principle. He could fill the house no matter what film he showed. Why look for trouble? I submit, however, that real trouble was bred by the shallow, biased, repetitious, and un-challenged materials that monopolized the silver screen in Providence.

If this were an isolated, freakish episode, I would not bother to tell it. Unfortunately, this is the usual state of the movies—and sometimes the libraries—of most of America. There are few New York Cities. In such cultural capitals, censorship invariably arouses thorough debate. Every attempted movie or book ban in *these* cities ensures thousands of additional sales for the material in question. A court case is almost certain to follow. Thus, at a minimum, the issue is in the public domain.

**The Illusion of Freedom**

But for most of America there is only a dangerous *illusion* of freedom. The people in all too many towns do not miss what they do not know. A firm and clear precedent has not yet been set here. And that is what is needed.

A great part of religious freedom, also a bulwark of liberty, is also actually protected under the same provisions made for speech, press, and assemblage. But this matter of individual conscience was so important to the men who drafted the Bill of Rights (the first ten amendments to the Constitution) that it was given first place in that statement. Thus the practices of religious worship that might transcend mere speech and assemblage (display of symbols and so on) are given explicit protection. Freedom of worship and religious advocacy has generally had the Court's full support. But even here there is equivocation. A very limited number of exotic practices deemed inimical to the public health and morals (snake cult rituals, religious refusals of medical care, polygamy) have been enjoined by the Court. Otherwise it has conscientiously upheld most individuals and groups in their varied religious pursuits. Even the refusal, on religious grounds, of schoolchildren to salute the United States flag in time of war has been upheld.[22]

Further expansion of the rights of individual conscience and free expression are also now appearing in those decisions that have upheld conscientious objectors' refusals to participate in war, first under the guise of religious freedom[23] and more recently under the guise of freedom of conscience.[24] It is no longer necessary to support one's individual belief system by a belief in a conventional God, much less of a particular church, in order to claim the status of conscientious objector.[25] But there are still chinks in the armor.

As I pointed out earlier, there is little doubt in my mind that there is an inherent logic in resolving this entire area of conflict unequivocally in favor of liberty of speech, thought, and dissent. Not only are there no intrinsically valid methods of arriving at supposedly reasonable cutoff points; there is a long catalog of historical evidence to document the fact that the curtailment of these fundamental individual liberties have always proved ultimately more dangerous to the security of the nation than have the supposed threats entailed in the cultivation of freedom. The failure of the Court to oppose censorship in *principle* puts it in the curious and undignified position of giving its explicit imprimatur to a long series of patently prurient publications. At the same time, this ambivalence over principle permits local jurisdictions the freedom to enjoin (at least for a while) works of such authors as Mark Twain, Ernest Hemingway, and William Shakespeare. The list of occasional bannings also includes textbooks of various kinds, pamphlets of the NAACP, *The Nation* magazine, and in some localities anything at all that appears to have been banned by the Catholic Legion of Decency. And that is a very long list indeed. Thus the record surely contains enough evidence to convince any rational man that the heresy of one time and place is the dogma of another.

Moreover, failure to grant free expression *absolute* protection puts the Court in the equally untenable position of prophesying. Where change is inevitable, security must be somewhat tenuous and the ultimate nature or value of any change unpredictable. The best we can do in such potentially dangerous situations is to keep the marketplace of ideas as open as possible. Surely this calls for a priority commitment to free speech. Perhaps I can let the matter rest with Milton's eloquent plea from the *Areopagitica:* "Give me liberty to know, to utter, and to argue freely according to conscience, above all liberties."

Nowhere is the high value placed on individual liberty more clearly pronounced than in the constitutional privileges extended to persons accused of crimes. Guarantees (within the national jurisdiction) include the following safeguards: grand jury indictments, speedy and public trials, prompt information as to the accusations, defense counsel, and procedures to compel witnesses on behalf of defendants. There are also explicit prohibitions against self-incrimination, coerced confessions,

**Clauses
Bestowing
Specific
Privileges
and Safeguards**

being tried twice for the same crime, excessive bail, ex post facto laws, bills of attainder, and cruel and unusual punishments. The writ of habeas corpus, protecting a person from detention without a formal public explanation, is also explicitly guaranteed by the Constitution. Most of these constitutional safeguards for accused persons referred originally only to actions by the *national* government. There has been, however, a steady judicial trend toward reading many of these items into the due-process clause of the Fourteenth Amendment, which pertains to state actions. Thus the right to defense counsel and the prohibition against unreasonable searches and seizures and against forced confessions (all of them specifically mentioned in the first eight amendments and all of them clearly within the Fifth Amendment's ideal of "due process of law") have already been extended, by interpretation, into the realm of state government.[26] There is also a general predisposition on the part of the Supreme Court to scrutinize state judicial proceedings that are brought to its attention in light of a general standard of fair play, which is inherent in the Fifth Amendment's due-process clause.[27] Thus, although the Constitution shies away from explicitly *requiring* the states to uphold every one of the specific commitments outlined in the first eight amendments, nonetheless an overall protection against state action does prevail.

**Law versus Order**

Today, however, some inroads, as yet constitutionally unchallenged, are being made against these bastions of individual right. The national crime-control law and recent state crime-control statutes—all enacted within the rhetoric of national and community security and under the misleading banner of "law and order"—contain many questionable provisions concerning the right to bail, preventive detention, and police entry without the usual safeguards. The proponents of these statutes are quick to point out that in this era we are not dealing merely with individuals accused of crimes, but often with syndicates and mobs. They therefore ask for special privileges to fight fire with fire. The outcome here is not yet known. But clearly where law is irreconcilably pitted against order, the law should take precedence in virtually every circumstance. Order can be achieved in concentration camps.

The argument for insisting on the primacy of safeguards for individuals who stand accused of crime is eloquently put by former Attorney General Ramsey Clark. He asks no quarter for security where liberty is at stake. Indeed, he says: "You *cannot purchase security at the price of freedom,* because freedom is essential to human dignity and crime flows from acts that demean the individual. We can enlarge both liberty and safety if we turn from repressiveness, recognize the causes of crime and move constructively."[28] Here too resolution of our ambivalence seems consistent with both logic and evidence.

Liberty is, finally, also protected by those sections of the Bill of Rights that guarantee us against the arbitrary intrusion of the state upon our personal privacy. This individual privacy is guaranteed in Amendment 3 ("No soldier shall, in time of peace be quartered in any house, without the consent of the owner . . ."), Amendment 4 ("The right of the people to be secure in their persons, houses, papers, and effects, against unreasonable searches and seizures, shall not be violated . . ."),[29] and Amendment 9 ("The enumeration in the Constitution, of certain rights, shall not be construed to deny or disparage others retained by the people"). But despite these clauses, any actual right to privacy has received specific judicial notice only in a few very recent cases. One case involved a Connecticut law that banned contraceptives. The decision held, among other things, that this law was a violation of our "right to privacy."[30] Privacy was also given judicial notice in a case concerning the publication of an account of a family held terrorized by gunmen. The family felt its privacy had been invaded, and the courts so held.[31]

Protection of Privacy in the Constitution

And, of course, the right to privacy is often cited in cases involving eavesdropping. Congress, particularly in the person of Senator Sam Ervin of North Carolina, is using its constitutionally derived investigative powers to scrutinize the computer mystique and what many believe to be the unprecedented and dangerous mass surveillance and dossier techniques of the Justice Department, the FBI, the CIA, the Customs Bureau, the Department of Health, Education, and Welfare, the Internal Revenue Service, and the U.S. Army.

While the right to privacy certainly underlines the high premium put here on liberty, it also illustrates again the cleavages that exist between individual rights and national security, as well as between one individual's rights and another's.[32] We cannot afford ambivalence in this matter of liberty versus security. This is not a matter for compromise. Liberty must take unequivocal precedence, since it is in truth not in opposition to security, but rather the only firm basis *for* security.

One of the most dramatic strains on the American community is the unresolved tension between liberty and equality. Both liberty and equality hold positions as moral absolutes in the hearts of typical Americans. Few citizens would admit a preference between the two—at least not in their general open rhetoric. Our citizens seem deeply and simultaneously attached to both ideas. They want, in the words of C. Herman Pritchett,

LIBERTY VERSUS EQUALITY

protection for the "right to be different" (liberty) and protection for the "right to be the same" (equality).

Nevertheless, the staunch affirmation in the Declaration of Independence that "all men are created equal" has found only faint and relatively recent echo in the world of white men's actions and even in the U.S. Constitution itself. The principle of equality has been constrained not only by contradictions between it and the principle of liberty, or by the shifting interpretations of the courts, but also by the ambivalence many Americans feel toward equality itself. This ambivalence is intensified by the breadth of the gap that separates myth from reality, by the countervailing pull of the Protestant ethic, and by the actual ambiguities in the myth of equality itself.

Clearly equality is a myth widely separated from reality, and this is a situation that inevitably breeds extreme behavior: violence on the one hand and apathy on the other. History is replete with such examples. Over a century ago Alexis de Tocqueville pointed out that if the American nation ever foundered, it would be over the matter of slavery, a condition that so blatantly flew in the face of our egalitarian values that in 1835 he was able to predict: "If America undergoes great revolutions, they will be brought about by the presence of the black race on the soil of the United States; that is to say, they will owe their origin not to the equality but to the inequality of conditions."[33] Abraham Lincoln also alluded to the dangers of a nation "half slave and half free." We did indeed fight a civil war over it, and yet the gap between myth and reality persisted so dramatically that Gunnar Myrdal, the famous Swedish economist, had to remind us in 1930 that this "American dilemma," as he called it, might again tear us apart. The more recent riots and the sulky alienation of the 1960s bear witness to the extensive gap between the equality myth and our reality, and to its potential dangers.

As a principle, equality is also challenged by the deep pull of our so-called Protestant ethic, which stresses individual achievement and unrestrained economic exchange. This ethic is based on a fundamental conviction that one's lot on earth is predestined and ordained by God. (At least this is the Calvinist Puritan tradition.) This causes considerable moral strain; for if godliness can be best demonstrated by thrift, sobriety, and productive enterprise, then the poor are not merely unfortunate, they are immoral. It makes it seem that *inequality* is the very stuff of the kingdom of heaven.

Tensions are further exacerbated by the ambiguity that accompanies the ideal of equality. The Constitutional phrase "equal protection of the laws" might well be construed, and indeed is construed on occasion, to mean differential and thus unequal treatment for unequal classes of people. Children, for instance, are given special treatment in our courts of law. But should inherent inequalities of age, birth, strength, and so on, go unrecognized by law and policy?

Equality is, of course, explicitly belied and strained by the opposing stress of liberty, which, as Daniel Patrick Moynihan reminds us, ensures inequality.[34] Few patriots stop to consider the easily demonstrated proposition that genuine and full liberty breeds inequality by leaving people unrestrained to develop themselves, to express themselves, and to choose among alternative educations, careers, and consumer goods. Thus liberty brings quantitatively and qualitatively different life styles, which in turn reinforce the inequalities of succeeding generations. If, on the other hand, we wished to achieve substantial equality of individual achievement, expression, and life style, we could do so only through the imposition of many restraints, the elimination of choice, and the confiscation of various forms of property. For example, we curtail the freedom of parents to arrange for the education of their offspring in order to assure some degree of equality in that education. State prescriptions about the number of years required, the accreditation of schools, their curricula, and so forth are clearly infringements of liberty in the name of equality. Or consider the Hobson's choice between a biology professor's freedom to present what he believes is evidence of innate racial differences in intelligence and the quite obvious damage this sort of teaching inflicts in the battle for social equality.

What should we do about all these dilemmas? Perhaps we should begin by more carefully dividing the scope and meaning of equality into separate components, each of which might be treated differently. That part of equality which concerns itself with equality under the law, equality of voting privileges, and equality of initial opportunities—political equality, in short—I contend should be placed above any countervailing pulls and should be unequivocally a reality.

The part of the equality myth that would require a total equalization of life styles, on the other hand, might well be discarded. There is evidence that this is a goal virtually impossible to achieve, and more than that, there is evidence that most people do not even want it. Robert Lane's study of working-class men, for example, discloses that these men, contrary to what many have guessed, have little taste for egalitarianism except in some very vague sense. Most pronounced among them is what Lane calls a "fear of equality."[35] The recent strikes of college professors and higher civil servants in Sweden, to take another illustration, make the same point. These are strikes, according to their social analysts, against the growing egalitarianism of Swedish society. It is, in the words of one such commentator, "a class struggle with academic and civil servants seeing the lower classes creeping up on them and not liking it at all." So it appears that at all levels of society there is a deep-seated and ineradicable resistance to total equality of life style. Furthermore, this type of equalization would surely fly in the face of free speech, press, and assembly, and, as I argued earlier, these freedoms must be granted a preferred position on the basis of both logic and evidence.

## Equality and the Constitution

Let us put aside my suggestions, however, and examine how we actually *have* dealt with equality. This can be illustrated by the history of constitutional treatment. In essence, equality rests on those constitutional clauses protecting essential human dignity, those conferring political equality, and those that move toward establishing social and economic equality.

## The Established Basis of Human Dignity

Certainly a belief in the inherent dignity of man is a main support of the ideal of equality; yet it was not fully recognized by our original Constitution, and it is still in need of amplification. The post–Civil War Thirteenth Amendment states what is patently a bedrock necessity for the achievement of equality: "Neither slavery nor involuntary servitude, except as a punishment for crime whereof the party shall have been duly convicted, shall exist within the United States, or any place subject to their jurisdiction."

It is hard to believe that for so many years we were able to live as a nation without recognizing the inherent worth and dignity of every human being. Yet the constitutional allusions to slaves as well as Indians makes it more than clear that we did just that. Even now the record is not clean. There are, for example, treaties (which have a rather special relationship to the Constitution)[36] and special laws made pursuant to the Constitution which set up the various Indian reservations that are still home to close to a half-million Indians. By their very existence these instruments often denigrate the dignity of the continent's original inhabitants. More specifically, they often contain provisions that quite directly bear unfavorably on the status of Indians.

The remainder of the Constitution's affirmation of the basic equality of all Americans lies in the Fourteenth Amendment's grant of citizenship to "all persons born in the United States and subject to the jurisdiction thereof" and in the consequent rights and privileges guaranteed to all Americans by that amendment and its subsequent interpretations. Some of these interpretations have already been covered in our discussion of liberty. Others will be covered below. Neither political nor social nor economic egalitarianism automatically followed from these general pronouncements. Whatever equality we have did not arrive swiftly or spontaneously. Much more was needed in the way of judicial review. This is the history we shall now pursue.

An understanding of the political rights of disadvantaged groups in America has no more dramatic sequence than the story of the struggle of black Americans to gain the vote.

Black Americans not only had no vote during their period of bondage, but were counted as only three-fifths of a person.[37] (I mention this only to dramatize the degree to which the educated society of that era could absorb the idea of "non-persons.") Subsequently, when blacks were "freed," their commensurate suffrage rights were supposedly fixed by the Fourteenth and Fifteenth Amendments (1868 and 1870). Section 2 of the Fourteenth Amendment tried to enforce black enfranchisement by mandating Congress to decrease the legislative apportionment of any state that denied the vote in national contests to any citizen by the size of the group so denied. But Congress never did enact any such penalizing legislation. The Fifteenth Amendment, which directly prohibits denial of suffrage on the basis of "race, color, or previous condition of servitude," was likewise flouted. Here the story was one of "grandfather clauses," which were quite bald attempts at evading black enfranchisement by requiring literacy tests of those persons whose grandfathers had not voted. This meant that blacks alone were required to take literacy exams (designed, of course, to be impossible to pass). This form of discrimination was outlawed by the Supreme Court in 1915.[38] The battleground then shifted to "white primaries" in the states where victory in the primaries was tantamount to election. These devices slid along on the marvelously unexamined premise that political parties were private clubs and could thus control their own membership and voting without regard to constitutional sanctions. This notion was rejected by the Supreme Court in 1944.[39] Then came a long history of poll taxes. These were, in general, cumulative taxes that had to be paid before a citizen was entitled to vote. Political parties often paid for white citizens but never for blacks. This practice was finally wiped out by constitutional amendment in 1964, legislation in 1965, and judicial decision in 1966.[40]

The Voting Rights Act of 1965 has been the strongest effort to date to redress the imbalance of political privileges. This act requires the use of federal registers in any southern county where less than half the voting population has been registered. In such communities, the spurious literacy tests that were still administered were likewise suspended. As a result of that act, black registration in this region rose from 43.3 to 62 percent.[41] In 1970 this act was extended to 1975 and broadened to include in its provisions those states throughout the nation whose registration figures are suspect. Moreover, it suspends the use of literacy and character tests throughout the country. In this same year, moreover, the Supreme Court broadened the franchise for all groups, but particularly the poor, by holding that property ownership could not be used as a criterion for voting on bond issues.[42] New York and thirteen other states have had such laws. Inroads have also been made against repressive residency laws and unrealistic absentee ballot requirements.[43]

The voting privileges of ethnic minorities other than blacks (Chicanos, Puerto Ricans, Orientals, and Indians) should, of course, also be greatly enhanced by these acts. Indians, by the way, did not receive the blessings of citizenship through congressional statute until 1924. Whether on the reservation or off, however, their voting status is not yet fully ensured. As for the largest group of the politically deprived, women, they had to wait for a constitutional amendment in 1920 to remove sex barriers to voting. Today women are suppressed only by the subtle but nonetheless real erosion of their rights through community pressures, debased self-images, and intimidation. These same subtle factors, along with occasional gerrymandering,[44] also persist for the ethnic minorities. While the Court will undoubtedly deal with gerrymandering, only time will wash away the other effects and leave us, as we must be left, with *genuine political equality*.

**Social and Economic Equality: The Fourteenth Amendment**

If political equality comes hard, economic and social equality comes harder still, if it comes at all. The story here is still unfolding.

For a long time the principle of liberty embraced economic license and as such held priority over other competing principles. Indeed, for over half a century the Supreme Court interpreted the Fourteenth Amendment to the Constitution in precisely such terms. States were enjoined from passing minimum wage laws or maximum hour laws or laws governing conditions of work (all of which could have moved us toward some degree of economic equality) precisely on the grounds that this would be a deprivation of liberty or property without **Due Process of Law** due process of law.[45] Liberty and property merged in the judicial mind, and an amendment designed to bring both freedom and equality was destined for many years to bring neither. It was this idea of property freedom, for example, plus a somewhat strained notion of egalitarianism, that impaled two legislative attempts at imposing an income tax law. The Constitution originally forbade any direct taxation except in proportion to the census.[46] This simplistic notion of "equal" taxation, of course, completely overlooked principles of marginal utility, comparative sacrifice, and so on. Since the passage of the income tax amendment, however, taxation policies for the general welfare have gone further than any other government policy in attempting to mitigate income inequalities. Yet in a stricter sense, many of these laws deny both the liberty principle and the equality principle by trying to serve the interests of a more general principle of "common good."[47]

And the battle between countervailing views continues. Indeed, the mutually contradictory thrusts of freedom, equality, and security make for strange bedfellows. The extreme right and extreme left are often indistinguishable on certain policy matters. Full economic equality, as I pointed out earlier, cannot be attained without doing violence to certain areas of liberty. It would require not only the confiscation of property, but also the denial of many other personal liberties that lead to individual development at different rates and along different lines. So long as people are permitted "equality of opportunity" (a reasonably equal chance to become doctors, technicians, or gardeners, each by his own choice and at his own pace), to this degree subsequent inequalities—if not of income, certainly of life style and status—are fostered. It is at this juncture, therefore, that I believe equality must bow to liberty. We can, however, continue our own search for some sort of justice in our distribution of goods by rethinking and reordering our basic values. More of the ambiguities of this difficult terrain will be described below as we trace certain other constitutional clauses that have been used in pursuit of economic and social equality, and this matter will receive further attention in Chapter 10.

The Fourteenth Amendment also directly prohibits any state from denying "any person within its jurisdiction the equal protection of the laws." Until 1954, however, the Supreme Court accepted state actions and laws providing for public facilities that were separate but presumably equal. While such a doctrine could perhaps have been used to segregate any group in our society, in actual use it was confined to blacks (or at least to non-Caucasians). In 1954, however, the Supreme Court finally took the position that mandatory classification on the basis of race as a condition for receiving the benefits of a state's educational system was in itself a denial of equal protection of the laws.[48] Racial classification was viewed as patently inappropriate to the purposes of education, irrational in genesis, and psychologically damaging to the individuals involved. "Separate but equal" was no longer "equal."

In the ensuing years, both the courts and the educational bureaucracies moved all too slowly to enforce this new standard. At last various moves on the part of the executive

**Equal Protection of the Laws**

branch and further amplificatory decisions of the Court put some teeth into the original decision.[49] In 1971 the Supreme Court upheld the constitutionality of busing (which had been previously challenged) as an appropriate method of dismantling dual school systems in the South.[50] But in the remainder of the nation, where de facto segregation persisted in many areas, the situation was not entirely clear.

Invigoration of the equal protection clause, moreover, made it unnecessary to continue to rely solely on such spurious devices as the interstate commerce clause to redress racial grievances in the courts.[51] Previously, in education as well as in certain other areas of civil rights (public accommodations and employment, for example), interstate commerce[52] was the hinge for judicial findings in favor of equality.[53] By 1970 the Court was squarely using "equal protection of the laws" to ensure equality in public recreation, public accommodations, and public housing. But some of the greatest advances in this arena have stemmed from the Civil Rights Act of 1964, the Civil Rights Act of 1968, and their subsequent judicial interpretations.

Both acts were upheld as constitutional and provided the means to mount a sweeping assault against racial, ethnic, religious, sex, or age discrimination in public accommodations, recreational facilities, employment, and labor unions. The 1968 act provided special safeguards for civil rights workers and offered the first national "open-housing" law. Access to housing, even to single-family homes if they are offered for sale or rent by brokers, cannot legally be denied to any person on the basis of race or ethnicity or religion. In 1971 the equal protection clause was invoked to test the constitutionality of unequal municipal services such as garbage removal, sewage disposal, and the like.[54] It has also figured in cases testing the propriety of zoning ordinances that have the effect of enjoining the building of inexpensive housing.[55] There are new frontiers opening here almost daily. For instance, the use of job tests that appear systematically to screen out blacks (and, by implication, others) without realistically assessing their qualifications actually to do the work at hand has been challenged.[56] Even requiring a person to hold a high school diploma as a fixed condition of employment is, under certain circumstances, now prohibited as a denial of equal protection of the laws.[57] Finally, racial discrimination in the private sector controlling mortgage financing has come under investigation. Ways of reconciling equality and liberty in these arenas will be discussed at the close of this section.

**Privileges and Immunities**    One must also see the equality principle in a perspective broader than race and broader too than the "equal protection of the laws" clause. There might someday, for example, be a liberalized interpretation of our now narrowly construed "privileges and immunities" clause. This too is part of the Fourteenth Amendment and has so far been used solely as a barricade for a few quite rarefied "national" privileges, like one's rights on the high seas. Yet I foresee a day when this too may be a vehicle for fulfilling appropriate parts of the equality dream.

We must also broaden our perspective on social and economic equality to include many minorities other than blacks, Indians, and similarly vocal groups. There are, for example, many lesser known ethnic groups that suffer grievous injustices. Gypsies, to take one exotic example, are often the butt of patently discriminatory licensing legislation. And of course women are notoriously singled out for unequal treatment in so-called protective state legislation. Less well publicized is the victimization of "illegitimate" children, students, and minors in general. There are also the aged, homosexuals, aliens, military personnel, persons with arrest records, convicts and former convicts, patients in mental hospitals and persons who have previously received treatment in such hospitals, persons labeled mentally incompetent, and even persons who are unkempt or odd-looking. Most notably there are the poor. All of these persons in one way or another, in one place or another, are in danger of being deprived of fundamental equality and liberty in their social and economic lives. They have unequal opportunities for marriage, sex relations, education, recreation, housing, employment, welfare, union membership; they receive unequal treatment in tests used for qualification for these activities, and they have unequal access to legal services. In regard to all of these privileges or resources, one or another of these groups is in some way disadvantaged.[58] We have a long way to go before equality is reached, and we require a clearer beacon than we now have if we are to get there.

As the Congress and the Court have moved fitfully along the road to equality, they have often, as I have already pointed out, had to confront what some citizens felt were their basic liberties. Thus the classic dispute over liberty versus equality. Interference in selling a home and in choosing one's neighbors and schools seems to many persons an unjustified invasion of basic rights. Properly understood and employed, however, equal protection of the laws does not of necessity have to erode any genuine areas of liberty. What is enjoined by our Constitution and our antidiscrimination laws (and properly so) is simply *irrational prejudice*. Indeed, one might say that true discrimination and thus true liberty have been permitted for the first time in matters such as the choice of neighbors, em-

**The Unpublicized Minorities**

ployees, and schools. That is, as people are released from the enslavement of ignorance, fear, and superstition, their liberties are actually enhanced. They are truly free to *choose*. In fact, it would serve the interests of clear thinking if these laws were called, as they properly should be, antiprejudice laws. That is, discrimination is sound and healthful. It is prejudice (the inability to discriminate) that is unsound and unconstitutional.

It must also be made clear that all the situations in which equality under the laws is properly invoked involve direct or indirect use of *public funds* and/or *public sanctions*. Private choice still operates.

In sum, it is only when flagrant inappropriateness marks the criterion of choice that certain practices are enjoined. This is the only justification for infringing on liberty. The tensions between liberty and equality can therefore best be managed by a very careful definition of what is actually meant by each principle, and by a willingness to grant a preferred superordinate position to the *free expression of ideas* and to the natural development of human differences. In those areas where the liberty involved is patently spurious, however, or where the equality sought is a basic political and human equality, then equality must be given preference.

**INDIVIDUAL-ISM AND ACHIEVE-MENT VERSUS GROUPISM AND ASCRIPTION**

Closely related to the tension between liberty and equality is the pull between achievement and ascription. The United States is invariably viewed as the "achievement society" par excellence. And indeed, with its deeply entrenched Protestant ethic and its broad spectrum of safeguards for individual liberty, this appellation seems appropriate enough. Yet in recent years we have been giving not only lip service but constitutional service to a quite contradictory trend: a movement toward class and caste, toward a society in which status is ascribed rather than achieved. I believe that while both principles deserve some fulfillment, priority should be given individual achievement when the two cannot in good conscience coexist.

Historically, most societies conferred status by ascription, and even today there are many that bear some of the chief characteristics of this type. That is, there are societies in which individuals are born into clearly designated groups to which they may be bound for life. The groups may be based on kinship, economic class, occupation, or religion. In such societies the group is clearly dominant over the individual, whether in the Zulu kraal or the Punjabi village. While American society has its share of ethnic and class differentiation, it has historically tried to turn away from caste. It abolished slavery and embarked on the road to racial equality. Moreover, a strong current of individualism is discernible not only in our national oratory, but also in the general attitudes of most of our citizens. The individual in America has generally been regarded as a source of strength rather than as a potential political liability. Our frontier living conditions and our abundant natural resources might account for the fact that the individual has been traditionally viewed as the cornerstone of our social order. While we cannot claim to have completely woven the ideal of individualism into our constitutional fabric, we can point to many original clauses, early amendments, and recent interpretations that move in this general direction. We grant citizenship (in the Fourteenth Amendment) to "all persons born or naturalized in the United States, and subject to the jurisdiction thereof," and we grant to these citizens certain "privileges [and] immunities," though the meaning of this clause is not yet clear.

The other mention of privileges and immunities in the Constitution, in Article IV, has also had only limited interpretation. The article provides that a state must extend to citizens of other states the same "privileges" (concerning marriage, morals, taxation, and so on) as it bestows on its own citizens. This provision has less cogency than one might think, since every state has the right to establish its own rules of residency as a precondition for its many privileges. In this area of privileges and immunities, however, we may hope to see considerable expansion of constitutional meaning in the future.

**Privileges and Immunities**

But whatever citizenship may come to mean, it is clearly an individually held status. We do not have classes of citizens. Along with those basic civil liberties previously described as protections of the "right to be different," and with the safeguards provided for individual privacy and for persons accused of crimes, these clauses are commitments to individualism.

Quite recently, however, we have embarked on a very different tack. It is one that not only contradicts the principle of individual achievement, but ultimately, in my view, denies the principle of equality as well. We have begun to shore up class and caste through much of our well-meant and perhaps essential social welfare legislation. When you have laws, for example, that provide benefits contingent on "maximum feasible participation by the poor," you must inevitably designate, circumscribe, identify, and contain a group known as "poor." Indeed, the political privilege of voting in certain neighborhood elections for federal planning projects has been tied to precisely this criterion. You had to be poor to vote. When you build housing for "senior citizens," to take another example, you must give birth to such a group. If there are "welfare mothers," "dependent children," "black capitalists," we are staking out rather broad and often inescapable boundaries for large segments of our population. Moreover, many of the groups we thus designate are not ones that our society truly celebrates. In honesty, we are not a society that honors either age, poverty, race, or dependency as such. Quite the contrary. Why, then, promote these factors in our politics? The ills suffered by the aging or the poor might be as well handled on an individual or societal level. Social security and income maintenance system covering *all* persons do this. Short of this, our very efforts to wipe out psychological and other forms of inequality may turn out quite ironically to have the opposite effect of entrenching castelike enclaves that by their very existence denigrate both individualism and equality.

Our new reliance on quota systems, which have so far been upheld in our courts, are doing the same thing. A requirement that educational, business, and other institutions maintain any type of fixed quota based on race, sex, or ethnicity is not only an infringement on certain areas of reasonable liberty, but an assault against individualism and achievement. It is the promotion of an unhealthy caste system. One might, of course, argue that all law is based on classification, and these laws do no more than set up new classifications. There are classes of cities, classes of businesses, farm classifications, criminal classifications. But I honestly believe that it is no semantic strain to posit a very real difference between artificial groupings like cities, businesses, and lawbreakers, on the one hand, and social designations based on color, sex, wealth, and age on the other—the very criteria we have been at pains to establish as intrinsically *inappropriate* to work, learning, and other benefits.

**Promoting a Caste System**

Of course, some of the very guarantees that preserve our individualism also protect our penchant for groups. Freedom to publish, for example, can be a group protection as well as an individual one. Freedom of assembly is by definition a group protection. So too the right to be protected in one's membership in organizations.[59] Moreover, those parts of the First Amendment generally known as the doctrine of separation of church and state certainly represent the pull of groupism. Here we generally come up against the intramural struggle among Catholics, Protestants, Jews, atheists, and others. Indeed, a long line of decisions has resulted in the use of tax money for buses, textbooks, and other secular educational materials for students in parochial schools. Here too we have been promoting the cause of groupism.

The overall constitutional burden of legitimizing class and caste legislation, however, falls primarily on the broad powers reserved to the states by the Tenth Amendment. It is through the constitutions and subsequent laws of the individual states that we can and do heed the voices of our many countervailing groups. It is here that we find zoning laws, community development laws, and special education laws. Any one of these may be used as a vehicle to promote specious race and class interests. Americans should be more wary than they are now of the double edge of some of the so-called social gains made by promoting group interests over individual interests. Many a victory here is short-lived and phyrric. The campaign of black militants to promote school decentralization and community school control may work out well for a short time in Bedford-Stuyvesant, but in Scarsdale it makes for a quite different picture. If you try to forge a class- or castelike weapon by means of laws regulating zoning, community development, planning control, or whatever, there is great danger that in time it will be used against the very group for whose benefit it was originally designed.

In this very sticky situation people should grope toward a method of fostering groupism only when it is necessary to permit a catching-up period for any group that has been legally disadvantaged for a long time, and only in ways that permit the healthful development of purely cultural qualities among the various races and ethnic groups of our nation. The development of cultural qualities, in fact, not only enriches the entire country, but psychologically strengthens all people who live (out of both necessity and choice) in what must remain an essentially achievement-oriented society. It is advantageous to virtually everyone to accept the great gifts of cultural pluralism: the variety of foods, dances, clothing, ceremonies, holidays, and personality characteristics of many peoples. The notion that black is beautiful, Irish is beautiful, Greek is beautiful—this is the stuff of which a rich national life is made. It is also the stuff of which a rich personal life can be made. It is psychologically strengthening to know that one's Italianism, for example, is unearned, a beautiful gift of birth. No climbing up a greasy pole for that! Whatever drama and glamour derive from each ethnic pattern, it is an unearned increment for each individual member of the group. In all these ways the hyphenated American is the healthy American.

But there are other fundamentals that must be faced. We are not yet prepared—and perhaps we never should be—to award all the large and small benefits that make up a life style on a group basis rather than on an individual basis. Political rights, I believe, should be awarded individually. In this arena the battle of America has been fought. And now, just as victory is within sight, it would be ironic and foolish to turn away from it. Political rights on a group basis are the building blocks of totalitarianism. So too are group economic privileges. While

**The Use of Groupism**

it is true that individual achievement breeds social and economic inequality, its converse, group achievement, has bred the same, and with less justice and more violence. What we need here are laws and processes to temper inequality and constantly to adjust and make fair the starting rules of the race. Let me use education as an example. We have made it the coin of our realm, and no matter how we try, it remains a difficult coin to obtain. By its very nature it tends to exacerbate rather than mitigate individual differences. It invariably rewards the swift more than the slow. Its ultimate reward cannot and should not be allocated on a group basis. While we have tried to make the race more fair by properly enjoining racism and by exercising increased sensitivity toward those whose minds and bodies are disadvantaged at the outset, we will never turn the trick of making education anything other than a race won by individual achievement. We cannot, therefore, permit "higher" education in its traditional sense to remain the only basis on which the nation's rewards will be distributed. Perhaps the notion that a college education brings with it a bonus of $100,000 during a lifetime should be reexamined. Perhaps college should not be the only road to the good life. Perhaps we must find other tracks along which more people can achieve and thus earn equally attractive sums and statuses. While I argue that we must permit and reward individual achievement, we can certainly reconsider and readjust our notions of what kinds of achievement deserve what kinds and amounts of reward. And under all circumstances, we must provide a decent level of life for those for whom accident has made almost any achievement impossible. This, rather than a return to a feudalistically ascribed society, should be our goal.

**PROCE-DURALISM VERSUS VIGILANTISM**

The final ambivalence to be discussed is that between proceduralism and vigilantism or appeal to violence. Proceduralism is a term used here to describe the Constitution's commitment (and that of American society in general) to the application of its provisions through the rule of law and through duly authorized legal procedures. Commitment to this principle was cogently described throughout the *Federalist* papers. No one man in our system, or even any group of men, is permitted by our Constitution to attain absolute power or to evade the rule of law. Individuals accused of crimes are assured of their rights to "due *process* of law." This includes specifically designed legal devices to protect them from the abuses of powerful accusers. And the assurance of these rights is not left to simple goodwill or intelligence. Our rights are quite carefully delineated. Our redress against all the possible grievances of a complex society is circumscribed with legal procedures. The Constitution is interpreted with care by lawyers for a community essentially committed to the rule of law. The most stunning changes in our society are most often brought about by laws and cases. Such dramatic changes as a complete reversal of accepted tax policy and a reversal of accepted methods of regulating agriculture, labor unions, and education have hung on legal decisions always carefully hedged by procedural niceties. For example, when the "nine old men" of the Supreme Court declared unconstitutional the whole complex of industrial regulations known as the NRA (National Recovery Act of 1933), millions of businessmen immediately affected by these provisions quickly removed their blue eagles (the symbol of this act) from stores and factories and accepted this fundamental change as peacefully as they had accepted the original legislation. The battle for racial integration has taken place in courtrooms as well as legislatures. The weapons have been legal briefs involving tactical arguments about sophisticated and abstract ideas such as "interposition" and "states' rights."

**Procedural Niceties**

Even when we deal with problems as personal as divorce proceedings we require rules. A reluctant husband in New York who is served with a subpoena while he is skiing across the Massachusetts state line will be permitted to evade testifying in a New York divorce proceeding on the ground that the subpoena was jurisdictionally invalid. When a court must decide whether an adopted child is to remain with the adoptive parents or be returned to the natural parents, procedure is expected to supersede sentiment. Such sophisticated restraint is a basic hallmark of American constitutionalism.

Indeed, this dedication to procedure transcends the language of the Constitution and permeates all aspects of our governmental process. The history of most of our governmental reform movements, constitutional and otherwise, is a history of changes in procedure. When we wish to "reform" the caliber of men in public service, we think of new procedures like civil service merit exams, direct primary nominating systems, or secret-ballot voting machines. We believe, in other words, that form can alter substance. The fact that each legislative house can and does make its own rules of procedure has a profound effect on the ultimate content of all our statutes, both in the nation and in the states, but we jealously guard the sanctity of these procedures.

During the sixties, however, campus confrontations, ghetto uprisings, police excesses, and other less than peaceful demonstrations began to erode the political landscape. We witnessed the beginning of contempt for the procedural style of thinking and a concomitant advocacy of the use of violence. The National Advisory Commission on Civil Disorders noted this in its report. Among the causes of the disorders of the 1960s it named "a climate that tends toward approval and encouragement of violence as a form of protest." It went on to condemn both "white terrorism" directed against nonviolent protest and the "resort to violence by some protest groups."[60] This report makes clear that violence cannot be tolerated, no matter who purveys it.

Violence on the part of any agent of the government is particularly reprehensible, since it is the government that maintains a monopoly on the legal use of force. Only the polity can legally take life. It is incumbent on those who monopolize such power to be doubly sure that all their agents meticulously honor the letter and spirit of due process. We have witnessed open assaults upon our court systems, public evasion of our punishment systems, abusive rhetoric against our schools, jails, hospitals, social service centers, and city halls. The procedures of our merit systems, our election processes, our draft registrations, our bail-bond methods, our juries and judges, our union negotiations—all of these procedures and the very notion that procedures are important per se are now being questioned. There is no quarrel here with the idea that all such matters should be open to debate and subject to change. But the young, the militant, the dissatisfied, both inside and outside the government, are also coalescing around the idea that what counts

**A Counter-principle? Ends versus Means**

is simply the outcome. The means no longer matter, only the ends. If this counterprinciple were to prevail, it would probably spell the end of the American political system as we now know it. It is not quite a principle yet, since it has little constitutional grounding and therefore does not hold the weight of due process; but it is clearly a trend. It is the theme of those who see violence as "American as apple pie." The only constitutional language in point here is the Second Amendment's guarantee of the "right to bear arms." This has been the theme of the various groups that rally to prevent passage of gun-control laws, carefully ignoring the fact that the Second Amendments ties the right to bear arms to a militia. While many are simply sportsmen, others are the neofascists of every stripe who believe that vigilantism should supplant vigilance. Successful change, they would have us believe, requires violence. It is a growing style and it should be carefully noted and studied. Indeed, it is my contention that if we do not resolve our ambivalence concerning this contradiction, we may lose all the other principles and benefits that our admittedly less than perfect system can and still does confer.

These, then, are the five pairs of contradictory principles that need to be rethought. Despite constitutional bases for each side of the conflict, I believe, priorities should now be clearly assigned. Majority rule should supersede minority rights when these two principles conflict. Liberty should obtain over security. Political equality should override certain possible freedoms. But in other situations liberty takes precedence over equality. So too with individualism in relation to groupism. And most clearly proceduralism must prevail over violence.

# CHAPTER 4

# THE CONSTITUTION AND CREATIVE CONFLICTS

There are three constitutional controversies that seem to me to have been fought to a draw. I cannot suggest with any degree of certainty that one or another of the principles involved has a logical right to absolute priority. In some circumstances flexibility seems clearly in order, in others, stability. Centralized government? Perhaps. Limited government? Maybe. These are the areas where the evidence does not yet seem to be clear. There are many ambiguities. I have therefore designated these as creative conflicts. They are competing biases. Perhaps the reader will be more ready than I to resolve these tensions.

**FLEXIBILITY VERSUS STABILITY**     The U.S. Constitution manifests a great capacity for both flexibility and stability. It is my view that no final resolution is necessary. Both principles have long competed and this competition has produced the essential compromise between our very human need for change and our equally human need for permanence. The specific procedures by which the Constitution demonstrates its flexibility are the amendment procedure, the use of language necessitating interpretation, the specific delegation of amplifying and modifying powers to certain branches of government, the explicit omission of certain matters, and the application of judicial review.

The provision for amendment allows four possible systems by which succeeding generations may change the Constitution. There are two methods of proposing amendments—one through Congress, the over by way of conventions within the states. These must be coupled with one or the other of two possible ratification processes: ratification by three-fourths of the state legislatures or by conventions in three-fourths of the states.[1] Each of these procedures has considerable flexibility, arising from the failure of the Constitution to specify many details (such as how the state constitutional conventions are to be called or the time limit within which an amendment shall still be considered alive for possible state action).

The Constitution also maintains flexibility by delegating power. While the Supreme Court, for example, is directly established by the Constitution, Congress must provide for the remaining national court system and for the enlargement or reduction of the Supreme Court itself.

Another example of constitutional flexibility through delegated power is the provision that the executive shall appoint "other officers of the United States whose appointments are not herein otherwise provided for."[2] This broad language in the Constitution has fathered an establishment of 2.33 million civilians who make up the administrative branch of the federal government (the much challenged political "Schedule C" as well as the merit system of our national civil service). These appointees are constitutionally noted only by the words that the President "may require the opinion, in writing, of the principal officer in each of the executive departments upon any subject relating to the duties of their respective offices."[3] When such economy of language can produce the extent and variety of bureaucratic action that we have witnessed over the past generations, the principle of flexibility is certainly well demonstrated.

Actual omissions in the Constitution also help maintain the necessary flexibility anticipated by the Founding Fathers. The omission of regulations governing political parties and nomination procedures, for example, has permitted the development of institutions more responsive to the changing needs of new generations than would otherwise have been the case.

Another important omission was corrected by the Supreme Court's decision in the case of *Marbury* v. *Madison*[4] in 1803. In delivering the Court's opinion, Chief Justice John Marshall established that the Supreme Court would be the final arbiter of the meaning of the Constitution whenever difficulties arose over its intent. There are innumerable examples of the use of judicial review to fill out omissions. The enactment of our national social security system in 1936 comes readily to mind. The Constitution does not use any language that could be clearly construed as directly authorizing Congress to provide old-age assistance payments to states or old-age benefits to individuals. The remedial steps that Congress took in this direction were therefore challenged. Eventually the case reached the Supreme Court. By interpreting the tax power of Congress to mean "spending for the general welfare"[5] and by freely reading the Tenth Amendment (which reserves all powers not specifically delegated to Congress for "the states or the people thereof"), the Court actually put into effect a major piece of legislation.

**Judicial Review to Fill out Omissions**

Many ambiguous clauses in the Constitution have also come to be defined through Supreme Court decisions. This collateral series of Supreme Court decisions, called constitutional law, has kept an eighteenth-century document alive and responsive to the needs of the twentieth century.

On the other hand, the very fact that the nation insists on the preservation of the Constitution and holds it in such reverence is itself a force that tends toward stabilization and the status quo. It restrains forward motion and in this sense certainly leads to the opposite of flexibility. While vast changes have indeed occurred over the centuries, many other possible visions have not been realized. With the exception of the slavery issue, great issues have been settled in the courtroom rather than on the battlefield. The other episodes of violence that dot America's landscape have rarely in themselves brought conclusive change. More often than not they have simply stimulated the constitutional process. In sum this underlying commitment to a constitution—indeed, to a series of constitutions—is the crux of a *stability principle* that delays certain actions when it does not actually defeat them. The time lag between conception and construction in the political system of the United States is ubiquitous and dramatic. In the fall of 1971, for example, the House of Representatives passed an amendment to the Constitution guaranteeing equal rights to women; the following spring it was approved by the Senate. By the fall of 1972, a year after the amendment had first secured congressional approval, it had been rejected by five states and passed by twenty; twenty-three states had taken no action at all. Such an amendment was first submitted forty-five years earlier.

**The Stability Principle**

It is, of course, always a matter of degree. Medicare is indeed here—but it took over twenty years from idea to reality. The Constitution frustrated child labor legislation for more than a decade, and the income tax required three separate legislative attempts and a constitutional amendment before it finally blossomed. The time lag and labyrinthine ways of the amendment procedure itself reveal our ambivalence in this matter. Most proposed amendments simply fade away. The story of U.S. race relations is the prime example of the way the Constitution in all its majesty can be used to thwart change. The Civil War, no less, presumably settled not only the slavery question but also the question of equal rights. Yet the constitutional battles over every inch of the territory of voting rights, education rights, economic rights, and civil rights for black Americans is eloquent testimony to the huge cost of delay.

To this day, moreover, we do not have as comprehensive a system of social security as those long since achieved in other Western industrialized societies. We do not have an integrated system of education or even common standards of performance—not because of our regard for the wisdom of the educators, but because of our regard for constitutional niceties. The same may be said of voting requirements, police systems, the very definition of crimes, and all the other police powers guarded by particular constitutional fiat. All these things testify to our attachment to stability and our very human resistance to change and flexibility.

Thus ours is a constitution dedicated to both change and resistance to change, to both flexibility and stability. Perhaps it reflects a wise recognition of our mutual need for receptivity to change along with our need for some fixed points of reference by which the value of these changes can be measured. The key to resolving this tension lies, therefore, in the ingenuity of the citizenry, rather than in any firm commitment to one principle or the other. It lies in trying out new methods that may speed change along without completely abandoning some fixed agenda. But in essence it can be viewed as an essentially creative controversy.

**PLURALISM VERSUS CENTRALISM**

The term "pluralism" covers considerable ground. In one sense it is meant to convey all the group life of America, both natural and contrived. This is a sort of sociological pluralism: the mix of races, ethnic groups, classes, ideologies, income levels; and the clubs, churches, political parties, and other associations that derive from these groups. But in another sense, the word can also convey our multifaceted political system; that is, a system of federated powers and divided powers, of states, towns, townships, cities, and villages, of executives, legislatures, courts, and parties. And finally we must note that "pluralism" has today taken on an ideological meaning as well. It is now often used to describe the philosophical outlook of political scientists who not only describe America in terms of overlapping interest groups, but also prescribe a polity devoted to the solving of problems by means of the "automatic" working of some sort of "invisible hand" among these groups. That is, the pluralists are seen as apologists for the American status quo. As an ideology, pluralism tends to see America in terms of a "happy game ecology" in which everyone has a chance to play, and in which there are different prizes—but nonetheless prizes—for everyone. I am not here using the term in this latter sense, nor shall I dwell on the descriptive facets of our population heterogeneity. Let us rather consider pluralism in its governmental or constitutional sense.

The first aspect of this view of pluralism is the uniquely American device called "federalism." While this was known in history before the United States came into being, no nation before ours had experimented with it so fully and so broadly.

Federalism is our essential division of power between nation
and state. It is a system in which sovereign power branches
out from its ultimate source, the electorate, to more than one
center. Each of the various foci of power is permitted to act
independently in different areas of social concern. The Constitution gives certain powers to the Congress (see Article 1,
Section 8) and reserves others to the states (see the Tenth
Amendment). Of the powers reserved, a number belong exclusively to the states. Among them are the power to regulate
state and local elections, the power to determine the degree of
authority of local governments, and the power to regulate
morals. Then there are powers, such as the power to levy taxes,
which belong concurrently to both national and state governments. Article 4 of the Constitution places three restrictions on
state power: (1) on the manner in which states are to recognize
acts and procedures of other states, (2) on the manner in
which they are to exchange fugitives from justice, and (3) on
the levying of tariffs against the products of its sister states. In
general, a reading of the Constitution itself, and even of the
early Supreme Court decisions, would give one the impression
that the states held the balance of power here. But the pendulum has long since swung the other way. The Court has had
to determine continuously where states' rights have been infringed by national actions and vice versa. It has had to determine where congressional action may be taken exclusively,[6]
and where it must act concurrently with related state powers.[7]
The Court has decided where states have abrogated rights
guaranteed under the federal Constitution as well as the
propriety with which states have engaged in their constitutional relations with other states. In balance, an examination
of the key to independence—control of the largest funds—reveals where the greater power now resides. It is in Washington.

**Separation
of Powers**

The Court has also had a busy time with another aspect of
our governmental pluralism—the "separation of powers." Here
too the Constitution provides for pluralism by attempting to
define three distinct and more or less equal centers of power
within the national government itself. All of our state constitutions, moreover, follow this same practice. Article 1 of the
Constitution (Section 8), establishes a legislative branch and
assigns to it a list of some eighteen specific powers. Article 2
establishes an executive branch in which *all* executive powers
are given to the President. Article 3 states: "The judicial power
of the United States, shall be vested in one Supreme Court,
and in such inferior courts as the Congress may from time to
time ordain and establish." Section 2 of that same article
elaborates on the specific areas of jurisdiction of this judicial
power. This artificial attempt to break up the power necessary

to perform the functions of government is again testimony to a deep distrust of monolithic power, and a desire to keep it fragmented. The Court's interpretive role in regard to separation is most clearly seen in the cases in which Congress tried to check the President and keep him from becoming a virtual despot.[8]

Despite the wealth of evidence, constitutional and decisional, of an attachment to pluralism, we have often flirted with its opposite, the pull to centralism. Centralism too has its obvious attractions. There are always the presumed benefits of increased speed and efficiency, the elimination of duplication and waste, and the occasional need to pull through some impending disaster by means of firm, swift, and unified action. Consolidation of power is the unvarying advice of the reformers on all levels of government. The host of reorganization commissions that constantly dot our governmental landscape at federal, state, and local levels virtually unanimously cry for functional consolidation, for more power for the chief executive, and for varying devices to integrate and centralize government service. They are joined, moreover, by those reformers whose chief passion is intergovernmental analysis. These reformers quickly become the protagonists of Washington, of regionalism, of county consolidation, and of many other devices that would in one way or another curtail the number, spread, and powers of our welter of decision-making units.

Yet the essential wisdom of this nation, I believe, has been its reluctance to resolve this dilemma clearly and firmly. Flexibility has permitted us the luxury—costly, I admit—of continuing experimentation in many areas where experimentation is clearly needed. There does not yet appear to be persuasive logic for abandoning pluralism in terms of either units of government or distribution of power within each unit. Again, it is an area of profound ambiguities. Yet there are certainly occasions when common sense as well as common disaster have required some greater degree of centralization. So far we have permitted the pendulum to swing in accordance with both Supreme Court decisions and the flow of tax revenues. The principle of centralization may well have reached its apogee during the New Deal era.

We then used every possible constitutional ploy to allow the national government, and in particular the President, to act in order to meet a depression and later a war of unprecedented proportions. Indeed, all wars have brought with them centralizing and consolidating waves. Today, however, there is a countervailing sentiment in favor of states' rights and community power. The Nixon administration has proposed new, somewhat generous, and unrestrained revenue sharing, for example. There

**The Pull to Centralism**

is also a drift in recent Supreme Court decisions toward enhancing the role of the states. Chief Justice Warren E. Burger has demanded that the federal courts restrain themselves from "undermining a keystone of federalism" by permitting litigants to short-cut the state courts and come directly to federal courts. When he first espoused these views in actual Court rulings, his voice was heard as part of a minority dissent.[9] But by March 1971 he led an 8–1 majority on this same principle. He also refused to use the Court's "original jurisdiction" powers to hear a water pollution controversy that crossed state boundaries.[10] Moreover, he carried the Court's majority in certain decisions that restrained federal courts from interfering by barring state prosecution of defendants who had asserted that their constitutional rights were being violated.[11] Without arguing the merits of the decisions, we can recognize that they do reassert the propriety of state action, whenever that is constitutionally possible, in an era that may be suffering in various ways from overcentralization and a concomitant growth in bureaucracy.

Perhaps, then, the better part of wisdom is to allow these contradictory tensions to continue to operate as they historically have. The only logic that might be applied to the swing from centralization to decentralization, or from unity to pluralism, is simply the observation that as one leaves the realm of certainty and unanimity (and one leaves that realm quite frequently) there seems to be an outward pull toward decentralization. Variety, in other words, is needed when there is uncertainty. And variety is best achieved by multiple decision centers. This will be discussed further in a later chapter. At this point I would argue that it does not seem sensible to abandon a traditional network of governments, with all the heavy costs involved, for results that are highly problematic. What evidence we have at hand is far from conclusive, and the logic that might be applied is similarly tenuous.

**RESTRAINED VERSUS UNLIMITED GOVERNMENT**

We come now to the tension between the principle of limited and restrained government and the countervailing pull toward unlimited, all-powerful government. The former principle is still clearly the stronger in our system. And this is probably a happy circumstance, although I suggest that neither one should be unequivocally enshrined. The idea of limited government rests not only on certain constitutional phrases, but on the whole underlying spirit of the document. This has always been a nation that relied on business, the free enterprise system, the market economy, to supply most of its wants, both private and public. It was therefore the experience of the Founding Fathers that the least government was the best government. And while we have traveled a considerable distance from that starting point, we have never gone the entire route. To begin with, there are certain constitutional protections for the idea of limited government. The Ninth Amendment specifies that "the enumeration in the Constitution, of certain rights, shall not be construed to deny or disparge others retained by the people." Thus American governmental units can, in general, do what they have specifically been granted powers to do. The Tenth Amendment also clearly reserves all those powers not delegated to Congress "to the states respectively, or to the people." And since the state constitutions also contain the same spirit of specific delegation, the reservoir of power is still—at least theoretically—the domain of the people at large.

There are also direct prohibitions on government. For example, the government is enjoined from enacting ex post facto laws (retroactive laws that inflict punishment on activities that were legal when initiated) and bills of attainder (legislation that denies judicial procedural rights or attempts to inflict punishments on succeeding generations). The First Amendment, moreover, states that "Congress shall make no law respecting an establishment of religion," and the Constitution specifically provides that there be no religious test for the holding of national office in the United States. This concept of separation of religion and government was later extended by judicial interpretation to cover state as well as national acts. All of these prohibitions illustrate the fact that there are spheres of life in the United States—and religion is a dramatic case in point—that substantially transcend the realm of any government action. As Thomas Jefferson put it, the First Amendment was intended to erect "a wall of separation between Church and State." In view of past ecclesiastical influence over authoritarian governments, this was seen as a necessary limitation by the authors of the Constitution.

**Direct Prohibitions on Government**

Even this wall, however, is not without breaches. The Supreme Court has upheld the right of a state to pay parochial school bus fares and it has permitted local schools to "release" students from school for religious instruction.[12] The Court has also sustained lunch and book payments to parochial schoolchildren, allowed members of religious orders to teach in public schools, and upheld tax exemptions for religious properties.[13] On the other hand, the Court does not permit the use of public school facilities for actual religious instruction, and in 1963, in its most far-reaching decision to date, it banned Bible reading and prayers from public schools.[14]

The principle of limited government is also carried out through the previously described devices of separating powers among different branches of the federal government and through its corollary principle of checks and balances. Thus each separate branch of government—legislative, executive, and judicial—acts as a watchdog over the other branches. The President, for example, is given power to veto legislation; the Congress can override with a two-thirds vote. The President can make a treaty; the Senate must approve it. The President may appoint federal judges and certain other officials, but only with the consent of the Senate. The President executes laws and the Congress may investigate their execution. The President may conclude executive agreements, but Congress alone can appropriate the money to carry them out. On the other hand, the House may initiate a move for impeachment of the President, and the Senate may try him when such charges are brought against him. The Supreme Court may set aside congressional acts as unconstitutional, but Congress may expand the size of the Court or initiate an amendment to alter the Constitution. There are also checks *within* a single branch: the bicameral (two-house) structure of the legislature requires that each house approve every bill before it can become law.

There is further restraint implicit in the overlapping terms of office between the two houses of Congress and the President (which ensure that a substantial number of the members of government will always be in office when others are obliged to campaign for reelection); in the life tenure of the Supreme Court justices and their limited areas of jurisdiction; and even in the four alternative procedures for amending the Constitution, each one of which has built-in checks against the seat of national power and even against the will of the majority.

On the other hand, there is also some constitutional basis for seeing the power of government as *plenary*. Take as examples all those Supreme Court decisions that have given rise to what some citizens see as "Leviathan government." These decisions make it appear as though there were no limits to what government can do. Social security, medicare, the Aid to Education acts, the Model Cities Program, the regulation of banks, the enforcement of safety codes, the regulation of wages and prices—virtually every major piece of social legislation of the past generation has had in it a strong dose of government activism and the consequent enjoinment of a laissez-faire, market-mechanism approach. And all such legislation is passed with due regard for the United States Constitution, and occasionally the legislation even survives explicit Supreme Court review. Most of it, moreover, not only bears constitutional imprimatur, but also seems to enjoy wide popular support. Indeed, there are many who frankly pronounce the whole idea of limited government anachronistic and see the pluralist doctrine with its restraints and limitations as a masquerade for privilege and a sop to the status quo. The enthusiasts of plenary

"Leviathan Government"

government see limited government as a similar sop. In their view the government should be able to provide for the general welfare directly and explicitly, with no strings, no limits, no subterfuges. Full power to call the tune and get things moving holds little terror for the protagonists of a strong unlimited government. On the contrary, they are more afraid of the stalemates and delays of our ritualistic system and its checks and restraining ploys. They see the problems of the next few decades as too big for anything less than "big government" solution. Yet the balance between restraint and activism continues to shift and shift again, and I for one am not sorry. This arena appears to me to be best managed by continuing compromise rather than forthright resolutions. The logic that favors variety over uniformity is again in point here.

So far our analysis has been concerned primarily with the national Constitution. But since we are a federal system of government with power divided between national and state governments, we must also examine the fundamentals of state constitutions. Under the United States Constitution, as noted earlier, the states have an area of "reserved powers." In general, these represent a range of activities frequently called "police powers." Such activities as public education, public health and hospitals, welfare programs, intrastate highways, road lighting, waste removal, public housing, public hospitals, public recreation, election procedures, regulation of intrastate businesses affecting the community health and welfare, intrastate franchises, and the general area of civil and criminal justice—all of these activities are the concerns of state governments. Though the last four decades have seen a shift in the balance of power in favor of the national government, it is significant that these decades have also brought about an overall increase in the functions of government at all levels. American citizens tend to look more and more frequently to the public realm to solve problems that in earlier years belonged to the private sector.

All of the original thirteen colonies had charters resembling constitutions long before the birth of our nation as an independent entity. These charters, a number of which were adopted with small changes as constitutions when the colonies became states—that is, upon their ratification of the national Constitution—reflected by and large the same underlying conflicts among principles as the United States Constitution.

It is almost impossible, however, to generalize successfully about these fifty constitutions, since they are often long, detailed, archaic, confusing, and repetitious. Many of them contain so much detail, so many special political ends and politi-

**THE STATE CONSTITUTIONS**

cally transient policies, that one easily loses the thread of their basic philosophies. It is therefore possible to describe only a few overall characteristics, and to note that they reflect the same ambivalences about basic values as our national Constitution. Like the federal Constitution, state constitutions are subject to amendment and review so that they may reflect changing values, but at the same time they remain bastions for the forces of delay and stalemate. They are ambivalent about liberty and equality, about liberty and security, about centralism and pluralism, and about limited and unlimited government.

**State Constitutions as Statutory Codes**

Most states long ago lost track of the generally recognized difference between a constitution and a statutory or administrative code. The California constitution, for example, concerns itself with the length of wrestling matches; Mississippi with dueling; New York with formulas for controlling the public debt of its municipalities. The excessive length and detail of most state constitutions can be traced to a spirited discontent with state legislatures during the muckraking era of the twenties. Fearful of what state legislators during that era might have done, constitutional conventions in many states whittled away their power to do anything at all by trying to make all decisions part of the constitution itself. This resulted, however, in simply substituting the judiciary for the legislature in many instances when decisions were required.

This cynical attitude, coupled with the rigidity of state amendment procedures, makes most state constitutions far less flexible than the national Constitution. Yet the fact is that except for the constitutions of the two newest states, Alaska and Hawaii, they all have managed to acquire many amendments—too many and often about matters inappropriate for constitutional concern. All fifty state constitutions also implicitly rely on the judicial review process to provide change and flexibility.

A deep-rooted concern for individual freedom can be found in the "bill of rights" of every state constitution. These lists, far more detailed than the first ten amendments to the U.S. Constitution, tend on occasion to confuse an appropriate concern for necessary liberties with attempts to provide the good life for all people at all times. This again reflects ambivalence about priorities. For example, a section of the bill of rights of the New York State constitution declares that the drainage of swamps and agricultural lands is a public concern and affirms that general laws may therefore be passed permitting owners of such lands to construct dams on the property of others under specific procedural conditions. This somewhat esoteric clause, moreover, precedes the section protecting freedom of speech and press. What does that say about New York's priorities?

Some states include assurances of the right to fish in public waterways, to organize labor unions, and to bargain collectively. There are bans on lotteries, regulations concerning workmen's compensation, and conditions for the sale of liquor. Such elaboration occasionally blurs the effectiveness of many state bills of rights where fundamentals are concerned.

The principle of plural government can be seen in those sections that grant "home rule" to municipalities within every state's boundaries. Indeed, attachment to the philosophy of plural government is a central principle of state governments. The tradition of state constitutional and political defense of states' rights (the sovereign power of the states in appropriate areas) gives evidence of this attachment. Yet in their day-to-day dealings with their own subdivisions as well as in the constitutional provisions for home rule, there are so many strings attached that the spirit of pluralism is often lost in the details.

The states' commitment to popular government, including the principle of majority rule, is often as ambivalent as the nation's. More than two-thirds of the states have constitutional amendment procedures requiring ratification by a majority of those voting on an amendment. The other states, however, specify three-fifths votes, or ask for a majority of all votes cast in the election, whether or not all voters cast ballots for an amendment. And Delaware requires *no* popular ratification of amendments. State attachment to the contrary principle of elitism may also be seen in the almost universal state constitutional sections specifying suffrage requirements. Five states made the payment of a poll tax a requirement for voting, some as recently as 1964. (As we have seen, the poll tax has since been outlawed by a Supreme Court decision.) Twenty states imposed literacy tests right up until the 1970 Civil Rights Act. Every state makes some requirements concerning registration; although these procedures were adopted to guard against voting frauds, they inevitably curtail the suffrage. And all states require a period of state residence for voter eligibility, which is also a voting deterrent. Furthermore, state constitutions universally make provisions for legislative apportionment and districting. Many of these provisions have built-in voting inequities. Rural counties frequently receive much more representation than urban ones, mainly because the country was largely rural and agricultural when districts were originally defined. But this picture is in the process of change following recent Supreme Court rulings. So in these many ways the states too reflect their ambivalence about the principle of majority rule.

The fifty state constitutions are, finally, dedicated to the ideal of restrained government. Yet at the same time they too keep enlarging their range of activities and their percentage

**Constitutional Impediments to Popular Government**

of public expenditures. All of them operate on a system of separation of powers, and checks and balances. Some legislatures have the power to balance and limit the executive branch. Each state also has a court system with implicit or explicit power to review state legislation. While there are innumerable variations in the precise details, overall the structures are remarkably similar in their attempts at restraint. But all states are today operating in more areas and in greater depth than they were a generation ago. In this sense the states too participate in promoting Leviathan government.

**The "Civic Culture"**

Given these fundamental controversies over basic values, can we discover any areas of consensus in America? Some evidence in this direction was provided by a cross-cultural study done in 1963 by Gabriel Almond and Sidney Verba.[15] Answers to a few key questions put to a sample of citizens in five countries indicated that there was an underlying pull that held Americans together, in contrast to other national samples. The authors called it the "civic culture." It manifested itself in the overwhelmingly affirmative responses Americans of various socioeconomic categories gave to such questions as "Does your government have a 'great effect' on your daily life?" "Do you receive 'equal treatment' from the government?" "Do you receive 'serious consideration' from your civil servants?" On these items there appeared to be a more generally trusting and salutory view of the political system in the United States than was found in Germany, Italy, or Mexico. But that was in 1963. The 1970s may require a more explicit rationalization of basic principles to realize any germ of such a "civic culture." Indeed, I suggest that the basic values of Americans need to be more carefully analyzed and possibly reordered so that they *can* be consciously accepted. As I have demonstrated in the previous pages, our principles are often inconsistent, even contradictory. We can, however, reorganize them and define them in such a way as to salvage a more coherent American ethical code. A continuing state of totally unresolved and often unrecognized ambivalence is far too burdensome and costly, and keeps us from choosing meaningful approaches to problem-solving. A rigid structure, however, in which all ambivalence and ambiguity are eradicated by some spurious "final solution," is equally dangerous. We must choose a middle way. That is not necessarily a "muddle way." If we make a few fundamental decisions about *essentials,* the more detailed goals and strategies can then be worked out by sweet reason, through devices that will be discussed later. Our firmest resolve must be to keep the marketplace of ideas as open as possible, and to keep everybody's access to the market as fair and equal as possible.

# BASIC CONFLICTS IN THE AMERICAN JUDICIAL PROCESS

There are a number of reasons why the judicial process should be given first place in a discussion of the institutions and procedures of the American political system. The judiciary has come to be the guardian of our many constitutions and the chief architect of our fundamental law. "The Supreme Court is the Constitution," Mr. Justice Frankfurter reputedly said. This was also the judgment of one of the most cogent analysts of the American scene, Alexis de Tocqueville. Over a century ago he wrote: "Scarcely any political question arises in the United States that is not resolved sooner or later into a judicial question."[1] This observation has been confirmed time and again by other foreign writers, as well as by American events. The idea of judicial supremacy may be further corroborated by noting that it is the judiciary—particularly the federal judiciary—that appears to command ultimate respect in our nation. Consider, for example, the rejection of Franklin Delano Roosevelt's plan to "pack the Supreme Court." Despite FDR's popularity at the time, Congress was besieged with letters from constituents vehemently protesting what they felt was an affront to an institution they held dear—dearer, indeed, than the laws FDR had forged for their economic salvation. The Court-packing plan was, after all, the President's attempt to reverse the trend of judicial decisions, which at that time were obstructing regulatory laws he had pushed through Congress to stem the tide of the depression. But the people wanted no tampering with the Supreme Court. And in this event, the Court changed only as its justices died and were replaced by others with different understandings of the Constitution.

It is to the judiciary, moreover, that Americans look for the arbitration of most of the disputes that inevitably arise in a complex society. There are suits between individuals (civil cases), suits brought by the nation or the states against individuals (criminal cases), and suits asking for resolution of the conflicts inherent in a political system with multiple jurisdictions and committed to adversary proceedings. When the President appears to have overstepped the boundaries of his power, for example, or when the Congress appears to move into the

**The Role of the Courts in the United States**

**Judicial Supremacy**

orbit of the states, or when the states themselves are thought to be rejecting an area of nationally supreme law—in all such instances the society relies upon the judicial system, and ultimately the United States Supreme Court, for the resolution of conflict.

This piece of machinery, more than any other, breathes life into the conflicting constitutional principles previously described. The courts are often the major instruments of policy flexibility or restraint, the prime balancers of pluralism and centralism; ultimately they protect or reject individualism, class interests, and the majoritarian process. It is the courts that weight the pendulum swinging from the demands of liberty to those of equality or security. We can thus see the conflicts of our entire governmental system mirrored directly in the operation of judicial review (which I shall discuss below) and in the other procedures of judicial politics.

There is some inevitable overlap between the value controversies previously explored and those with which we are dealing here. But there are certain institutional characteristics that require special consideration. The ambivalence mirrored in the American judiciary can be outlined as follows: (1) There is a pull between what I call analytic justice and sociological justice. It is expressed primarily in controversies over the proper role of judicial decisions. (2) Next there is the conflict over unified and simplified court systems as against more heterogeneous and complex ones. This reflects the argument between centralism and pluralism. (3) The tensions between majoritarians and elitists are mirrored in the struggle over the use and selection of judges as against the use and selection of jurors. (4) Arguments over the role of courts versus the role of quasi courts reflect conflict over the proper extent of judicial powers, which in turn reflects the conflict over limited versus unlimited government. (5) Finally, there is ambivalence over the ultimate goal of our judicial system: should it strive for retribution or rehabilitation?

**Ambivalence in the American Judiciary**

**Judicial Review**

Before we pursue these judicial conflicts, a brief explanation of judicial review will be helpful. The term in its precise usage refers to any action in which one court reviews the work of another. But it has come to have a special meaning, and it is this special meaning that most political scientists have in mind when they use the term: the power of the U.S. Supreme Court to review congressional, presidential, and state actions to determine their "constitutionality." This procedure is more peculiarly American than any other in our judicial system. Its unique character was noted with great interest by Alexis de Tocqueville in 1830. He pointed out—and this is a most important key to the understanding of our judiciary—that judicial review gives American judges a political influence not encountered elsewhere.[2] That is, justice here is clearly understood as politics.

While the United States Constitution itself says nothing about judicial review, or about who shall have the final word in disputes among the various participants in our complex system of government, it is generally agreed that most of the Founding Fathers assumed some degree of judicial review, certainly over state legislation if not over national legislation. There is at least evidence that the authors of the *Federalist* papers viewed the Supreme Court in this light. In any event, a situation arose in the early days of the republic which put the matter to a practical test and resolved the issue in favor of judicial review. That test was the case of *Marbury* v. *Madison*,[3] in which Chief Justice Marshall, through legalistic legerdemain, established the idea that the Constitution, as the supreme law of the land, required that congressional laws (and by implication state laws too) be interpreted by the Supreme Court. Further, Marshall successfully argued that it was the judiciary, rather than any other branch of the government, that was uniquely capable and suited to make this final determination. This decision for judicial review has become hallowed by time and remains to this day an integral part of the American governmental system.

It is the Court's own view of how and when this essentially political power is to be used, however, that provides the broadest of the conflict areas in American jurisprudence. The ease with which a justice assumes this political role, his preference for emphasizing it, reducing it, sidestepping it, or pretending it isn't there, becomes the cutting edge of our judicial system.

**ANALYTIC JUSTICE VERSUS SOCIOLOGICAL JUSTICE**

In every important case when the Supreme Court has set aside a congressional law or a state law, it has in effect added some meaning to the Constitution or subtracted some meaning from it, and has affirmed one or another of the conflicting values described earlier. It has thus made a political decision. There has always been a contrapuntal interplay between those justices who tend to take a restrained and ostensibly purist view of the law and those who see the law as an instrument to shape social policy directly. The former are always searching for the "will of the legislature," for the clearest set of precedents, or possibly for some variant of "natural law." This school of thought is best illustrated—perhaps founded—by John Austin. It has been the hallmark of such eminent justices as Felix Frankfurter, John Marshall Harlan, and Warren Burger.

A far more "sociological" view of the law has been attributed to Roscoe Pound. He frankly viewed the Court as an instrument of social engineering, and his views were followed by such justices as Oliver Wendell Holmes, Louis Brandeis, and Benjamin Cardozo. The opinions written by these justices offer many clear illustrations of social engineering. Indeed, the phrase "Brandeis briefs" was coined to suggest this style of thinking. If this basic philosophical split is not frankly recognized by all justices and potential justices, it seems more than clear to the U.S. Senate. The Senate Judiciary Committee hearings on candidates for Supreme Court vacancies bear witness to the senators' keen interest in determining the side of this particular fence on which a judicial candidate is likely to stand.

**Attitudes of Supreme Court Judges as Reflected in Key Cases**

Moreover, it is possible that this basic conviction provides a crude test of some of the crucial attitudinal differences that distinguish individual justices. Ever since Schmidhauser did his pioneering work on the political and social background of Supreme Court justices, political scientists have been willing to concede that early background as well as later role-playing influences justices' attitudes, and justices' attitudes in turn influence their decisions.[4] But whatever the conscious or unconscious motivations of individual Supreme Court justices, the Court has given meaning over the years to such necessarily vague constitutional phrases as "the executive power," "such laws as are necessary and proper to carrying out the foregoing power," "treaties under the jurisdiction of the United States," "privileges and immunities," "equal protection of the laws," "due process of law," "regulate interstate commerce," and many other ambiguous constitutional phrases. Each determination has underlined one or another of the principles of jurisprudence described here. The sociological view of law can be illustrated, for example, by the way in which the power to "regulate interstate commerce" has been stretched to cover all sorts of activities. The word "regulate" has been stretched to mean "prohibit."[5] The word "interstate" has been stretched to cover even local activities that impinge, however lightly, on what has come to be called "the stream of commerce."[6] And even the word "commerce" has been stretched to include such activities as manufacturing.[7]

So too with the "due process" clause of the Fourteenth Amendment. This clause was given broad proportions in efforts to bolster the laissez-faire economic system in the first half of the twentieth century.[8] In the second half of the twentieth century, the Court went on to accept within its public philosophy quite different interpretations that have permitted the development of what many persons call a "semi-welfare state."[9] This elastic accommodation to differing economic and social tenets and conditions is evidence that the Court often plays a political role in the establishment of law and policy. The same well-worn words have served both to restrain and to justify the regulation of labor and manufacturing. In all events, the Court's decisions have had the effects of social engineering.

The greatest vacillation between the two principles of restraint and reform has probably occurred in the decisions determining the meaning of "federalism." Here again we find the Court wavering from a commitment to strict control of legislation and precedent to a commitment to some particular social reform. In its continuing determinations concerning the infringement of states' rights by national actions and vice versa, the Court inevitably affects actual policy. The Court has had to determine, for example, when congressional action may be taken exclusively and when it may act concurrently with similar state powers.[10] The Court decides when states have abrogated rights guaranteed under the federal Constitution, and the propriety with which states have engaged in their constitutional relations with other states. When the Agricultural Adjustment Act of 1933 was set aside, for example, Mr. Justice Roberts relied in his arguments upon the idea of the reserved powers of the states as expressed in the Tenth Amendment.[11] He claimed that if Congress were not specifically delegated the power to regulate agriculture (or if specific delegation could not reasonably be implied), this power was to be left exclusively to the states. This is a clear example of "strict construction." So was the decision that set aside the National Recovery Act of 1933.[12]

In a contrary vein, but still in the spirit of a broad view of social engineering, are those cases in which state law that presumably infringed upon a federal power or right has been set aside by the Court in an effort either to maintain balance in a plural system of government or, more probably, to permit some type of social action. Thus in *McCullouch* v. *Maryland*, a tax levied by the state of Maryland upon a branch of the United States Bank was held to threaten the sovereignty of the national government and was therefore declared unconstitutional.[13] This doctrine was later expanded to protect state institutions from national taxation as well.[14] Other cases have also served to clarify the areas in which state and national governments may legislate.[15]

On the other hand, the Supreme Court has adopted at least three practices that usually serve as judicial *restraints* and which have generally operated to illustrate the Court's conservative and legalistic side—the side of "analytic justice." First, the Court has always been the sole arbiter in the selection of cases to be heard from among the thousands that come to its attention each year. Except for the relatively few cases

**Methods of Judicial Restraint**

in which there is a right to appeal in law, these cases may be heard or not, at the Court's discretion. The usual practice of the Supreme Court has been to move into controversial areas with great restraint. It took the Court more than fifty years to reconsider its judgment on the meaning of "equal protection of the laws," even though during this interval there were hundreds of cases that could have provided an opportunity to act. But it chose to wait until lower courts and public opinion had crystallized the issues.

The Court has also decided to act only on actual controversies. While certain state courts do give "declaratory judgments," the common practice throughout the United States (and the Supreme Court has not deviated from it) is for a court to act only when actual situations and injuries are involved; that is, real cases. This is a form of self-restraint, since it permits a court to see how a law appears in action rather than in speculation. When the Supreme Court has felt that no serious injury has actually occurred, it will not hear a case. This too commits the Court to the narrow "analytic" role rather than to social reform.

**Legal Fictions**     Finally, the Court has invented a series of legal fictions that limit its reformatory role. For example, it considers taxpayer cases nonjusticiable. These are cases in which a taxpayer tries to test a law's propriety or constitutionality on the grounds that he has a pecuniary interest at stake through his tax payments. The Court has held this interest insufficient, since an individual's tax dollars cannot be traced to any particular action, but are lost in a pool of activity. Recently, however, a state court in Michigan has explicitly held that any taxpayer can bring suit against either the state or another individual on the grounds that a particular policy is endangering the environment. Once again, the role of social engineer crops up. Other states have also broadened their views on this question.

Political questions have provided another convenient escape hatch for the narrow constructionists of the analytic school. Whenever the Court has felt that a particular controversy would too seriously strain the fabric of the governmental system, it has avoided the issue by calling the matter a "political question." Thus the Court has chosen to view the following questions as political: the meaning of a "republican" form of government;[16] when a sufficient emergency exists to justify the mobilization of the militia to put down an insurrection;[17] the assignment of legal titles to properties subject to foreign dispute;[18] what constitutes a reasonable amendment procedure on the part of states seeking to act on an amendment to the Constitution;[19] and whether extradition is a mandatory duty for a governor.[20] These questions have been left undecided, under the fiction that they are political. Those judges whose style is what I call "sociological" would in general be willing to make such decisions. They would recognize frankly the political nature of *all* questions before the Court.

The question of whether state reapportionment of congressional districts following a census is mandatory was also confined to this category of nonjusticiable matters for many decades. The matter of redistricting had long been seen as the sole prerogative of state legislatures, and to this view Justice Frankfurter strictly adhered.[21] This is the apogee of the analytic view of justice. In 1962 he was overruled by those who saw the Court as a last resort for those seeking basic political reform when the election process was incapable of reforming itself.[22] Reapportionment was at last no longer "political."

As a final example of the controversy over the essential role of the Court, consider a case in which the state of Massachusetts sought a decision from the Supreme Court on the constitutionality of the war in Vietnam.[23] If the war was unconstitutional, as the state contended, Massachusetts wished an injunction from the Court enjoining the Secretary of Defense from raising troop levels and from ordering any inhabitant of Massachusetts to serve in Vietnam in the absence of effective congressional action. The government claimed, among other things, that this was a nonjusticiable issue, a political question subject to resolution only by the executive and the Congress. The case never reached the Supreme Court; it was dismissed by a federal district court in June, 1971, to the despair of those who saw court action as the only rational response to a crisis situation that the other branches of government were unwilling or unable to resolve, and to the satisfaction of those to whom interference in the issue seemed a violation of the court's proper analytic role.

Many observers contend that the analytic style is mere subterfuge, that it too is a form of sociological movement. Refusal to act is itself a form of action. All this is the stuff of genuine conflict. It may be a conflict between liberalism and conservatism, or among certain other basic attitudinal elements present within all judicial breasts. But it is a real and fundamental conflict area within our judicial system, and as such it requires careful public attention.

Of course, judicial review and the Supreme Court and the argument about judicial roles encompass only part of the judicial tensions in this nation. There are many other conflicts. One of them centers on the relative merits of centralized and localized justice. At this point in history we operate under a highly decentralized system. Only at the national level is there

**LOCALIZED VERSUS CENTRALIZED COURTS**

**The Structure and Jurisdiction of the Federal Court System**

any semblance of unification. The fifty state court systems provide bewildering complexity. The national system consists of eighty-six district courts located within the fifty states, four district courts in national territories, and one in the District of Columbia. Each of these courts has at least one judge, but some have as many as eighteen. At present approximately 240 federal district judges hold office. These courts have primarily original jurisdiction. This means that most federal cases start here. If the case is criminal in nature, a "grand jury" is used for indicting and a "petit jury" for trial. A petit jury is also used in all civil cases in which more than a specified minimum amount of damages is sought. Whether one or three judges hear a case depends on the nature of the case. Federal courts try only two types of cases: (1) those involving nationally defined crimes—treason, kidnapping, smuggling, tax fraud, security fraud, counterfeiting, and a few others; and (2) those in which the office or residence of the litigants requires federal attention—cases involving foreign officials, federal officers, litigants from different states, or two or more states themselves. Aside from these instances, civil and criminal controversies are handled by the states. The federal district court has appellate (review) jurisdiction over the decisions of a number of quasi-judicial bodies, such as independent regulatory agencies, and it also hears certain cases of claims against the United States.

The United States federal court system is further divided into eleven judicial circuits for the circuit court of appeals, each consisting of from three to nine judges. These judges have only appellate jurisdiction and serve as the only intermediate body between the district courts and the Supreme Court. They review decisions from the district courts within their respective circuits. In addition, there are a few special courts in the federal system: the court of claims, the customs court, the court of customs and patent appeals, and the court of military appeals.

All the federal judges that preside over these courts are appointed by the President, with the approval of the Senate, and serve for life during good behavior. Aiding these judges are certain assistants: clerks, bailiffs, law assistants, court reporters, and others. In general, they are appointed by the judges they serve. There are also other ancillary officials associated with the federal courts. These people help not in deciding cases, but in prosecuting them: United States marshals (who guard prisoners, make arrests, and carry out court orders) and United States attorneys (who investigate and initiate criminal and occasionally civil actions under national laws and then prosecute the cases). There is one marshal and one United States attorney in each of the eighty-six districts. They are appointed for four-year terms by the President with Senate approval. In fact, the Senate wields a rather heavy hand in these appointments. This is called "senatorial courtesy". Assistant United States attorneys are generally appointed by the Attorney General, who is a member of the President's cabinet and head of the Department of Justice. The FBI is a special investigating agency that works independently but is an arm of this department.

And there is another court system, or rather set of systems—those of the fifty states and their subsidiary local governments. Few of these systems could be described as unified. These state and local courts deal with a far more common range of crimes and civil suits than do the national courts. It is here that persons charged with murder, assault, burglary, embezzlement, morals offenses, and the entire gamut of criminal activity are tried. It is also within the state jurisdiction that most accident, contract, divorce, libel, and other civil suits are tried. Since each system is somewhat different from its counterparts in other states, we can do no more here than suggest a very general outline. Every state has a court of highest jurisdiction, generally called its supreme court. This is a court of almost exclusively appellate jurisdiction, and it is the court of last appeal unless a constitutional question is involved. In that instance, further appeal is directed to the United States Supreme Court. The state supreme court is responsible for the final interpretation of the constitution and the laws of that state. There is an appellate level, and almost invariably a system of county courts constituting the next to the lowest level in the state jurisdiction. Most counties also have probate or surrogate courts that handle wills, estates, and guardianships. In the rural and semirural areas of all states except Ohio, justices of the peace preside over trials involving traffic violations and minor offenses, perform marriage ceremonies, and administer oaths. They also occasionally have to "hold over" persons accused of more serious crimes—misdemeanors and felonies—until the cases are remanded to their proper jurisdictions.

In cities, the courts of justices of the peace give way to other minor courts that are often separated according to civil and criminal jurisdictions or assigned certain special problems: family courts, children's court, traffic courts, and so on. About half of the states also have a special court of claims to hear suits against the state itself. (Although neither a state nor the federal government may be sued without its consent, such consent is almost always granted.) While all American courts are to some degree bound to ultimate standards of fair play, each state is still free to develop its own common law (judge-made law). The principle of *stare decisis* (following precedent), moreover, does not extend from one state to another

**The Structure and Jurisdiction of State Courts**

except in occasional situations. All of these practices, plus the individuality of each state's criminal statutes and legal procedures, make for a complex and confusing system. Many specialists as well as laymen would prefer a simpler, more manageable and unified system. Such people tend to support policies that enhance federal judicial power; they prefer national resolution of jurisdictional conflict, and would like to see national rules of court procedure made mandatory. Those who prefer simple and unified courts usually support movements for uniform state laws, for enlarging the scope of such constitutional phrases as "equal protection of the laws" and "full faith and credit," and for any other measures that minimize the heterogeneity now characteristic of the American judiciary. Even the class-action suits concerning environmental problems are a wedge in the door toward greater nationalization of our court system.

In this arena of conflict between localism and centralism in the courts, judicial problems abound. Critics of localism contend that it breeds delay, uncertainty, and expense. The advocates of localism claim that, quite to the contrary, the dual system, with its variant practices, differing interpretations of civil and criminal law, and separate sets of precedents and procedures, gives our courts their unique flexibility, their resilience, and their experimental character, and guards the nation against the danger of degenerating into a police state. These people extol diversity as a good in itself and faithfully defend the state courts from the least threat of even statewide unification and centralization, not to mention nationalization.

Indeed, statewide reform has been an uphill battle since the early 1900s. To this day only about fifteen states are sufficiently centralized to control judicial manpower allocation and judicial appeals procedures within their borders. Advocates of centralization claim that it will reduce calendar clogging and delays. But each reform is opposed by some vested local interests whose spokesmen are ready to fight. Centralism versus localism remains a lively area of controversy. Even the judicial reformers, however, urge that we maintain a dual federal-state system, and merely centralize and unify procedures within each separate system. They also believe in clarifying the two jurisdictions sufficiently to reduce duplication, congestion, and delay. This, therefore, seems to be a conflict that demands resolution, and the most rational resolution favors those who propose such moderate measures of judicial simplification.

**JUDGES VERSUS JURIES**

Although all judges are by definition above the common herd, many Americans feel that they should conform as closely as possible to the least common denominator in the population. In over two-thirds of the states, therefore, most judges, justices of the peace, and even police magistrates are elected rather than appointed. Most states also allow for nominations at party conventions, but some states are considering the selection of judicial candidates by the voters in primary elections. Both systems, however, involve political considerations and patronage, which usually masquerade as concern for keeping the judiciary close to the people. Sometimes the machinations are so blatant that judges' "contributions" to party coffers are openly sought and actually scheduled on the basis of a percentage of salary. This type of practice and the scandals it causes quite naturally give rise to open conflicts between those who defend the system of elected judges and those who press for an appointive system. The former generally argue that, however faulty, the elective systems are inherently more democratic and yield judges who are more in tune with the common man. Those who advocate some form of judicial appointment modeled on the federal system emphasize the need for professionalism, independence, and a high moral tone. At the root of these arguments lies the fact that judicial selection touches on the socioeconomic status of judges. Members of an appointed judiciary are likely to be affluent, educated at prestige schools, and WASP (white Anglo-Saxon Protestant). The elective system is more likely to produce "ethnic" judges, persons from less prestigious law schools, and those with longer, steadier service to the political party dominant in a particular area. This is an important area for public discussion since recent research has made it clear that a judge's own value system is the greatest single determinant of his judicial decisions.[24] His value system in turn is clearly colored by his socioeconomic status. It is only after the primary motivational forces are accounted for that such secondary determinants as group pressures, politics, and professionalism enter the picture. For this reason a selection system that favors one or another type of social and economic class is clearly a major consideration.

**The Value Systems of Judges**

A popular reform model in this arena of controversy is the so-called Missouri Plan. Basically it provides that a slate of names for each judicial vacancy be submitted to the governor by a professionally competent (and elitist) nominating group— a bar association, for example. The governor selects his appointee from this limited, professionally acceptable list. After one year, the judge appointed runs unopposed in a general election. If he survives this test, he serves for a designated period, usually reasonably long, before having to run for reelection, again unopposed.

The assessment of a judge's values, background, and status

impinges directly on a related conflict, the use of judges versus the use of juries. This, again, is an argument of very long standing. There are those who zealously seek to guard and enlarge our rights to jury trials whenever possible. Others are convinced that jury trials add little to justice but much to delay, uncertainty, and expense—the antitheses of justice. The debate over juries in turn involves a series of related questions. How, for example, is a defendant guaranteed a jury of his "peers"? The notion of a jury is, of course, the notion of a peer group, and the advocates of juries rely heavily on the thesis that justice is more readily discerned by a group of persons of ordinary common sense than by a remote professional. But who is a "peer"? Must each individual jury box be filled by persons of both sexes and of various races, ages, and ethnic origins in proportion to their representation in the population at large, or should the proportions reflect the particular judicial district? Or should each jury be composed only of persons of the same race, sex, age, class, and ethnic group as the defendant? Or is it sufficient to ensure that no particular race, economic group, or sex has been systematically excluded? And how many jurors does one need? A few cases have fleshed out some basic ground rules about juries per se (and also grand juries, which are an interesting special problem). These cases have made it clear that, at a minimum, a trial cannot be construed as fair when any jury system systematically excludes persons of a particular race.[25]

But of course this does not really join the basic argument. The question of what constitutes a jury of one's peers is still unresolved, and so is the fundamental question of whether, in the final analysis, justice is more likely to come out of any jury box, no matter how it is filled, than from an elected or appointed judge. This is an area of conflict which I believe can best be determined on a state-by-state basis by means of majority decision. Only enjoinment of irrational prejudice need be given special priority. For the rest, continued experimentation is probably necessary. There is a great need here for empirical research. We do not know the degree or direction of skew connected with, let us say, decisions of appointed judges as against elected ones. Is one group predisposed to give lighter sentences than the other? To convict more often? To set high bail? Similar predispositions of juries as compared to different types of judges need also be tested. When the evidence is in— and it is not now available—we can perhaps make a better informed judgment.

**COURTS VS. QUASI COURTS VS. NO COURTS**

Another basic controversy concerning the U.S. judicial system is the pull between an ever-increasing use of the courts and the view that social problems should be dealt with *outside* the courts, either by governmental administrative bodies or by nongovernmental groups with professional expertise. The advocacy of judicial problem-solving has become so widespread that Chief Justice Warren Burger felt the need to comment on it in an address to the American Bar Association on the state of the judiciary. He asked on this occasion that "the public examine carefully each demand that they make on that system" (i.e., the courts). "People speak glibly of putting all the problems of pollution, of crowded cities, of consumer class actions and others in the federal courts."[26] To be sure, the Chief Justice advocated only that these problems be siphoned off from federal courts to state and local courts. But there are many others who advocate more extreme measures, such as the use of tribunals altogether outside the judicial system. Former Supreme Court Justice Arthur Goldberg has publicly called for the transfer of some court matters to other agencies. I call these nonjudicial channels "quasi courts."

The oldest and most familiar type of quasi court is the administrative adjudicatory body. These abound within all regular line departments of government, at both federal and state levels, as well as within the independent agencies that have also been spawned at all levels of government. Many line departments, for example have hearing boards to decide "security-risk" cases and other personnel matters. Their procedures are often essentially indistinguishable from court actions. Such hearings occur regularly in the Justice Department. The Department of the Interior, another regular line agency, uses special hearing panels for adjudicatory purposes of a quite different nature. Here the cases often involve claims made by Indians. All six of the major independent federal regulatory agencies, moreover, act as administrative courts. The Interstate Commerce Commission hears rate cases. The Security Exchange Commission hears and adjudicates charges of transgressions in stock exchange transactions. The Federal Trade Commission hears cases involving unfair trade practices, and is empowered to issue orders to "cease and desist." Most states have public service commissions with similar duties and powers. On the local level we have boards that issue licenses and adjudicate alleged infringements of licensing conditions preliminary to revocation.

There are classical arguments for and against the usefulness of these agencies. On the one hand, they are designed to be more efficient and more expert than the courts, and equally independent. But even as far back as the forties the unprecedented growth of these administrative adjudicatory bodies aroused concern in many quarters. One result of these early

**The Administrative Adjudicatory Body**

fears was the Administrative Procedures Act of 1946, establishing special rules to ensure at least some of the elements of judicial fairness in these administrative tribunals. Persons appearing before them were now guaranteed adequate notice of hearings, right to counsel, written publication of rules of both procedure and substance, availability of records, and certain other amenities. But these early reforms left untouched some of the basic problems of these agencies, in particular the extent of their supposed independence, efficiency, and expertise, and their genuine capacity for regulation. It was quite clear even before 1969, when a presidential advisory council began a study on these problems,[27] that the use of a single body both to prosecute and to judge any important question belies our ordinary concept of justice. Moreover, the supposed advantages of speed in decision-making have similarly not been realized. The expectation that these cumbersome, many-member commissions would be truly efficient was short-lived. Most important of all, there have been far too many instances of basic conflicts of interest between the persons called upon to regulate some of the nation's largest economic interests and the powerful companies involved. The regulators have too often been the pawns of their presumed subjects. One of the most consistent recommendations that have emerged from the many studies of these agencies is that the adjudicatory functions of the regulatory bodies be lodged in separate and independent agencies. Others would go further and return these matters to the courts.

**Alternatives to the Judiciary**   In addition to administrative quasi courts, a growing number of professional groups also serve as alternatives to the judiciary. Some states and localities, for example, have boards of mental health that commit people to mental hospitals and order their release. These activities so closely resemble the administration of conventional justice that many lawyers and citizens argue that the courtroom is the only proper place for them. The use of mediation boards, arbitrators, union hearing officers, and many similar groups that negotiate and also hear charges against employers, employees, and unions can also be placed in this category. Occasionally some fairly serious school offenses are handled by administrative officers or by lay boards, even though the actions charged could be viewed as legal offenses requiring court action. The work of parole boards and even health boards comes under this heading too. Finally, self-regulating industrial bodies, such as the Motion Picture Association, which polices the motion picture industry, however ineffectively, also play quasi-judicial roles.

The arguments in favor of putting all procedures requiring the hearing of evidence and the meting out of punishments or penalties into courts of law stress the American commitment to canons of procedural fair play. For most citizens these refinements are best played out in courtrooms. On the other hand, the long delays in court calenders, the chronic shortage of judges, and widely publicized courtroom travesties have contributed to a growing movement toward problem-solving outside the courts. This is a controversy that requires further research before resolution.

There is one other dimension to this broad conflict over the use of courts. It has been suggested that we might avoid the overuse of courts by redefining criminal action. Citizens are joining scholars in suggesting the removal of "victimless crimes" from our statute books. This not only would go far toward reducing calendar congestion in the courts, but would also solve many of the problems involved in police work. Victimless crimes are those that are usually called morals offenses: homosexuality, prostitution, public drunkenness, narcotics addiction, and vagrancy. This is still an area of experimentation but the battle lines are being drawn, and I feel the preponderance of evidence is on the side of withdrawing morals actions from the courts.

There is often very flimsy moral sanction for certain of these laws. Is drinking immoral? What about smoking? On what grounds is polygamy immoral? Is the Bible to be the source of our morality? If so, which Bible? Is common practice the source of morals? These questions themselves point up the absurdity of the possible answers. But more than that, how can laws successfully curb people's appetites in matters of sex, food, and amusements? It is far worse for the community to support laws that are openly and widely flouted than to withdraw from such areas. More harm is done to children and adults by the daily spectacle of policemen shutting their eyes to numbers runners than by the numbers game itself. This racket, after all, is nothing more than the poor man's horse race. We have managed to legalize off-track betting without bringing the world to an end. But open disregard of the law and the consequent corruption of the law enforcer are deadly in a complex society. Equally deadly is "selective enforcement," which is merely another variant of lawlessness. In some instances the police may be lax because they are being paid by underworld figures to overlook certain practices in certain areas; but they are often in the even more remarkable position of being *ordered* by their superiors to overlook certain violations in deference to somebody's view of humane consideration, or to ethnic sensitivities or for very practical reasons arising from the budgetary restrictions of police or court facilities. And so the word goes out to take it easy on Mah-Jongg

**Redefining Criminal Action**

in New York's Chinatown, on numbers in Harlem, on adultery in the East Fifties, on prostitution on the Upper West Side, on polygamy in certain upstate communities, on marihuana in Scarsdale.

Nonenforcement, selective enforcement, and syndicate enforcement are the real demoralizers. Some victimless crimes are better handled by hospitals: alcoholism, narcotics addiction. Others might better yield to income reforms: vagrancy and panhandling. Still other problems should be left to churches and self-help groups. But, most certainly, these are activities that should not be pursued in the courts.

Alexander M. Bickel, professor of law at Yale University, has succinctly stated the various facets of the problem of judicial overuse:

> We overuse—to the point of vanished returns—the criminal law as an instrument of regulation, and the civil law suit as the basic, all-purpose instrument of social and individual justice. We overuse all our courts, and the Federal courts above all. We clog them, for example, with automobile negligence, employers' liability, and bankruptcy reorganization cases. Not to speak of patent litigation.[28]

Restraint, then, might be the prevailing principle to be applied here. This would not mean yielding any fundamental liberty. The civil liberties of accused persons must remain paramount. But when we talk of how best to handle competing economic interests or select judges and juries or deal with public morality, then at the very least we need frank recognition and open discussion of the ambiguities and ambivalences involved. Without them we cannot hope to resolve specific problems within these areas of controversy.

**RETRIBUTION VERSUS REHABILITATION**  Although, strictly speaking, prison systems are not part of the judiciary, they are commonly considered in tandem with our court systems. This is understandable since the courts are clogged mainly by recidivists: most offenders are multiple offenders. Indeed, estimates of recidivism run as high as 80 percent, and even the most conservative estimates concede that half the prison population is made up of repeaters. So the judicial-penal system is a kind of revolving door. We are involved in a stalemate, and we seem unwilling to face the fact that our methods of dealing with offenders cancel each other out. We will never have a sound system of "justice" until we stop using the courts as conveyer belts that move people into institutions that virtually assure their reappearance in the courts. What ought we to do, then, with persons convicted of crimes? Most Americans at least give lip service to the goal of rehabilitation, but there are still many who flatly demand retribution. Neither of these goals is currently achieved, and part of the problem may well be the high degree of ambivalence with which we approach the situation. Perhaps we are unwilling to face the extent to which we have let our feelings run away with our minds here. Unquestionably there are large areas of ambiguity, but we frequently do not even get to this level of the problem.

The experimentation done on New York City's bail system is a case in point. It took years to persuade the city's judicial authorities to permit an extensive study, which disclosed that ambivalence about bail was rampant. People were at the mercy of vague visceral notions that public safety required defendants to be locked up if they could not post bail. How otherwise could their appearance in court be guaranteed? The public at large had no idea how many people were locked up because of inability to post bond, nor did they know how long such people might be held or for what crimes this procedure was followed. Even the judges themselves did not know. True, even with the facts clearly presented there might have been ambiguities: the data might not point to any safe and fruitful substitute system. But the first order of business was to allow some experimentation. When this experimentation was concluded, it not only presented some astonishing data, but it also yielded incontrovertible evidence that, indiscriminately applied, bail was less of a deterent to nonappearance than the judicial practice of releasing defendants on their own recognizance. As many as seventy-five persons then being held for lack of bail had been in prison for one year or more and the median time spent in jail without trial was 5.6 months.[29] Indeed, a 1970 federal census of persons in city and county jails showed that 52 percent had not been convicted of any crime. Of a special group of 3,505 who were released on their own recognizance, only 1.5 percent failed to appear for trial. This contrasts with a normal rate of 3 percent forfeiture of bond.[30] According to these figures, a judge may dispense with bail in many cases with very little risk of nonappearance. This in turn bears heavily on the possibility of a subsequent fair trial for the defendants in question. Yet even now bail procedures remain quite unsystematic in most jurisdictions. In sum, it is only through the experimental testing of alternative procedures that our judicial-penal system can begin to serve its true purposes. Its failure is often preordained by our own failure to understand what such purposes are.

Consider what is actually happening. Most penitentiaries supposedly aim at rehabilitation but the reality is totally different. Few observers question the fact that our prisons are not doing the job they should do. Former wardens as well as

**Bail and Nonappearance**

former prisoners are in agreement here. Their warnings are underlined by the statistics cited earlier. Job training is either inappropriate or nonexistent, and in either case there are no jobs in which to place former prisoners when they are released on parole. Sexual assault inside jails is not prevented and proper medical and psychiatric care is not provided. Prisons are overcrowded and many guards are brutal. But worst of all, in my view, there is a total failure to experiment with release without bail, certain types of indeterminate sentences, and other devices that would provide to our prisoners the most vital ingredient of all—hope.

I suggest that our dismal record here may lie in part in our quite incomplete commitment to the ideal of rehabilitation.

**Retribution versus Rehabilitation**

There still lurks in us a conscious or unconscious desire for retribution and more than a little willingness to cast out people whom we see as society's dregs. Perhaps we should deliberate a little more on what retribution implies and how well we are achieving *that*. At a minimum, retribution demands that the punishment fit the crime. But the jails are filled with people who have not yet been convicted of any crime, and among them are many who will be found innocent when at last they are brought to trial. And what about the jail cells that house debtors and husbands who are unable to pay alimony? Surely imprisonment is a dysfunctional method for dealing with these cases. Even when the crime is an act of unmitigated sadism, does jail provide proper retribution?

If the seekers of rehabilitation win the debate over principle, it will still be a hard job to work out the costs and benefits of the various methods that may be proposed to achieve that end. But at no time should we see rehabilitation and retribution as anything but mutually contradictory goals.

A final word about the judicial system as a whole: Any student who wishes to put flesh and blood into this outline of judicial controversies can do so by wandering into any nearby courthouse to watch the proceedings. This might well be the best way for any reader to resolve his ambivalence and to clarify the many areas of ambiguity here. Ambivalence within the courts themselves will also fade if the public can decide on the proper role of judges in the decision-making apparatus of our political system.

# AMERICAN
# LEGISLATURES

Traditionally the legislative process has been viewed as central to American democracy. In our national folklore it is the heart of popular government. In national practice this may no longer be true. The Congress is undergoing some basic conflicts, and the outcome of these conflicts will shape the future of this institution. As I see them, the basic controversies are these:

**The Legislative Role in the United States**

1. There is a struggle over the proper role of a congressman. Should he be a delegate, a representative, or a broker? Essentially this conflict reflects American ambivalence over whether or not the Congress should be the voice of the people in any shape or form. The voice of most of the people? Or perhaps the voice of just some of the people? This type of imagery is implicit in the word "delegate." "Representative," on the other hand, conjures up an image of higher ideology and wisdom, which the legislator uses in the "best interests" of the people. Still others see the Congress as a vehicle for compromise between constituents and colleagues. This is the broker role. The debate over this fundamental matter spawns a few secondary but related controversies. One is the pull of peers versus the pull of policy; another is the strain manifested between the House and the Senate.

2. There is controversy over the proper role of Congress as one institution among others in our national government. Should it be "first among equals"? Should there be legislative supremacy or simply legislative assent? This question too involves subsidiary conflicts, such as the controversy over the style of congressional investigations. Should the Congress be hound dog or watchdog, or neither, or both? What should be the style and limits of these investigations?

3. Finally, there is ambivalence among Americans over questions of political ethics. Is there a "public morality" that runs counter to private morality? Should one ethic reflect the other? Or does the public ethic require more rigor than the private one?

In order to analyze these basic controversies we must evaluate the nature of the day-to-day legislative process that has been in operation in the United States for nearly two hundred years.

**CONGRESS: The Voice of the People? Which People?**

Our legislative chambers, filled as they are with men and women elected by an increasingly varied, informed, and properly counted electorate, ought logically to be the central forum for the "voice of the people." One might suppose that most congressmen see themselves, and in turn are seen, as delegates. Yet it is doubtful that this is true, and it is equally doubtful that many Americans want it to be true. Most scholars as well as citizens feel that the proper function of the legislator is either to express moral truths, or at least better informed opinions (the representative style), or to effect compromises among the competing minorities and institutions (the brokerage role). Further, the delegate role is virtually prohibited by the antimajoritarian bias of the Congress itself—a bias so pronounced that it is rarely even debated. It may be optimistic, therefore, to include the delegate role in this part of the legislative controversy. But I believe it should be considered part of the controversy—a very important part.

As things stand now, the election process, the resulting demography of the Congress, and its structure, rules, informal procedures, and leadership styles, even its party proclivities— all are individually and collectively stacked against any realization of true majoritarianism. If the voice of the people is heard at all, it is surely heard very faintly. It is doubtful whether the voices of the legislators themselves can be heard inside or outside their own walls. I therefore intend to take up each of these elements—elections, demography, structure, rules, procedures, party proclivities, and leadership styles—in the context of the existing antimajoritarian bias. It is my belief that Congress should represent majority views (as expressed in Chapter 3), but that it cannot do so because of the way it is structured. Whatever we may ultimately conclude in regard to this conflict, we should at least be aware of the way the cards are now stacked.

**Who Gets to Congress and How?**

Consider first the impact of our election system on this question of the proper role of a congressman. Do the elections themselves permit a forum for the voice of the people? No, they don't. First there are the difficulties of enfranchisement and apportionment. Despite the newly recognized need for Congress to reapportion itself after each decennial census, there remain pockets of malapportionment both accidental and contrived (some districts contain many more persons than others). Occasional instances of gerrymandering (the skewing of districts into peculiar shapes to protect one or another party or interest group) still manage to escape legislative and judicial notice. While the electorate is now very broadly based, less than half of those eligible to vote normally do so in a typical congressional election. Why this apathy? It may reflect some cynicism on the part of at least a portion of the electorate, who notice that election contests are based on personalities rather than on the policies that concern them. America's traditional two-party politics has not been long on issue orientation or on educating the voter to grapple with issues. Nor has the escalation of campaign expenditures done much to democratize the process or to bend congressional ears toward rank-and-file voters. Many voters are cynical enough to believe that large campaign contributions speak more loudly than small ones. All of this induces a kind of Gresham's law of congressional issues: bad issues drive out good ones.

Even after Election Day congressmen are not encouraged to take clear policy positions. The next election campaign is just around the corner, especially for members of the House; meanwhile they are caught up in the politics of House or Senate, and they must thread their way carefully through the pitfalls of legislative voting. Before a complex bill is voted upon it has usually acquired a series of amendments, often irrelevant. In 1971, for example, the controversial and highly significant Welfare Reform Bill, providing for a "guaranteed base income," came to the House of Representatives hitched to social security and medicare items, and hedged by a rule that permitted no amendments. Thus there was no opportunity for genuine debate or for reworking the provisions into any ordered set of priorities. It was a take-it-or-leave-it proposition. The usual omnibus bill, with its peculiar rules for debate and its other rites of passage, never permits any thoughtful ordering of personal or collective priorities. There is no method, in other words, for the "transitive ordering of preferences." Indeed, the Congress occasionally finds itself in the paradoxical position of finally voting out a bill that represents a conglomerate position favored by far less than a majority of its voting members.[1] Thus the evidence suggests that the electorate seldom can and seldom does translate its views on issues to the Congress, and that congressmen themselves seldom are able to translate their own views into legislative policy. There is clearly no majority rule here.

But even though the vagaries of our election system both for and in the Congress are neither mathematically nor morally majoritarian, it might still be argued that a sort of invisible hand is at work to make the Congress fundamentally "representative" in spite of itself, in some visceral way. There remains a possibility that the Congress might be a true mirror of the population at large as far as significant demographic factors

**The Background of Congressmen**

are concerned. It's possible—but it isn't so. I don't mean to imply that the voice of the people can issue only from the statistically average voter; I am talking only of demographic representativeness. For what it's worth, we can state unequivocally that Congress is *not* representative of the majority in socioeconomic terms. On the contrary, sociologists who have studied the backgrounds and attitudes of American political leaders have documented the elitist character of most of them.[2] We have come a long way since 1831, when Alexis de Tocqueville observed of our House of Representatives: "One is struck by the vulgar demeanor of that great assembly. Often there is not a distinguished man in the whole number. Its members are almost all obscure individuals . . . mostly village lawyers, men in trade, or even persons of the lower classes of society."[3] The upper house appeared very different to him. "The Senate," he said, "is composed of eloquent advocates, distinguished generals, and statesmen of note, whose language would at all times do honor to the most remarkable parliamentary debates of Europe."[4] There is still some degree of difference between House and Senate members, but not much; and most of our national legislators, in one way or another, can be said to belong to the higher echelons of society. In no way is the majority of citizens reflected in either house.

To begin with, Congress is almost entirely male. In 1972 there was one woman senator, Margaret Chase Smith of Maine, and there were twelve congresswomen. In the House of Representatives, there were thirteen blacks, one Puerto Rican, and one Mexican-American; there was one black senator; and there were one senator and one representative of oriental ancestry. In 1969, 76 percent of congressmen were Protestant, 20 percent were Catholic, and 23 percent were Jewish.[5] While more and more senators and representatives come from large urban districts, the number who grew up in small towns is still impressive. More important, the members in positions of greatest influence are more than likely to be white Protestants from small communities. In 1967, for example, the chairmen of all sixteen Senate standing committees were from really small towns. Persons over forty are also heavily represented in both houses of Congress. Though the figure varies from year to year, the average age of congressmen appears to hover around fifty-one, while the average age of senators is about fifty-eight. The leaders in each house tend to be much older than this, in their late sixties.[6]

We also know that a very high proportion of legislators have some prior experience in public office, and that only a small percentage has not gone to college. Most members of both houses of Congress are lawyers, and this has been true

**Dispropor-
tionate
Representation
in House
and Senate**

throughout our history as a nation. Almost all of the other legislators are from the upper echelons of business and the professions, with a sprinkling of farmers. As for income, official salaries are in the public record: $42,500 for both houses along with an annual $50,000 staff fund for members of the House and substantially more for senators. The additional outside income of legislators is a matter of popular conjecture and occasional scandal, but no sound research. Again, the "representative" citizen is not reflected in these figures.

The only systematic study of the social background of national legislators was done in 1960 on the Senate,[7] and it too documents the elitist nature of this body. Any reasonable portrait of the average member of either house would therefore have to show him as quite unrepresentative of his constituents: he is far more affluent and always has been; his social background is of a higher order than that of most of his constituents; he is older than they; and he is, of course, male. All this certainly sets him apart from the "typical American." On the other hand, no responsible investigator has yet concluded that the national legislature is itself a citadel for any *particular* elite. Thus sociologist G. William Dumhoff concludes that "members of the American upper class do not *control* the Legislative branch but rather have influence."[8] Nor does Dumhoff paint the membership as being heavily from the upper class—just from the upper middle class. But in all events, our man in Washington is hardly the man in the street.

Finally, some observers of Congress feel that a sense of party counters any tendencies toward elitism. Those who share this view feel that the two-party system provides a genuine voice for the majority through firm party leadership. In the legislature, however, party operations are essentially confined to the original organizing session of the Congress; in the party caucus, where committee memberships are assigned, you do indeed see some disciplined party voting. Later there are occasional displays of power on the part of party officers called whips and in the party steering committees, which round up votes for partisan issues. But these are relatively frail devices, and they operate only on the few occasions when purely party issues are at stake. Moreover, party leverage usually requires control not only of the Congress, but also of the presidency. Most of the real leadership of each house is in the hands of the respective formal officers—the committee chairmen, the majority leader of the Senate, the Speaker of the House. The actual party affiliation of most congressmen and senators also fails to reflect the citizenry a good part of the time. Note that the Republicans controlled Congress for only four years between 1932 and 1972, although Republicans held the presidency for twelve

**The Party Role in Congress**

of those years. This has in no way necessarily reflected the partisan interests of the majority of citizens. Party labels are frequently misleading. Congress usually appears to be dominated not so much by party as by what some observers have called a "conservative coalition" consisting primarily of midwestern Republicans and southern Democrats. Stephen Bailey has called this an "inverted coalition."[9] These are the congressmen from the "safest" constituencies, who are returned to their seats year after year from one-party areas. Thus the men most likely to influence legislation are also the least likely to be responsive to the winds of change. In 1970, for example, the five largest and most volatile states, containing one-third of our population, controlled only six committee chairmanships. The others went to far less populated areas and to those with little party competition. Of course, there have been efforts to organize a countervailing force, particularly within the Democratic party. Some Democratic legislators have formed an organization called the Democratic Study Group, which tries to map out strategies both to offset the inertia of the system and to counter the power of the inverted coalition. There are

**Forging a Benign Coalition: The Need for Internal Reform**

also a few other informal arrangements of ad hoc liberals designed to overcome the power of the "old boys." One is called the Hard Core and another is called The Group. Both work to use party machinery, including the party caucus, to their own advantage. But I am afraid that those who look forward to what Bailey calls a benign coalition—that is, one that is more truly representative of the people—will have to await some far more basic changes. They will have to wait for the resolution of the delegate-representative-broker controversy. Before it can be resolved we must face our own ambivalence about these roles. A benign coalition will not emerge from congressional reapportionment and redistricting alone, nor will it automatically follow from the impact of the newly enfranchised youth group. It will require changes in the internal rules of the game: reform of congressional procedures. And this will come about only when there are some very powerful signals from the people that they really want such reforms. The impact of reapportionment and enfranchisement of eighteen-year-olds is uncertain at best. The benefits stemming from these reforms may well serve to increase the influence of the suburbs and the sun states rather than the cities. Not all young people are college students and poor blacks; we have given up the struggle to keep 'em down on the farm, but those who leave are as likely to head for Arizona as for Chicago. Once again, the voices of some of the people may find louder echoes in Congress than the voices of others.

At present the structure and processes of Congress push its

members toward the broker role. The desire of many citizens for an ombudsman in Congress contributes here too. Services to constituents, such as redressing real or imagined grievances, requires the congressman to do favors for bureaucrats and bargain with fellow legislators. Career imperatives also force him to assume the bargaining role. The delegate or representative style is far harder to come by. The average citizen, however, clings to some textbook image and becomes a cynic when his heroes turn out to have feet of clay. He seldom understands that it is he himself, Mr. Average Citizen, whose conflicting and ambivalent demands shape the legislative figure he mocks. In general the formal rules of Congress, along with its informal traditions, are instruments of self-preservation, and self-preservation today demands brokerage.

The committee system, the rules, the formal processes, the informal conventions, and the leadership style of Congress all tend further to produce the broker type. The pressure of a congressman's peers is almost always greater than the pressures of ideology and policy commitment.

**PEERS VERSUS POLICIES: COMMITTEES, RULES, PROCEDURES, LEADERS**

Of these forces, the most significant is the highly decentralized structure of Congress. Both chambers must of necessity work through committees in order to cope with the twenty thousand or so bills that are proposed each year. The committees in turn are controlled by a handful of chairmen. And the chairmen are dedicated to increasing their own power, which requires them to be responsive to certain sectional and specialized groups. All of this produces brokers rather than representatives or delegates. Consider the basic structure of the committee system. The Senate has sixteen standing committees with from seven to twenty members each, and the House has twenty such committees with an average of about thirty members on each. Both senators and representatives may and do serve on more than one committee, but in general an attempt is made to limit any individual's membership to two or three committees (a goal more strenuously pursued in the House than in the Senate). When Congress last reorganized itself, in 1946, the number of committees was reduced, but over the years the work load and human behavior have operated to produce a host of subcommittees. Thus multiple membership is still the order of the day and new fiefdoms of power continue to proliferate.

Each chamber has ad hoc committees that normally dissolve after making specific investigations. There are also conference committees made up of members of both chambers, which work out compromises between House and Senate versions of legislative bills. Joint committees are also composed of mem-

**Structure and Organization of Congress**

bers from both chambers, and may be permanent (like the Atomic Energy Committee) or temporary. Joint committees are obviously more economical than duplicate committees holding duplicate hearings, but political pride and intramural jealously dictate the sparing use of joint committees, no matter how sensible they may be. Each chamber clings to its own prerogatives and its own committees.

There are many prerogatives in Congress, and almost all of them manage to obscure the voice of the people. They include the operations of the standing committees, the special privileges of the House Rules Committee, the pomp and power of committee chairmanships, and finally the peculiar potentials that derive from a thorough knowledge of floor procedures.

Consider first the House standing committees and their chairmen. They follow the functional lines of congressional business (Post Office, Agriculture, Education, Ways and Means, and so forth) and are organized at party caucuses following congressional elections. Committee assignments, like committee chairmanships, follow the principle of seniority. Only occasionally is professional expertise recognized in a particular appointment. Most often, committee assignment is a question of party discipline and congressional tenure. And the tenure of many House members is notably long. Indeed, a number of political scientists have commented on the degree to which House membership is becoming a closed-circuit career.[10] This trend not only works against effective influence by constituents, but moves the House toward some strangely bureaucratic practices. There is an increasing respect for tradition and for long and loyal service. The increasing length of a typical session also moves Congress in the direction of peer orientation rather than issue or constituency or even party considerations. Finally, the need for Congress to protect its prerogatives against the pull of the executive branch provides an "outside enemy" situation that further cements intramural relations. In sum, the sheer power and autonomy of committee life is an incentive to mutual respect, clubby reciprocity, and out-and-out logrolling.[11]

**Congressional Procedures**

Committees have a life-and-death hold on legislation, and chairmen have a life-and-death hold on committees. The typical chairman appoints the members of his subcommittees and their chairmen, refers legislation to those subcommittees completely at his own pleasure, and arranges the agenda of the full committee. He and his subcommittee chairmen then have the power to call meetings or not, to hold hearings or not, to decide when to go into executive (secret) session, and to determine who shall be witnesses at these hearings. They select their own committee staff and designate the studies they will make.

Finally, they decide what bills will be submitted to the full membership, and they manage the bills that are reported out of committee. That is, they determine the procedural rules that will guide consideration of these bills on the floor of the House. According to the general regulations of the House (which are adopted by the House each year, and which tend to remain the same), most public bills are received for floor consideration only when they come out of regular committee and only with an attached rule or order from the Rules Committee. This rule—which is only a procedure—can actually make or break a bill. For example, if the Rules Committee attaches to a bill the "wide-open rule," the bill can be amended without restraint on the floor of the House. Depending on the nature of the bill, such a rule may have the effect of crippling or even killing the bill. Conversely, if certain bills are let out with a "gag rule," which prohibits any amendments, this too may augur certain defeat. Of course, in fairness, I must also point out that the House as a whole can theoretically defeat a rule. But in practice this is difficult to do, and it does not happen often. This is also true of the discharge petition, which may be invoked by the House against the Rules Committee or any other standing committee. Such a petition, signed by a majority of the House membership, forces the committee against which it is used to report a bill to the floor of the House. This is obviously difficult to the point of improbability. In practice, therefore, committees decide the life or death of most bills, the Rules Committee has an additional hold on them, and the chairmen have the firmest grip of all. It is no wonder, then, that the "old bulls" who survive to inherit committee chairmanships command so much respectful attention both in and out of the House.

**The Grip of the "Old Bulls" and the Effect of Ordering Procedures**

House procedures also tend to make Congress a citadel of compromise among special interests, rather than a forum for the people. Before a bill is sent to any committee it is put into a hopper and from there it goes to its proper calendar. In the House, this means that financial bills go to what is called the Union Calendar. Other bills of a public nature go onto the House Calendar. And bills dealing with individual problems (such as a bill to grant citizenship under special circumstances) go on the Private Calendar. There is a numbering system that is supposed to ensure order and fair play, but there are methods for considering bills out of order. In the House, this business is in the hands of the Rules Committee. By the time a bill reaches the floor, consideration may be purely perfunctory, or of a political nature (that is, designed for consumption back home through the reportage of the *Congressional Record* or the local press, or the congressman's own propaganda sheets). Most of the real work on a bill has already been done behind the scenes in the committees and the necessary votes have been bargained for by energetic committeemen or by members of the party steering committee. In sum, floor procedures cater to horse trading, not to representation.

**Voting Procedures**

Voting, when it finally occurs, can be by voice (viva voce), by a standing count, by filing past the tellers, or, if there is a demand for it, by roll call. The particular method of voting is determined by the maneuvering of proponents and opponents of a bill. The recording of a vote is another important matter. Until March 1971 the House had never recorded the names of members voting on important amendments to bills. This secrecy was a great advantage to individual members and made policy positions close to invisible. A demand for a "teller count vote" makes it possible to institute a check on individual records, and enables the people to be informed of the exact size of the vote. It has become increasingly apparent that important issues are often determined by less than one-fourth of the actual membership.

This blatant exercise of minority rule along with dramatization of the number of instances when a larger than majority vote is required (and when control is thus in the hands of a minority) should stimulate some debate about the incidence and wisdom of congressional antimajoritarian practices. Senate confirmation of a presidential appointee, for example, requires a two-thirds vote. So do certain parliamentary maneuvers like the use of special rules and cloture (the cutting off of debate so that a vote may be taken). The requirement of a two-thirds vote in these instances is patently antimajoritarian, but it never arouses more than token opposition either in or out of Congress. The coziness of committee life, augmented by the psychological variables that come into play in small groups and work to produce conformity, counter any movement for issue-oriented majoritarianism.

**The Speaker**

The formal leadership of the House is also a factor in the brokerage role of Congress. The Speaker is the chief political figure in the House and a person to be reckoned with at both ends of Capitol Hill. Many strong personalities have held this post and they have all had at their disposal a formidable array of rights and privileges. It is the Speaker, for example, who recognizes persons on the floor, settles parliamentary disputes, appoints members to special committees and conference committees, and in general directs the business of the House. He acts as the leader of the majority party in the House. He also uses every possible political weapon to exert his leadership within his party's caucus.

The Speaker's importance and prestige are well known; the importance of his second in command, the House majority leader, is not so well recognized. Yet according to a well-known journalist, the majority leader is also a "king among dukes and princes. The job is limited only to the extent that the man holding it invokes limitations, or perhaps a stronger Speaker may."[12] The majority leader is in charge of pushing through his party's programs, and to do this he is given a large voice in committee elections and in direct presidential and Cabinet-level meetings. On and off the floor of Congress—even in the press, where most House members tend to be ignored—he is a man who must be reckoned with.

To rise to either of these pinnacles in the congressional career system is to have mastered well its most cherished traditions. Woe to him who has not properly served his time, his elders, and his peers. To have put some principle of government or some matter of policy above the time-honored principle of loyalty is to risk disaster. This was dramatically illustrated by the career of Morris K. Udall of Arizona. Udall was a promising younger liberal who, in the interests of congressional reform (that is, in the interests of democratizing House procedures), challenged the incumbent Speaker, John McCormack of Massachusetts, for the post in 1968. The elderly McCormack was not to be dislodged. In 1971, thinking that the old wounds were healed, Udall ran for majority leader. It was at this juncture that he came to realize that he was politically dead. He found that insurgents do not live to make comebacks in Congress. If you do not win the first time around, you are very unlikely to be given a second chance.

In the final analysis, what counts in Congress, in the words of Jim O'Hara (a representative from Michigan), is "old friendships, personal favors or dislikes, rather than ideology, geography or leadership potential."[13] Or as Udall himself said:

> The leadership-ladder bit—tradition, promotion, seniority—was stronger medicine than I originally thought. The House apparently just insists on people getting in line, and serving time. Boggs [Hale Boggs of Louisiana, who was the victor in the race for majority leader] knew this and exploited the sentiment very effectively. He worked his ass off and he used all his tools. In the South, the Boggs people put the heat on recalcitrants through lobbyists for various industries: oil, tobacco, textiles, and so on. He snatched six or eight votes from me there. He played the freshmen like a virtuoso: he could pass out more goodies than I. The big city boys came to him through a combination of his contacts with mayors and other politicians I didn't know externally, and through such guys as [Dan] Rostenkowski [of Illinois] and [Hugh] Carey [of New York] and a few old deans. Boggs had people all over Washington: lawyers and lobbyists and bureaucrats dating back to the New Deal—and almost all of them knew somebody to pressure for him.[14]

At the end, Udall's remaining hope was that maybe "we've scared a few of the old bulls so that individual committee rules are being loosened and may provide a bit more of a participating democracy."

I suspect he was too optimistic. To borrow the terminology of Stephen K. Bailey again, the centrifugal forces of Congress are still stronger than the centripetal ones; and this, in the final analysis, means that the chance for a majoritarian voice is extremely slight. The committee structure, the formal rules, and the floor procedures all combine to permit a whole series of entry points for small minority obstructionist groups. The protagonists of any reform measure must fight long and hard through a series of skirmishes. The antagonists, on the other hand, usually need to rally their forces only once, and in a quite limited arena, or in an arena where the informal pressures of the institution easily persuade individual congressmen to allow the usual "courtesies" to their peers. The rules, the structure, the procedures are very effective tools in the hands of a small number of experts. In view of all this, the voice of the people is not likely to be heard soon in these legislative halls.[15]

**Senate versus House**

One of the traditional tensions within the legislative arena is the rivalry between the House of Representatives and the Senate. Although the two bodies operate through similar committees, rules, and floor procedures, the variations in their formal structuring and informal norms produce actual differences as well as different images. These differences too have an impact on policy. In balance, the advantage accrues to the Senate. Thus the less representative of the two bodies is the more powerful.

The presiding officer of the Senate is the Vice-President of the United States. His closeness to the President gives him an occasional advantage. He is expected to conduct meetings impartially, and he himself cannot vote except to break a tie. He is not himself a member of the body and may not even be a member of the majority party in the Senate. Any influence he has, therefore, is completely informal. One might easily conclude that he is less powerful than the Speaker of the House, and in general he is. It is the majority leader that commands the real influence in the Senate. This influence varies considerably with the style and capacities of the incumbent, but its potential, at least, is enormous, and fully equal to that of the Speaker. Former President Lyndon Johnson, for example, exerted a powerful influence on the Senate during his years as majority leader. He was a centralizing force that transcended both the autonomy of committees and the coalescence of parties. His successor as majority leader, Mike Mansfield, on the other hand, is a far less compelling force. He regards himself simply as "first among equals," and has therefore contributed to considerable decentralization of the leadership function.

There are many other important differences between the two houses of Congress. The Senate has controlling power over formal treaties with other countries and over executive appointments to high offices. A two-thirds vote in the Senate is required to ratify all treaties, and a majority vote to confirm presidential appointments to the Supreme Court, the Cabinet, and other important national posts. These are obvious advantages, but the unofficial power of the Senate in the realm of appointment is far greater than one might conclude from a reading of the Constitution. Through the custom of "senatorial courtesy" the President virtually cedes his power of appointment to most posts that theoretically come under his patronage. The appointment of U.S. marshals, U.S. attorneys, postmasters, federal district judges, and others is directly turned over to the senators from the states in which the vacancies exist, even when the President does not belong to the same party as these senators. This custom has come about because of an unwritten agreement among senators: they will not consent to any presidential appointment that is not totally acceptable to the senators involved. In comparison with this extensive array of privileges, the patronage that trickles down through the occasional courtesy extended to the House is small indeed. The constitutional requirement that revenue bills (and, by extension, appropriation bills) originate in the House does not go far toward balancing the power of the Senate.

And the Senate has certain other formal structural advantages over the House. Senators are elected for six years, congressmen for two; senators' terms overlap (that is, only one-third of Senate seats are up for reelection in each biennial congressional election); and the Senate is less than one-fourth the size of the House. These factors combine to make the Senate the more prestigious of the two chambers.

One of the most distinctive features of the Senate is its long history of unlimited debates. Until 1917 there were no limits at all; in that year the Senate adopted the famous Rule 22, which provides a theoretical means of putting an end to a filibuster (that is, endless talk by a handful of senators so as to defeat a majority's desire to take action on a bill) by permitting cloture (that is, the limiting of debate to no more than one hour per senator) on agreement of two-thirds of the senators present. In practice, however, the rule has never been successfully invoked. Rule 22 covers both procedural and substantive matters. Its precise effects and its genuine popularity within the Senate have been matters of great controversy. One of the most cogent analyses of this device and its predictable outcomes was made by Raymond E. Wolfinger, who concluded that "most Senators like Rule 22."[16] Most Presidents have not been too worried about it either. How the public feels is unknown. One thing is quite clear; the filibuster is a device that can be used by liberals as well as conservatives to their own advantage, and so no one is in a hurry to set a precedent against it by invoking cloture in any particular instance. Another thing that makes the filibuster attractive in senatorial eyes is the drama of it all: it dramatizes not only the senators doing the talking, but the Senate as a whole. It is a formidable weapon that the House does not possess; and of course it is a weapon that prevents majority rule.

Senators are older, on the average, than congressmen, though this difference is apparently shrinking. The socioeconomic variables reviewed earlier tend to make the Senate more "elite" than the House. Note the smaller proportion of women, blacks, and members of other minority groups. In an earlier era it was also seen as more conservative, but at present it appears to be the more aggressively liberal, as these rather loose terms are used. It is, in general, a more flexible body than the House, and its members tend to have shorter tenure.

**The Senate's "Inner Club"**  For a long time there was an unchallenged view that the Senate was dominated by an "inner club,"[17] heavily southern, very institutionally oriented, dedicated to the Senate's traditions and norms above any other principle or legislative purpose. This view, however, was recently challenged by Nelson Polsby. He suggests that the formal organization of the Senate, rather than any informal patterns, was the true basis for its power elites.[18] Whichever view one takes, there is no denying the operation of special norms. Nor can we overlook the great degree of visibility of the Senate, or its increasing role in the incubation of presidential hopefuls. While all of these forces have combined to make the Senate a far more issue-oriented body than the House, even a more liberal body, and much more inclined to see itself as national rather than parochial, still it is far removed from the voice of the people.

All things considered, the question of the Congress' role vis-à-vis the American people will not be resolved short of very fundamental changes. In the final chapter I sketch out the basic reforms we might make toward the objective of majority rule.

**LEGISLATIVE RULE VERSUS LEGISLATIVE ROLE**  Whatever the style of our legislative leaders, and whatever their efficacy as instruments of popular government, the key question in the minds of most students of Congress is not how well the Congress represents whom, but what its essential institutional role is. While the formal work of the Congress is described in Article 1 of the Constitution, there is more to it than passing laws. Congress also acts as an information and education conduit for the people at large; it is the overseer of the executive branch; it is the nation's chief investigative body (its power to investigate, of course, is used to implement the three previous roles); it serves as a tribunal for impeachment proceedings against civil officers, including the President; it judges the conduct of its own members; it proposes amendments to the Constitution; it admits new states to the Union; and most important of all, in the view of some students of Congress, it does favors and services for its constituents. What is at stake here is the question of legislative supremacy. Does it exist? Should it? Or has Congress (and by inference many state legislatures as well) strayed so far from its theoretical function that we may question whether it has any legislative power at all?

Those who claim that the legislature has lost ground do not mean that it has lost numbers, or lost any explicitly assigned prerogatives, or even lost its traditional hold on people's imaginations. But it may have lost actual power and prestige as a center of decision. This is the question at issue. It is the myth of legislative supremacy, for example, that drives many citizens to tour the chambers of Congress and even state assemblies in the wild hope that they will hear echoes of the Great Debates. But debates went out with Webster and Calhoun; an occasional monologue or a rather perfunctory roll call is more the order of the day. Today's American legislators are more likely to be manipulators than persuaders. The pressure of their work calls more and more for executive talents rather than legislative ones. This change may be an inevitable result of population and technological changes in our society; but there may be other factors at work here.

The Constitution specifies that Congress is endowed with "all the legislative power herein delegated." While the list of some twenty specific items in Article 1, Section 8 is in itself not vastly impressive, it becomes more so when read in the light of the meaning that each brief phrase has acquired through the years. Consider the power "to regulate interstate commerce." Taken together with that elastic phrase "to make all laws which shall be necessary and proper for carrying into execution the foregoing powers," the regulation of commerce, as we have seen, has given Congress entrée into business affairs not only in the transportation industry, but also in manufacturing industries whose products eventually move into what the Supreme Court has called "the stream of commerce." Such regulations include safety laws, legislation on minimum wages, laws providing for collective bargaining agreements, laws prohibiting immoral conduct (transportation of women across state lines for immoral purposes), and laws concerning certain criminal acts (provisions for the entrance of the FBI into

**The Constitutional Delegation of Powers and Its Limits**

kidnapping cases after a twenty-four-hour time lapse). The history of the expansion of congressional power is too long to be considered here in detail. There is power to tax and provide for the general welfare, power to borrow money, to establish post offices, and to regulate the armed forces, among others—and all of these clauses have fathered innumerable laws that might not immediately appear to be within Congress' province from the language of the Constitution itself.

Yet this great legislative power is belied by the many analysts who have concluded, along with Samuel P. Huntington, that "Congress either does not legislate or legislates too little and too late."[19] It is Huntington's view that "if Congress legislates, it subordinates itself to the President; if it refuses to legislate, it alienates itself from public opinion."[20] He supports this view by pointing to certain trends that have resulted in congressional isolation from national issues and in the dispersion of Congress' power to legislate. Congressional parochialism results from the increasing length of tenure of congressmen, the increasing importance of seniority, the dead-end nature of the House career, the decline of personnel interchange between Congress and the executive branch, and the provincial background of most congressmen. The dispersion of congressional power results from the seniority system and the rules described earlier, and from a tendency to substitute administrative oversight and private legislation for public legislative activities. This will be more fully investigated below, in the discussion of investigations.

While Huntington, among others, advocates swinging with these winds of change by explicitly recognizing the congressional role as one of administrative oversight and constituent service, there are others who wish to revitalize Congress so that it can resume the role of chief lawmaker.

**The Weight of Executive Power**

Probably a majority of political scientists concede that public legislation is increasingly being initiated by the executive branch. The hand may be the hand of Esau, but the voice is the voice of Jacob. They therefore conclude with Clinton Rossiter that the scales of power have tipped drastically and probably permanently toward the White House and away from Capitol Hill.[21] More than that, most of these scholars conclude that the scales *should* be so tipped. But there are a few studies that move in an opposite direction. Lawrence Chamberlain[22] in 1946 and later Moe and Teel[23] have purported to prove that Congress has been highly involved in great policy decisions as well as in the slower processes of policy modification. Along with Nelson Polsby and others, these scholars urge the members of House and Senate "to enhance the participation of these institutions in the process of policy making by improving their capabilities rather than destroying their power."[24]

Many legislators themselves see things this way. Senator J. William Fulbright, for example, said in 1969 that the war in Vietnam "is the culmination of decades of liberal over-reliance on the White House and the 'strength' of the men who sit there."[25] And even some chief executives, notably Dwight Eisenhower, have not included the role of chief lawmaker among the President's prerogatives. Thus the controversy over the basic style of the legislature—whether it should rule or merely play a role—continues unabated, and its resolution does not appear to be in sight.

There is considerable uncertainty surrounding what Stephen Bailey has aptly described as the hound dog and watchdog functions of Congress. The hound dog investigations are those that are ancillary to the legislative role of Congress. They include some of the Congress' proudest achievements: its reports on organized crime, the pricing of drugs, civil disorders, the munitions industry, and migratory labor.[26] The watchdog investigations, on the other hand, have been more uneven in quality and have included such disasters as the investigation of the Joint Committee on the Conduct of the Civil War. But here too there have been some triumphs: investigations of the lending policy of the Reconstruction Finance Corporation and of the inefficiencies in the Civil Aeronautics Administration. Both kinds of committee operations are often clouded by public ambivalence over congressional goals and methods. There is some concern, for example, over how close a watch the Congress should maintain over the day-to-day operations of the executive departments. In practice, the Congress can and does control the vast apparatus of government through budgetary scrutiny and consequent changes in resource allocations and appropriations. It also controls the executive branch through the scrutiny of personnel. Direct legislative confirmation of certain high-ranking officials is required, but in general Congress' control of executive personnel is exercised through its regulations concerning civil service operations and through the operation of informal restraints. All of these controls, both budgetary and personnel, are born and bred in committee hearing rooms. Indeed, in the opinion of Leiper Freeman,[27] Aaron Wildavsky,[28] Francis Rourke,[29] and many others, it is in the interplay of congressional committeemen and their corresponding numbers among civil service bureau chiefs that American policies are most directly hammered out. At issue here, then, is not only the extent of congressional hearings, but their style as well. A hearing may be simply an inquiry or it may be an inquisition.

The typical congressional hearing is an open affair to which administrative spokesmen, representatives of business and

**HOUND DOG VERSUS WATCHDOG**

labor organizations, professional experts, and many other interested parties are invited to present data and views on the legislation under consideration. Most of this work is singularly unexciting. People appear willingly and procedures are informal. It is in this way and in this atmosphere that congressmen come to learn about such matters as the intricacies of salmon spawning, the amounts of salmon processed each year by the canning industry, the number of sportsmen who fish for salmon, the general scientific consensus on the world salmon population, and so forth. The people who appear at such hearings are drawn heavily from those executive bureaus concerned with the matters under consideration and from related industries. This makes it possible for a group of laymen (that is, congressmen) who have been chosen for many attributes but hardly for any specific knowledge they may have about fish life (except perhaps in Oregon) to decide what constitutes a reasonably good bill for the conservation of salmon. In such routine committee hearings conflict often centers on the propriety of the interests represented, the time consumed, and the relative expertise of bureaucrats.

**Controversial Hearings**

The subject matter of some committee inquiries, however, is such that the hearings take on a more investigatory and correspondingly adversary flavor. Here it is often the style and the procedures of the hearing that are called into question. This type of hearing receives publicity that all too often causes difficulties. The more spectacular committee investigations tend to deal with the conduct of the executive branch of government (the dealings of the "independent" regulatory agencies such as the Federal Power Commission, for instance), the practices of certain business or labor groups that operate under national regulations (such as labor racketeering), or the possible prevalence of "subversive activities" in some special facet of American life (such as the movie industry or the universities). All of these investigations hang on Congress' legitimate power to make laws directly concerning the subject under consideration and to make sure that such laws are being properly executed. Unfortunately, congressmen may have ulterior motives for some of the investigations they conduct. A desire for spite, vengeance, political advantage, or front-page publicity can lie behind these high-voltage committee hearings. The subject matter, in other words, is explosive, and the hearings can pose real danger for many of the participants. In such hearings, therefore, the committee members generally use more formal procedures. Witnesses frequently have to be subpoenaed rather than merely invited. The committees may appoint special legal counsel to conduct the interrogations and the witnesses may be accompanied by their own lawyers. Thus, even though this is still a congressional hearing, it takes on something of the adversary aspect of a court trial. In this charged atmosphere, unfortunately, the allegations and data elicited at certain hearings have caused personal and economic ruin to some witnesses. In the hysterical aftermath of World War II and in the hostile freeze of the subsequent cold war, for example, public feeling ran high against people who in any way appeared "suspicious." Many citizens were all too ready to believe, as some congressional leaders implied, that their most pressing domestic problems were caused by "Communists" in Hollywood and in army dental offices. Private enterprise refused employment to persons who were called to testify at hearings of the House Un-American Activities Committee. It was a veritable witch hunt. We need not question congressional motivation, however, to recognize that there is room for legitimate complaint against some of the cruder tactics that certain of the committees have been known to employ: the irresponsible leaks to the press, the high-handed disregard for the rights of witnesses, and on occasion the cavalier contempt for proper procedure.

These congressional errors in judgment and procedure, however, need not be turned into a weapon against the committee system as such. Committee hearings are an integral part of the legislative process. What is needed is simply a sense of balance and self-restraint on the part of Congress, and the adoption of more stringent procedural rules. The use of executive sessions (from which visitors and the press are barred) might on certain occasions help relieve tension. (It is perhaps salutary to remind ourselves that the U.S. Constitution itself was the result of a closed meeting.) In any event, committee procedures must be continuously revised so as to reduce abuses without necessarily reducing power. In sum, Congress must resolve to make certain that its investigations conform to proper legal and moral standards. And the public must have a proper regard for both the hound dog and the watchdog functions of Congress, and a proper respect for the powers necessary to perform these two quite different but equally necessary roles. It is not appropriate to view them as antithetical to each other. They can and should be complementary. It is necessary, however, to resolve the basic question of style. Committee hearings must be understood by both the Congress and the public to be just that—inquiries necessary for the *legal* purposes of Congress. Neither the legislature nor the public can for a moment allow its prejudices to reduce these hearings to instruments of punishment. A congressional inquiry must not become an inquisition.

In sum, congressional investigations properly conducted are much-needed tools in the balancing act that Congress must perform to maintain its proper position vis-à-vis the executive branch.

**Committee Hearings: The Basic Question of Style**

**SELF-
INTEREST
VERSUS
PUBLIC
INTEREST**

Nowhere is American ambivalence about basic values more clearly seen than in the arena of public morality. Obviously there are two sets of ground rules here, one for the private sector and another for the public. In the private sector the ethics of self-interest and profit are quite acceptable. In the public sector, moral standards are clearly escalated. The picture emerges most sharply in the various proposals that keep cropping up for the regulation of legislative "conflict of interest." The best known attempts to keep lawmakers pure are those that deal with Congress, but many states and local units are also involved in these harangues. The most stringent of the federal provisions, however, deal with the members of the executive branch, rather than with the Congress.

**Conflict of
Interest**

In general, officials in all branches of government are expected to eschew outright bribery: they may neither accept nor offer bribes in any form. The statutes here are long and loud and clear. But when the quid pro quos are delayed or indirect, the situation becomes clouded. For example, is there a conflict of interest when a congressman intercedes on behalf of some group of voters whose properties are being threatened by an administrative action, and whose reward to the congressman will be their continued voting loyalty? Or is that just a part of the job of being a congressman? If an official comes to learn about some future government action and buys or sells property so as to make a profit on the basis of this information, is this corrupt or just clever? And while accepting outside fees for private work, such as a continued law practice, is by now generally agreed to be unacceptable, what about *future* fees? Or even future employment based on present actions? Is that bad? Is it avoidable? In business, companies frequently recruit employees from one another on the basis of their special experience and expertise. But in certain areas of federal employment, employees are enjoined from accepting jobs with companies with which they have been dealing until five years have elapsed. Congress has thus been reasonably zealous in legislating against the nefarious outcomes of executive conflicts of interest; it has been far less vigorous in regulating itself. Although there have been a number of major hearings into the matter, there is still a legislative void, traceable not to mere intransigence on the part of Congress, but to the very real uncertainty both in and out of Congress about the proper congressional role. We have noted before the many roles the legislator may adopt—the representative, the delegate, the ombudsman, the broker—and we have seen that most congressmen conceive of themselves as brokers, or negotiators among competing interests. Professor Norton E. Long makes the point vividly when he explains that a conflict *among* interests has always been acceptable. The broker role, in fact, is part of the

Madisonian creed.[30] Yet how can a man be expected to represent interests, or even maintain his electoral status without some cloud, particularly when his election depends so heavily on funds for campaigns that yearly grow more expensive and less rational? How is he supposed to arrive at a sense of pure public interest? And how then is he supposed to finance his campaign?

In 1964, for example, the California Democratic state primary race alone cost one of the candidates over $1 million,[31] and a 1970 New York senatorial race cost even more. There are state assembly races that reputedly cost in excess of $100,000. I must add that all of this flies in the fact of existing laws that purport to limit campaign expenditures. There is a $5,000 ceiling on House campaigns and a ceiling of $25,000 on Senate races, and various states have put similar regulations on their books. But the limits apply only to what the campaigner himself may *directly* contribute to his official campaign. Nothing is said about the contributions of special ad hoc committees that spring up in his support, and there is an endless stream of contributing individuals, including babies. It can hardly be expected that any average person would have available the huge sums of money necessary to conduct a successful congressional campaign. Yet we do not readily advocate that only the rich should run for public office. Of all the possible solutions offered for this dilemma, the most logical seems to be the restriction of the *total* amount that is permitted to be spent on all classes of campaigns, and a disclosure law that would require legislators to reveal both their total campaign expenditures and their total expenditures while in office. Public scrutiny of these figures might provide everyone, legislator and citizen alike, with the necessary impetus to straighten out the morality muddle. Yet it is doubtful that we will ever be able to deal with conflict of interest in the British style, with the simple and widespread expectation that "Members of Parliament act like gentlemen." Expenditure reforms are needed, but it would also help greatly if we were to discipline ourselves into a more reasoned attitude about what constitutes a proper public morality. We cannot expect public saints while we tolerate private sinners. We must recognize the probability that all men will act in their own self-interest, and make certain that the self-interest is adequately assuaged and that it remains congruent with the public interest so far as possible.

These, then, are the congressional conflicts. What about the other legislative bodies?

Our state legislatures reveal the same conflicts as Congress. They follow, after all, many similar practices. For example, all but one state legislature is bicameral, despite the fact that the

**Campaign Expenditures**

**STATE AND LOCAL LEGIS- LATURES**

states lack the essential prerequisites for this structural form. That is, there is no sound territorial, population, or any other basis for representation in the upper houses of state legislatures. The districts that underlie the state senates are arbitrary divisions without life or traditions of their own. There is little reason for anyone to represent them except to ensure the rural domination of the state legislatures. Yet only Nebraska has done away with the two-chamber system and conducts its business through a one-house legislature.

**Structure and Procedures of State Legislatures**

As for other structural facts, there are variations in detail but not in essence. All state legislators serve either two- or four-year terms (the upper houses claiming the longer terms). The most striking way in which state legislatures differ from Congress is that they are always part-time affairs. Three-fourths of state legislatures meet in regular session only once every two years, and the remainder serve for very limited time periods. In as active and populated a state as New York, the legislature meets only once a year in regular session, and for only three months or so at that. And even during the months of legislative activity, the houses sit only an average of two or three days a week. Indeed, only sixteen states operate without a fixed limit (commonly sixty days) on the extent of the legislative session.

**Powers of State Legislatures**

In their methods of operation, most state legislatures imitate the committee system, the calendar concept, the multiple readings of bills, and other procedural devices of Congress. The forum in which they wield their power is circumscribed not only by the United States Constitution, but also by their own state constitutions. The Tenth Amendment to the national Constitution reserves to the states "the powers not delegated to the United States by the Constitution, nor prohibited by it to the States." Among the nationally prohibited items are ex post facto laws, bills of attainder, titles of nobility, and the levying of imposts on goods from other states. States are forbidden to make alliances with other states, to conclude treaties, to coin or print money, and to keep troops in peacetime. States are also restrained by the Constitution from denying any person due process of law or the equal protection of the laws. They may not deny any citizen the vote because of race, religion, or sex. In addition to these explicit injunctions, there are a few other areas, such as the regulation of interstate commerce, where the courts have held that Congress holds preemptive power. There are more areas, however (such as taxing power), where the state legislatures and Congress may act concurrently.

While most state constitutions refrain from setting forth an explicit and exclusive list of state legislative powers, they do specify certain general types of authority, such as authority to tax, to appropriate land, borrow funds, to regulate business, to define crimes, and to set punishments. For the rest, it is generally assumed that the state legislatures will operate within the states' "police powers." Most state constitutions, however, are inappropriately restrictive of legislative power, as a result of turn-of-the-century disgust with the corruption common at that time in state legislatures. The impediments to firm legislative authority stem from a number of devices common to all state constitutions: (1) a tendency for the constitution to spell out a long list of details, such as workmen's compensation programs, which would be more appropriately covered by state statutes; (2) a tendency to prescribe too many powers and thus imply that others are denied; (3) a general use of specific sections forbidding certain designated types of legislation, such as prohibitions against laws concerning individuals or laws concerning specific localities; (4) a generous use of the initiative, the referendum, and the proposition, all of which carry policy matters directly to the electorate instead of leaving them in legislative hands; and (5) a tendency to hem in the financial powers of state legislatures with complicated formulas concerning limits on tax rates, on borrowing, and on purposes for loans. Add to this the states' own bills of rights, and one can see the straits in which the state legislators frequently find themselves.

Moreover, state legislators do not command the respect that congressmen do. The earlier tendency of state assemblies to serve as steppingstones to Washington has atrophied, and this exacerbates the problem of prestige. The state legislators are also less generously supplied with aides and services than congressmen. All of this has the effect of hampering their efforts. Yet these legislators must respond to an ever growing set of demands for government services. The American public is becoming increasingly urbanized and increasingly prone to look to government at all levels for the solutions to their problems. Suffering as they do from badly distorted districting, poor salaries (making them easy prey for unscrupulous lobbyists), low prestige and minimal services, rigid constitutional restraints and malapportionment, state legislators are involved in the same conflicts that plague congressmen: they waver between restraint and reform, between the roles of protector and prototype, between peer and policy. And the need for some degree of resolution is as pronounced at this level as in Washington.

Lawmaking bodies at the local level, on the other hand, bear little resemblance to national or state legislatures, either structurally or procedurally. For one thing, local legislatures are almost universally single-chambered bodies. They are frequently dominated by one party, and on occasion (particularly

**Local
Legislative
Bodies**

in certain villages) are nominally nonpartisan. Their major work is done during executive sessions; public sessions are devoted to hearings on property sales, zoning changes, and similar matters of local concern. All votes taken at public meetings are thus cast without benefit of debate and are the result of decisions obviously made during previous executive meetings. The political pathology of small-town America lies in the fact that there *are* no frankly acknowledged basic cleavages. Presumably there are only more and less efficient ways of performing necessary services. The public personality of most towns and small city councils, moreover, is carefully designed to perpetuate this myth. Much of the business of local government might well be improved by a frank facing of the essential contradictions posed here. Along with all the other legislatures that serve the American public, those at the grass-roots level are also under severe and often countervailing pressures. There are pressures concerning legislative role, intergovernmental relations, and basic ethics.

**Basic Cleavages in Small-town America**

If our legislators, national and local, are ever to serve as true spokesmen for the people, and if institutional power is ever to be balanced, legislatures must have the support of a citizenry that has come to grips with its own views on just what these assemblies should be. The people must be clear in their own minds about the proper relationship between themselves and their elected legislators. They must decide too what role their legislators ought to play vis-à-vis the executive and judicial branches of government. They must try to separate in their minds the issues that belong to each level of government (a subject I shall take up in a subsequent chapter). Finally, they must make up their minds about what constitutes "ethical" dealings and recognize that there cannot be two sets of standards, one for public office and another for private life. A failure to think these problems through puts us in the position of passing the buck and then blaming the other guy. As we resolve our own ambivalences about these conflicts, moreover, it seems to me that we must be resolute in pressing for a greater degree of majority rule and less of the existing pluralist brokerage system of competing minorities. The public might well also reconcile its desire for legislative ombudsmen with a willingness to pay for the supportive services and staffs this work entails. In short, we must work to resolve existing contradictions so that the voice of the people can be truly heard in the legislatures, and the voice of the legislatures heard in the land.

# CHAPTER 7

# THE AMERICAN
# PUBLIC EXECUTIVE

At first glance, the President appears to hold the reins of power in the American political system. He is therefore often thought of as the one person who can end the stalemates in our policy-making apparatus. But there is considerable ambivalence, ambiguity, and controversy about the presidency itself. Is the President really as powerful as he seems to be? Can the presidency actually serve as the ignition system, the continuing energy source, and the prime legitimizer of our society? *Should* the President be the sole arbiter of our national destiny? There are great uncertainties involved here, and public ambivalences over these questions are quite sharp. But at least the area of argument is limited. The strong-president–weak-president controversy is by far the most fundamental in American politics. Only two other secondary problems need detain us at all: the controversy over a proper method for selecting the President and the question of the proper style of presidential campaigns.

The President is the apotheosis of the American dream: the initiator, the inventor, the driver, the man at the controls. He is the very nerve center of the public decision process. At the same time, he is the antithesis of the American dream: a potential tyrant, a potential demagogue. Whenever he acts, he leaves behind him a widening circle of inertia. He minimizes the area in which others can fully participate in what most democratic theorists believe should be a system of interdependent decisions.

Viewed alone, the American presidency is awesome and even frightening in its potential. Many political analysts assess the U.S. presidency as the most powerful individual executive office in the world. Its power, in their view, stems not only from the internal mechanics of our system, but also from the position of world leadership that the United States now occupies. The increasing imperatives of foreign policy certainly press power on a man to whom the Constitution gives virtually sole initiative in that sphere. And in an era of continually rising expectations and continuing orientation toward government solutions, domestic concerns too thrust more power on the President than has been traditional. Finally, the pervasive influence of television,

**The Presidency:
Public
Ambivalence**

with its stress on personality and instant charisma, is also having profound effects on the presidency. It may well be, therefore, that the scales of power, which may once have been equally balanced among our three constitutional branches of government, has by now been permanently tipped in favor of the executive branch. Add to all this the widely held myths of public administration, such as "unity of command," "executive leadership," and the "scalar process," and the supremacy and power of the presidency seem unassailable. Indeed, I would venture to say that this is an almost unchallenged view of the office. Most people see the President as holding control over Congress in both foreign and domestic affairs.[1] It is an image made vivid in the daily newspapers and other media.

**Presidential Power**

After decades of accommodation to an increasingly powerful executive presence, some voices, particularly in the Congress, are now being raised in protest against what is seen as presidential usurpation of power. There are those who now see the President as a virtual dictator, overbearing in his relations with Congress, with the judiciary, with the press, and with the public. There are, some would say, too many secret decisions, too many secret papers, too many events in which neither the Congress nor the people participate. Indeed, there are events they do not even comprehend. The Congress has been denied not only its formal right to declare war and to advise, but even to have access to necessary information. The Pentagon Papers, a series of high-level documents that purport to describe how and when the United States became involved in Vietnam, were too long suppressed by means of "top secret" classification, a system entirely controlled by the executive branch.

There is ample evidence that the President influences Supreme Court decisions, not only through his appointment power but also through informal pressure. Finally, there is striking evidence that the President fails to seek the advice of the members of his own cabinet or even to inform them of the decisions he has made without them. These straws in the wind cannot be ignored.

Many other pieces of evidence, however, are being overlooked by those who are sure that the President's tremendous powers are ordained and inevitable. To begin with, there are many formal ways in which the Congress can frustrate the President. Congress has considerable leverage with his executive budget, for example—particularly since the President does not have an item veto. That is, the President must either accept or reject the budget that Congress approves; he cannot pick it apart. The exigencies of day-to-day government often force him to accept congressional items he does not like. And Congress alone can create or destroy new departments and "independent" agencies. The Congress is also able to embarrass and even harass the President by repeated investigation of one or another of his executive agencies. It can refuse to approve his ambassadorial, administrative, or judicial appointments. It can hold up appropriations for his pet programs and reduce the size of his White House staff. It could even decide to take some substantive initiatives of its own in policy-making. Congress is, after all, our formally designated lawmaking body. All of these ploys have been considered at various times when a President has persisted in going his own way without the advice or consent of the Congress.

The Supreme Court, of course, has every opportunity to act independently, since justices are appointed for life and are popularly expected to act with complete indifference to executive command. Indeed, history offers many examples of judicial independence. The Supreme Court hardly fulfilled the ambitions of Franklin Delano Roosevelt; it cut down every one of his basic programs. Lincoln was denied constitutional sanction when he suspended the writ of habeas corpus during the Civil War. President Truman felt the wrath of the Supreme Court when he sent troops to break a steel strike. And there are many other less dramatic examples.

Little attention is paid to the degree to which the President is inevitably constrained by the actions and decisions of previous administrations. No President can really do much about the forces that were set in motion yesterday. Budgets are already drawn up, personnel is hired, foreign policy commitments are made, and so forth. Moreover, the President is very much constrained by the recalcitrance of many members of the bureaucracy and the very incomplete controls he has over them. More than 85 percent of the executive establishment operate under merit systems that effectively protect them from executive carrot-and-stick operations. They move in and out and up and down on an escalator beyond his control. It is often hard for him to reach effectively even those in the politically appointed "Schedule C" group. Richard Neustadt tells a story about President Truman musing over Eisenhower's impending succession to office. Truman remarked, "He'll sit here and he'll say, 'Do this! Do that!' and *nothing will happen*. Poor Ike, it won't be a bit like the Army. He'll find it frustrating."[2] And he did.

**Constraints on the President**

The Twenty-second Amendment to the Constitution, which provides that "no person shall be elected to the office of the President more than twice," also substantially limits his power. In effect, any President who has been elected twice is a "lame duck" during his last two years in office: the *potential* of presidential influence, so crucial in the power game, is greatly weakened by the certainty of his removal from the scene on a fixed date. Top-level assistants seek out lucrative jobs while they still have maximum bargaining power, patronage plums fall away, leverage over Congress weakens.

Moreover, the President's strengths can themselves become weaknesses. As James MacGregor Burns points out, the presidency has already absorbed into its orbit all the institutions that once checked it, such as the Cabinet, the Vice-President, and the national party.[3] This absorption, coupled with our demand that the President be a charismatic leader, leads him more and more to become a captive of a type of consensus politics that is made up of small issues rather than large policies. It forces the President to be responsive to the pressures of parochial constituencies, and makes him highly manipulable by middle-level bureacrats with their middle-level concerns. And the lack of an institutionalized opposition with coherence and visibility increases the tendency on the part of the President to internalize a great many diverse and conflicting views. He will act only after he has estimated—perhaps overestimated —what the other forces in his all too necessary coalitions are likely to do. This too diffuses genuine leadership. In sum, this is not the stuff of real greatness, or of real power.

**Strong and Weak Presidents**

There is also a certain amount of historical evidence that must be accounted for by those who insist that the presidency is the seat of all power. If it is, how do we explain the all too many weak Presidents we have undoubtedly had? President watchers frequently lump Presidents together in two major categories: strong and weak. This is the practice, for example, of Professor Robert Hirschfield.[4] Others add a third category midway between strong and weak. In any event, there seems to be almost universal agreement about who the really strong men were: Jefferson, Jackson, Lincoln, Wilson, the two Roosevelts, and Truman. Among the weak Presidents we may surely list the two Harrisons, Fillmore, Pierce, Grant, Harding, and Coolidge. In the middle range we might find the two Adamses, Van Buren, Hayes, Cleveland, and Eisenhower. There is more debate about Polk and Kennedy.

Whatever we may conclude about the strengths and weaknesses of past Presidents, we must face the question of what a President *should* be. Weak Presidents might well have been weak because they believed this to be their proper stance. Many analysts of the presidency, including Professor Robert S. Hirschfield, explain our presidential ups and downs as primarily the responses of individual incumbents to the presidential role. A weak President is not necessarily a weak man, or one overpowered by circumstances; a strong President may be neither forceful nor fortunate. There is also the matter of self-image.

Does a President see himself as strong leader or respected chairman? We can find most of the pros and cons of this argument in the words of the Presidents themselves.

The essence of the strong President's self-image is contained in the words of Woodrow Wilson when he was still a professor: "The President is at liberty, both in law and conscience, to be as big a man as he can"; and in Teddy Roosevelt's description of the White House as a "bully pulpit"; and in FDR's first inaugural address, in which he said, "In every dark hour of our national life, a leadership of frankness and vigor has met with that understanding and support of the people themselves which is essential to victory"; and in Lincoln's words to his wartime cabinet: "I have gathered you together to hear what I have written down. I do not wish your advice about the main matter. That I have determined for myself"; and in the sign on Harry Truman's desk: "The buck stops here." These men viewed the office (and their views were essential determinants of that office) as the locus of initiative, of party and national leadership, and of the effective and ultimate resolution of almost all national problems.

Ulysses S. Grant held a dramatically different view of the presidency. He called the President "a purely administrative officer." Calvin Coolidge did not consider it good form to discuss "public business" with either congressional leaders, the press, or tne public at large. Eisenhower was very much concerned throughout his two terms with avoiding "executive usurpation of power." He held to the views that had helped him to rise to the top of the military hierarchy: a good officer relies heavily on his staff, disperses as much authority as possible, and minimizes his own convictions in the interests of organizational unity.

Scholars and political writers, as well as Presidents, have strong opinions on the propriety of these opposing views of the presidential office. There is little doubt that Professor Robert Hirschfield advocates a strong presidency; the journalist Tom Wicker, on the other hand, not only describes a weaker version of the presidency, but sometimes appears to prescribe it:

**Presidential Views of the Office**

> It is fair to ask what Presidential government of the Johnson type has done for us lately. Aside from that, it is necessary to ask whether the vast accretion in Presidential powers that took place from FDR to LBJ was entirely justified by the results —whether, indeed, the Presidency had not, by 1965, become almost a Frankenstein's monster that needed only the opportunity of Vietnam to turn on its creators.[5]

Perhaps the ideal of a dynamo in the White House prepared to set the country right on all fronts is not only impossible, but inappropriate.

Some analysts catalog the President's roles under as many as ten headings: head of state, commander in chief of the armed forces, chief organizer of foreign affairs, chief manager of the economy, first legislator, chief organizer of the civil service, ultimate judicial disciplinarian, chief banker, insurance agent, and social worker.

**Presidential Powers**

The administrative role of the President is obviously central, because it underlies and makes possible all of his other activities—legislative, judicial, political, even ceremonial. As the chief administrator the President has at his disposal many direct administrative tools and structures not mentioned in the Constitution. Indeed, the Constitution says only that "he may require the opinion, in writing, of the principal officer in each of the executive departments, upon any subject relating to the duties of their respective offices." Here we have the authorization for an eleven-member cabinet. From the equally vague requirement that "he shall take care that the laws be faithfully executed" come the more than sixty special agencies that complete his domain. The President has also been given certain statutory powers of appointment and dismissal within the civil service. (But he has also been denied others by both Congress and the Supreme Court.) Congress has vested in him "reorganization" powers that also help him manage the executive branch. In this reorganization enterprise Congress merely has veto power; the President has the initiative to increase, reduce, and rearrange his departments. This is a very broad power indeed.

The Constitution specifically grants the President certain other powers as well. The President is commander in chief of the military establishment. But the direction, policies, and commitment of the military are hammered out in the Defense Department, the State Department, and certain other civilian agencies of the administration. Even though the power to declare war rests with the Congress, the President's maneuvers and policies in this area can make the actual declaration academic. As the chief architect of American foreign policy, the President has traditionally relied on the State Department, the Council of Economic Advisers, and others in the administrative machinery. Before the President completes an executive agreement (which does not require confirmation by the Senate) or signs a treaty (which does), thousands of administrative man-hours have gone into its planning and negotiation, and thousands more will go into its execution.

As chief legislator the President calls special sessions of Congress to deal with urgent administrative plans and policies, submits budgets prepared by the Office of Management and

Budget for congressional approval, and presents an annual address to the Congress on the state of the union. In exercising his constitutionally prescribed veto power and his power to fill in the details of general laws passed by Congress (such as the trade agreements acts and the reorganization acts described earlier), the President must rely heavily on his administrative machinery for statistics, advice, and general planning. Many studies have pointed out that a large proportion of laws actually originate in some unit of this fourth branch of government—the "administration." The people professionally involved with running a social security agency, administering a highway grant, or deploying an army are the natural sources for most of the data and ideas on which Congress must ultimately base its bills.

The Constitution also gives the President certain judicial duties: "power to grant reprieves and pardons for offenses against the United States, except in cases of impeachment." In a typical year the President receives more than 1,500 applications for pardons; to deal with them he must lean heavily on the advice and data of the Justice Department—another bureaucracy. His ceremonial duties as chief of state also require the services of his White House staff, his press secretaries, and others in the administration.

**Judicial and Partisan Duties of the President**

Although political parties are nowhere mentioned in the Constitution, the President is also the chief officer of his political party. Even in this somewhat extracurricular role he uses the powers and machinery of his bureaucracy. He uses the administration to make the policies and the news that serve to tailor party designs and campaign strategies. He uses the administrative offices available to him for political patronage. This tool is helpful in controlling even local party politics. His political role, moreover, is a very useful support for his legislative powers. For example, he allows a state's congressional representatives to make judicial and postal appointments in their respective states, but in return, he demands their votes for his programs. His administrative staff helps him in these political ploys, and almost every department has its own liaison officers, who forcefully present agency policy to senators and congressmen. His press staff, legal advisers, and others on the White House staff also support him in his political role. Everything that the President does in his official capacity, in fact, is part of the record on which he will run for a second term, or on which his successor in his party will have to run. His administrative officers are well aware of this, and it is part of their every calculation. In sum, whether strong or weak, the President is most frequently an *administrative* man. Whether or not he chooses to supplant Congress, to influence the judiciary, or to absorb the power of the states, in any and all events he must manage with and through his bureaucracy.

Even so, the President's many roles and powers may still fail to equip him to be the unifying directional force needed in our political system. His necessary reliance on a vast staff of bureaucrats not entirely susceptible to his command and inherently disposed to work for their own parochial goals is hardly a sound basis for effective leadership. Indeed, if the presidency as it now operates were capable of dealing effectively with our basic social problems, we would not be caught in the crisis of confidence that grips us now. The image of a strong presidency is attractive to many, and has been for many years. Yet while I would agree that it is the critical question concerning this office, I do not believe a strong presidency is a proper solution to our basic problems.

**PRESI-**
**DENTIAL**
**SELECTION:**
**Politics versus**
**Policy**

The institution of the presidency is the focus of other (though lesser) controversies that must also be aired if we are to understand its proper place in our constitutional system. Whether we view presidential power as benign or threatening, the current debate over the way the President is selected has grave implications. An amendment that would abolish the electoral college is in 1972 bottled up in the Senate. This is not the first time such a change has been considered. Some five hundred constitutional amendments to alter or abolish the electoral college have been introduced in Congress since Thomas Hart Benton made the first such move in 1824. Even the Founding Fathers were ambivalent over this matter, and once again the Constitution's prescription represents a compromise. It is a matter of grave concern, since it has far-reaching implications for the nature of American democracy. Changing the electoral-college selection process would not only change the power of the presidency and the quality and style of presidential leadership; it would undoubtedly also have some effects on the nature of the political party system and on actual policy decisions. I believe the most profound change, however, would be in our political philosophy. If direct voting for the President is substituted for the present system, we will have gone a long way toward institutionalizing the philosophy of majoritarianism.

As things stand now, the President is elected not by a simple majority vote of all those enfranchised and voting, but by a majority of slates of electors, who meet in their state capitals some six weeks after the popular vote and, on the basis of their own possibly slim margins of victory, deliver *all* of the votes of their respective states. In other words, on election day the voting citizen actually chooses a list of electors who more or less promise to vote for one or another of the presidential candidates. When the count is in, the slate of electors that won presumably gives all of its votes to the candidate of its choice. In 1968, however, an elector in North Carolina, Lloyd Bailey, broke his pledge to vote for Nixon and voted instead for George Wallace. And there is nothing the electorate can do about this. Moreover, since the number of electors chosen in each state reflects the size of their congressional delegation, the same inequities of malapportionment obtain in the electoral college as in the halls of Congress. Furthermore, under this winner-take-all arrangement, the people's choice can be and is diluted. The degree to which this system can depart from true majoritarianism can be seen in the mathematical possibility that a candidate who receives only 30 percent of the popular vote may win a majority of electoral votes and thus be elected. (This requires very slim margins in a series of strategic states.) While there has not yet been such a gross disparity between popular and electoral votes, we have twice had Presidents who received fewer popular votes than their opponents: Harrison in 1888 against Cleveland, and Hayes in 1876 against Tilden. Moreover, in the event of a tie in the electoral college, the election devolves upon the House of Representatives, in which each state casts a single vote. This certainly defeats popular control, and it too has happened: in 1824, when John Quincy Adams was selected over his rival, Andrew Jackson, amidst many rumors of back-room politicking.

**The Defeat of Popular Control**

In any event, the current system is a far cry from the ideal of "one man, one vote," which presumes each person to be the voting equal of his fellow. To some persons (and I am one), this seems patently unfair and unjustifiable. The very logic of democracy is at stake. Yet the system, with all its inequalities, has its defenders. Indeed, the defense rests on those very inequalities. Irving Kristol, for example, argues that critical urban minorities can swing elections under the present system by delivering all the electoral votes in certain large urban states. And this ensures what he views as "liberal policies emanating from the Presidency."[6] Aside from its ethical impurities, the notion is fraught with uncertainties. To date, the record does not justify this inference. And even if it did, a system that allows any minority to outvote a majority is illogical as well as undemocratic.

The other arguments generally raised in defense of our present presidential selection system seem to me peripheral. For example, it has been argued that true majoritarian selection would increase campaign costs. This is doubtful, unimportant, and (if true) easily corrected. It seems laughable to worry, as Kristol does, about what direct election will do to the "drama" of TV coverage. The most cogent of these secondary arguments concerns the effect of direct elections on the two-party system. It is possible that state party leadership in certain arenas might atrophy a bit, but this too would not be altogether a curse, nor is it impossible to balance when and where it should occur. The questions involving party politics will be scrutinized more closely in a later chapter.

**The Nominating System**

There is also considerable debate about the efficiency and propriety of the presidential nominating procedure. Once again basic democratic theory is involved. Those who give first priority to majoritarianism are pitted against those whose primary attachments are to other goals, such as "maintaining the two-party system" or "supporting the rights of minorities." As things stand now, the nominating process is a marvel of complexity. The formal forum for the nomination is the national convention, called into being and supervised by the national committee of each of the two major parties. The national committee of each party (about which more will be said in Chapter 9) controls the place, rules, and size of the nominating conventions. Each convention is free to determine its own balloting rules. Republican conventions have, in general, permitted split voting; that is, members of each state delegation may vote individually. Democratic conventions have, in general, tried to enforce unit rule: the state delegation votes as a block for the candidate who is favored by a majority of its delegates. The conduct of the actual convention strikes many observers as colorful and uniquely American. In the minds of others, however, the conventions are not only unwieldly and undemocratic, but vulgar.

The present system of selecting the delegates to the national nominating conventions is another highly variegated enterprise. Each party is governed in the selection process by the party regulations embedded in the laws of the fifty states. There are many unique wrinkles, but in general two major methods predominate: statewide conventions at which the national presidential nominating delegates are chosen, or presidential primaries.

Fifteen states hold presidential primaries, and from 30 to 50 percent of the delegates at the last few conventions have been chosen in this manner. Actually there are several types of primaries. In some the names of those wishing to be delegates are listed under the names of potential candidates; some (as in Oregon) are accompanied by a presidential preference poll; in some no identification is offered, and the voter must find out for himself which would-be delegate supports which would-be candidate. In any event, it is actually impossible to "bind" a delegate, since there is no way of foretelling how long any individual candidacy may survive at the subsequent convention. Some primaries take place about a year before the convention, and all of them have some effect on subsequent events.

The convention method of delegate selection requires that members of a state convention, who themselves may have been directly or indirectly elected by enrolled voters, in turn elect a group of national delegates from among their ranks. In some instances there are also some delegates who represent no specific district, but are chosen "at large." They are usually selected by the state committees, which are at least twice removed from the rank-and-file voter. But the truth is that no matter which method is used, a convention or a direct primary, the delegates who finally surface at the national nominating conventions owe their selection to the party organization, working through a formal or more frequently informal caucus.

Now few things are as enthusiastically defended as this national convention system of ours. Its adherents point to our history of "adequate" to "great" Presidents; remind us of the many virtues of the two-party system, which is given great stimulus by this nominating method; and invoke the not inconsiderable blessings of compromise, which permeates the convention atmosphere. But today an increasing number of critics point to the malapportionment of voting strength in the conventions, to the continued seating of delegates from states whose party organizations are not truly open to blacks and other minority groups, to delegates who do not and cannot represent the views of their constituencies, and to questionable procedural rules. Stokely Carmichael, for example, has chronicled the plight of black members of the Democratic party, who were successfully disenfranchised at the 1964 convention.[7] The proponents of change lean in one or the other of two basic directions: (1) self-correction of each party's apparatus through changes in the party's rules and conscientious application of certain sections of the 1964 Voting Rights Act (the Democratic party went far in this direction in 1972); (2) federal regulation of national party life, including the nomination of the presidential candidates under national regulations. Until these controversies about selection are resolved, it is impossible to come to grips with the more fundamental ones about presidential purpose.

**The National Convention: Adherents versus Critics**

Behind the broader concern over the President's role, and behind the important question of selection (but intimately connected with both), is the matter of presidential campaigns. Here the controversy centers on the amount of money a candidate should spend, means of countering the advantages held

**PRESI-DENTIAL CAMPAIGNS**

by incumbents, the effect of television, and the possibilities of making the campaigns more rational. A presidential campaign now costs in the neighborhood of $35 million—and this in the face of laws that limit the expenditure of each national committee to a mere $3 million, and also limit the contributions of any single person to $5,000. As for media exposure, how do you ensure fair treatment for leading contenders? An incumbent always has the advantage. He can literally create news; his press briefings, his messages to Congress, his diplomatic maneuvers are fuel for his political campaign. These media mechanics, moreover, have a way of influencing the style and even the substance of candidates. Many persons today are worried about the "packaging" and "merchandising" effects of Madison Avenue on political candidates.[8] Is it possible that good looks can eclipse good ideas? Will sartorial elegance replace solid ability? Of course, personality was a factor in some presidential campaigns long before the era of television, and it is difficult to judge a man's ability in office until he has actually held the office. The use of television will not in itself necessarily guarantee either good or bad results. In some instances it might give unfortunate impetus to the personality trend, but it might also enhance the possibilities for genuine debate (which is in short supply). The medium need not replace the message, but the choice has certainly been considered.

In sum, the office of President does not and cannot now resolve America's basic political problems. Although it is the single unified branch of government in the country, it has not, for reasons already noted, generated sufficient power and a sufficient reservoir of undisputed legitimacy to carry us over the threshold into a new era. A respected political journalist, Douglass Cater, has written:

> I happen to believe that we would have a very serious domestic crisis, a crisis of confidence in leadership and in the Presidency today even if there were not a war in Vietnam. The problem of policy making in American government would certainly be just as great, war or no war. . . . The chief problem of policy making in modern government is to establish priorities which can override the priorities that are set by subgovernments (example: the defense industrial complex).[9]

It is precisely the President's inability to set such priorities that leaves the office inadequate to the needs of the people.

**STATE AND LOCAL EXECUTIVES: Integration versus Expertise**
In contrast to the President, state executives are dwarfed by the relative unimportance of their domains, their removal from the vital arena of foreign and military affairs, and their consequent inability to command coverage by the national media. Nonetheless, governors retain an array of roles and they are

commonly subjected to the same pull between legislature and executive that permeates government at the national level. The governors of urban industrial states, along with the mayors of large, heterogeneous cities, are experiencing the same trends toward increased powers that we have reviewed in relation to the President. (The movement is generally less pronounced, of course, in smaller and more rural situations.)

Occasionally governors have political and administrative tools that can outgun even the power arsenal of the President. Take, for example, the area of investigatory powers. Here most governors' weapons more than match those of the President. With grand juries, special attorneys, and other special investigatory agencies at their disposal to gather information and enforce policy within their states, governors are often in an enviable position. They also have certain powers over legislation that are denied the President. Thirty-nine governors have an "item veto"—they can strike out individual sections of appropriation bills—whereas the President is bound to accept or reject the entire package. Only the governor of North Carolina is at a disadvantage here; he has no veto power at all. The remainder of the governors' legislative powers are similar to the President's.

**The Powers of State Governors**

At times the party potential of governors can also outrun the President's in terms of internal politics. To begin with, it is easier for a governor to control a single state than it is for the President to control the entire nation. This is strikingly true in the considerable number of one-party states. Here a governor can be a true political despot. Furthermore, a governor in such a state can parlay his strength beyond his state's boundaries if he knows how to play presidential politics. The governors of the "undecided" states—states where either party may win—have a different sort of advantage in this game: they can themselves become nominees for the presidency. And they inevitably have considerable influence on the presidential nominating machinery. There is also the fact that a governor is the head of what is usually an integrated party organization, which is more than can be said for the President. The national parties are no more than an occasional and loose confederation of the machines of the fifty states. Finally, internal state politics is ideologically more homogeneous than national party politics. All of this helps a governor maintain party control.

The governors also have a broader array of judicial power and responsibility than the President. All governors have the power to grant pardons, commutations, reprieves, paroles, and extradition. The governor's power to pardon is the same as the President's, but it is more extensively sought (as are all other forms of judicial action), since the state is the arbiter of most crimes. Commutation is a reduction in sentence; reprieve is a postponement of sentence to allow time for additional appeals; and parole is a conditional release from detention. Most governors usually share the power of parole with special boards. Extradition (or rendition) is a governor's power (mandated by the United States Constitution) to return a fugitive from justice from another state, if he is requested to do so by the governor of the state from which the fugitive has fled. He is not obliged to comply with such a request; every governor retains complete discretion in the matter.

Despite all these advantages, a governor has vastly less impact than a President. He may be a big fish, but he is always in a relatively small pond. And within each state the struggle between the chief executive and the legislature remains classically lively and unresolved.

**Should the Executive Office Be Integrated?**

There is another conflict area that is unique to governors and mayors; that is the matter of whether or not the executive office should be integrated. "Integrated" here refers to an administrative principle. It means that the office should not suffer "loose ends." Authority must be commensurate with responsibility. At the presidential level, integration is not fully achieved, but there is little argument about it as a proper principle of application. This is not so at the state level. Our ambivalence concerning this matter is most dramatically demonstrated by the fact that all governors must share their executive power with other independently elected officials. Even within a political entity as large and complex as New York State, the chief fiscal officer (comptroller) and chief legal officer (attorney general) are elected separately from the governor. At the national level, these are presidential appointments, and they are not subject to the consent of the Senate. Not only does the state system permit considerable personal autonomy for the two persons who should be part of an executive staff, but it often permits a division in party control as well. During the entire decade of the 1960s, for example, New York had a Democratic comptroller, while all the other executives were Republicans. Many states also have independent election lines for their treasurers, secretaries of state, and school superintendents. A smaller number of states elect tax commissioners, public utilities commissioners, and agricultural directors.

The notions of unity of command and political responsiveness through responsible party government are clearly at stake in these states. Yet this piecemeal selection of officeholders caters to a countervailing and equally deep-seated devotion to independence, expertise, and nonpartisanship. These values underlie the vast proliferation of independent boards, commissions, agencies, and authorities that clog the administrative wheels of most states and cities. These offices reduce not only the unity but also the actual power of state and local executives. Virtually none of our state and local executives have reorganization powers commensurate with those of the President, or even with the scope and variety of their own problems. These limitations, coupled with their generally too-short terms of office and their inadequate executive staffs (for budgets, legislative relationships, and so on), more often than not make governors appear as victims rather than personifications of the American dream.

At the local level one particular ideological struggle is dominant. There is a very great strain between those who would rule by expertise and those who would rule by common consent. The first group is at home in the so-called nonpartisan systems of local government, frequently found in small cities and villages, and in some cities that have no mayor (or only a totally ceremonial mayor), but instead a supposedly politically neutral expert hired by the legislative body to run the government. City commissions also embody this drive for expertise instead of integrated and frankly political power. This attachment to nonpartisanship stems not only from a belief in expertise, but also from an even stronger lack of faith in politicians. There is a crisis of confidence all around.

The executive function continues to be weakened by these struggles in countless towns and townships. Some counties and towns have "supervisors," whose powers vary in the same way that mayors' powers do. A few urban towns and counties may have quite strong executives wielding considerable authority, but the usual pattern is extreme division of the executive function within a narrow range of authority under the state constitution. Most local executives share the state executive's hazard of having many of their administrative staff members placed beyond their direct control by the elective process or by the manner of their appointment.

A final solution does not need to be found for every one of these tensions and arguments. Surely the issues of nonpartisanship, city managers, expert commissions, and systems of election and campaigning might well profit from continued experimentation and variety of approach. But the larger executive issue—its proper role among the tripartite power system—does seem to me to require a deep searching of the public soul. We must set our compass or we will surely founder. It is my view that we should resolve our uncertainties in the direction of checking our executives—most particularly the President, in view of his enormous and far-reaching impact. No man can or should shoulder the burden of making and then legitimizing all the complex value judgments that our system requires. This is, at a minimum, the role of a popularly elected collegial body; at a maximum, it belongs to the people themselves.

**Local
Executives**

# CHAPTER 8

# THE AMERICAN PUBLIC BUREAUCRACY

At every level of American government—indeed, in most governments of the world—the strings of power are pulled by enterprises variously called the "administration," the "fourth branch of government," and the "bureaucracy." All of these terms refer to the departments and other agencies that perform public services at the national, state, and local levels. The importance of this group cannot be overestimated. One cartoonist in the early 1960s depicted the power of the bureaucracy by showing two agency heads in conversation, one saying to the other, "You know this guy Kennedy really thinks he's running the country." Because of the importance of bureaucracy, the controversies and ambiguities surrounding it run particularly long and deep. In the most fundamental way, ambivalence and conflict are involved in a great number of important questions: whether bigger is indeed better; whether the group or the individual is the key to bureaucratic strength and creativity; whether politics and administration are separable, and if so, whether administration should be on top or on tap; whether efficiency or satisfaction should be the primary yardstick for public enterprises; whether there should be administrative decentralization or devolution; merit and neutrality versus spoils and representativeness; speed and responsiveness versus accountability and predictability; whether products should prevail over participants; whether public bureaucracies should be restrained by management or by marketplace; whether, in sum, bureaucracy is a benefactor or a behemoth.

Before analyzing these basic controversies, let us make a brief survey of this somewhat complicated terrain.

**THE NATIONAL ADMINIS- TRATION: The Machinery for Today's Decisions**

Article 2 of the Constitution quite starkly specifies that "the executive power shall be vested in a President of the United States of America." After describing the details of his election and succession, Section 2 goes on to say that the President shall be the commander in chief of the armed forces and that "he may require the opinion, in writing, of the principal officer in each of the executive departments, upon any subject relating to the duties of their respective offices." The Constitution also specifies that the President shall make treaties and appoint ambassadors, "other public ministers and consuls," and Supreme Court justices, by and with the advice and consent of the Senate. Other officers may be selected by the President if the Congress so decrees. From these few references has grown an administrative branch of government comprising close to 2.6 million civilian employees distributed among twelve large departments, fifty or more independent agencies (depending on how they are counted), and over a dozen government corporations. If this giant structure is considered in terms of operating units, it comprises over two thousand divisions. Where do all these people come from? What do they do? Where do they work? And is the President really in control?

This giant bureaucracy is divided up somewhat naturally according to function, and somewhat less naturally according to certain ideas about structure. We shall first discuss the simplest and most commonplace federal administrative development—the department. Even in the early days of the Republic, the "faithful execution of the laws" required that the President somehow arrange to collect and account for the limited funds then needed to protect the nation from foreign aggression, distribute the mails, and regulate commerce. Logically, these tasks called for a treasurer, a Secretary of State, and a War Department, as a minimum. With expanded functions came expanded departments. As taxes and bills increased, the Treasury needed more personnel. As the number of employees increased, it became necessary to organize these people into "bureaus" according to the nature of their work. And so we have "T-men," who perform the police functions of investigating and enforcing federal laws, and internal revenue officers, who work out the necessary forms, make the necessary inspections, and send the bills needed to collect the federal income tax.

Occasionally a function creeps into a department which could just as logically have been placed elsewhere. The Treasury enforcement officers who work on narcotics investigations, for example, might just as logically belong to the Justice Department. History, accident, and personalities play their roles in the structuring of these functions. From its earliest days the Treasury Department had collected customs duties and inspected overseas goods to prevent smuggling; thus the drift to narcotics regulation can be readily understood. Occasionally a department may have unusually aggressive officers who grab up functions through their own initiative. Still more occasionally, a President will simply make a personal assessment of the people involved in existing organizations before he determines where he will place a new function. In any event,

**The Federal Department**

once an organization gets started—any organization—a great deal of pressure is needed to change it in any basic way. People get used to "the way things are," and any change seems threatening. The individuals who comprise any organization generally see change as a threat to their own survival.

**How New Agencies Originate**

We have recently seen the birth of two new institutions in our executive branch, the Department of Housing and Urban Development and the Transportation Department. The Department of Housing and Urban Development came into being as a response to a complex of problems arising from a new set of facts: over 60 percent of our population now live in urban centers, and this concentration of people breeds the type of situation that requires more community action than was necessary earlier. But this new department was also a response to certain political pressures. A new cabinet vacancy can provide an opportunity for the judicious appointment of a member of an unrepresented minority. The first Secretary of Housing and Urban Development was a black man. Of course, only a law of Congress can authorize such new cabinet posts or permit the President to appoint the new heads and assistant secretaries of these departments. Once these persons are appointed, Congress typically gives them the power to determine how the remainder of the department is to be organized and staffed. But all such delegated power remains subject to subsequent congressional specifications.

A new department generally blossoms with top-level plans, planners, and what are called "executive housekeeping" functions. That is, high-ranking specialists first have to be assembled to decide on the specific problems to be dealt with, the ways in which the national government can address itself to them, the best means of acquiring the necessary staff, and the individuals who should be hired. Executives start out with assistants and secretaries; as their plans grow, the assistants need secretaries and the secretaries need assistants. There is often such an abundance of staffing that many citizens wonder if all the jobs are necessary. The government has its share of sinecures and waste, but probably no more than its *proportionate* share. The tendency for large organizations to expand, however, is very well described by "Parkinson's Law": "Work expands to fill the time available for its completion."[1]

Most new departments rather quickly grow to look very much like their brothers: a pyramid of units, sections, branches, divisions, bureaus, and services, each with certain counterparts in possible field offices outside the central home office in Washington, D.C. (See Figure 1.)

**The "Independent" Agencies**

Occasionally Congress has faced special problems that seemed to require special treatment. When, for example, Con-

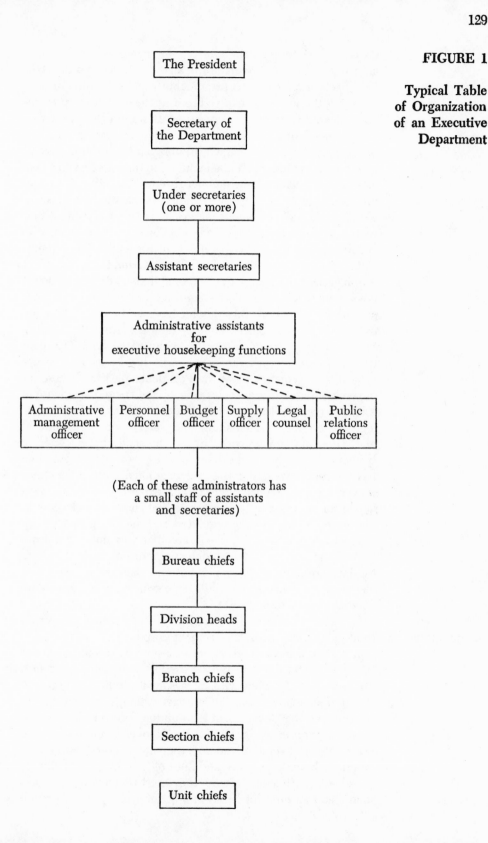

**FIGURE 1**

**Typical Table
of Organization
of an Executive
Department**

gress wished to regulate rates in interstate commerce, and later to organize and regulate the airways, it decided to establish special expert groups presumably capable of directly representing the interests involved, but at the same time presumably isolated from political pressure. It was in this spirit that the independent regulatory commissions were born. Depending on the way the term is defined, from seven to eleven important government structures can be included in this category; if lesser agencies are included, the number rises to about fifty-eight. The total number of employees in these organizations is close to 350,000. Virtually everyone agrees that the Interstate Commerce Commission, the Federal Power Commission, the Securities and Exchange Commission, the Federal Communications Commission, the Federal Trade Commission, the Civil Aeronautics Board, and the National Labor Relations Board belong in this group. These agencies are headed by plural executives (generally three) who have varying, overlapping, but fixed terms of office. Though they are appointed by the President, they are not generally removed by him. This contrasts, of course, with the department heads, who, once approved, serve completely at the President's pleasure. These independent regulatory agencies develop in general in response to a need to regulate large economic interests. They perform quasi-legislative duties (ratemaking and such) and quasi-judicial ones (deciding among competitors who shall obtain a specific benefit). Recently, in the face of many scandals, the public has begun to wonder if this organizational pattern functions as well as had been expected. The expertise that had been hoped for has frequently degenerated into mutual back-scratching by the industry being regulated and the group that is supposed to regulate it. The flexibility that was hoped for from this format fast froze into hidebound procedures that irritate the businessmen and lawyers who must deal with these agencies. Independence from political pressures has tended to degenerate into irresponsibility.[2]

**Government Corporations**

Similarly, the hopes that originally accompanied the structural experiment with "government corporations" has receded from the high-water mark of enthusiasm that accompanied the successes of the TVA in the 1940s. The government corporation was also designed with an eye to flexibility—to escaping the rigid mandates of the Civil Service Commission, the Budget Bureau, and the Government Accounting Office. In later years, however, such expert groups as the Hoover Commission have been critical of some of the government's corporate structures on precisely these grounds, and most of their original attributes have been shorn away.[3] Today they must budget and hire personnel and account for funds and acquire new funds in much the same manner as any other line agency, though they are still permitted business-style budgets in lieu of line budgets and somewhat different accounting procedures. Many are being turned into departmental bureaus in the hope that the parent structure may restore executive responsibility.

There are also a score of other independent agencies, ranging from the Battle Monuments Commission to the Advisory Committee on Weather Control. When these are lumped together, the executive department is seen as a rather formidable and complex conglomeration.[4]

**Reorganization**

Over the past generation, Congress has been generous (probably out of necessity, owing to the complexities involved) in granting the President broad statutory powers to reorganize his executive structure. With certain exceptions and limitations, the President can formulate, reformulate, reduce, consolidate, and reassign functions among his executive agencies. Congress may veto the plan if it chooses, but if Congress says nothing, the plan becomes operative. Every President, starting with Franklin D. Roosevelt, has used this executive reorganization power; President Nixon, for example, formulated a plan to restructure the Bureau of the Budget into a more powerful Office of Management and Budget. But no completely satisfactory reorganization formula has been found. Reorganization is therefore a recurring executive process. From time to time the legislature has itself initiated necessary reorganization and housekeeping improvements for the executive establishment.

**The Executive Office**

Over the years Congress has also given the President the authority and funds to build up a special "Executive Office" to handle the vast planning, administrative, and housekeeping functions necessary to run this giant executive machinery. The major components of the Executive Office are the Cabinet, the Office of Management and Budget, the White House Office, the Office of Defense Mobilization, the Domestic Council, and the National Security Council. The Cabinet is comprised of the eleven heads of the line departments: Secretaries of Agriculture; Commerce; Defense; Health, Education, and Welfare; Interior; Justice; Labor; State; Treasury; Transportation; and Housing and Urban Development. Occasionally the head of one of the other large structures, such as the chief of the Veterans' Administration, may be invited in. It is a totally different type of cabinet from those found in parliamentary nations. None of the men in the Cabinet are legislators. All are political appointees of the President, who is free to ignore their advice. They are appointed not only for their executive ability, but also with an eye to paying political debts and to balancing social, religious, and geographic interests. They necessarily have considerable influence, however, in day-today policy in their roles as executive directors of the large bureaucracies and administrators of important laws. In spite of the many oblique considerations that govern the choice of Cabinet officers, they are generally men of considerable competence, since they must perform in a very visible arena and any mistakes will reflect immediately upon the President.

**Office of Management and Budget**

The Office of Management and Budget employs more than five hundred persons to work with the budget officers of every department and agency in gathering the information necessary to prepare the overall financial plan that the President submits each year to Congress as his proposed budget. It also prescribes the forms and methods all agencies are to use in their budgeting, reviews all agency plans and statistics, and through its administrative management section occasionally tries to advise departments on reorganization and on special management procedures to increase the government's efficiency and economy.

Next in this top executive staff arrangement is the White House Office, staffed by some four hundred special legal advisers, military advisers, scientific advisers, administrative assistants to the President, press officers, personal secretaries, legislative representatives, and their staffs. Another sixty-odd persons constitute the Executive Mansion Unit. These people do the physical housekeeping connected with the White House. The Council of Economic Advisers (a group of three economists with a small staff), the Domestic Council (composed of the budget chief, the chairman of the Council of Economic Advisers, and a few key Cabinet officers), the National Security Council (the heads of defense and military operations with a small staff), the Office of Defense Mobilization, and the CIA constitute the remainder of the Executive Office.

**The Civil Service**

Unfortunately, the other housekeeping and management units that might logically fit into the Executive Office are left to float among the independent agencies: the General Service Administration (which deals with purchases, contracts, storage, public buildings, and archives) and the Civil Service Commission (the personnel office for this government Leviathan). The chairman of the Civil Service Commission does sit in the Executive Office as the President's personnel adviser, but this arrangement does not accomplish the degree of intimacy and control that many administrators believe should exist between a chief executive and his personnel officer. It is through the structure of the Civil Service Commission that all but about 10 percent of the civilians working for the national government are recruited, hired, trained, rated, promoted, serviced, and ultimately retired or dismissed. In general, the commission hires people through competitive examinations, rates them according to a uniform system, promotes them according to merit, and removes them only for specified causes and after proper procedures are followed. About half of the Civil Service personnel works for the Defense Department. More than 20 percent work for the Post Office Department and the rest are scattered among other departments and agencies. More than 80 percent of these people work in parts of the United States other than Washington, D.C., and some 10 percent work on foreign soil. They represent more than 15,000 personnel skills and most of them are blue-collar workers, administrative and clerical workers, and professional and technical experts. Top-ranking officials are hired politically by the President, and certain other lower-echelon employees, such as U.S. marshals and assistant U.S. attorneys, are also political appointees. In addition, a comparatively small number of people are hired by special merit systems run independently of the Civil Service Commission, such as those of the FBI and the Foreign Service. Ever since the establishment of the Civil Service Commission in 1881, its functions have grown as a natural response to the added complexities of government as well as to the growing pressure to maintain a merit system rather than a spoils system. Today, however, the greatest criticism of this commission is that its operations are too cautious, too closely geared to keeping scoundrels out rather than to getting good people into the service. All of this will be discussed later.

The government's recruiting practices have been the subject of a spate of studies. (There are also less complete ones describing state and local bureaucracies.) The most interesting and wide-ranging of these studies found that the national bureaucracy had an executive-level group of about 13,000 persons, fewer than 2 percent of whom were women, fewer than 5 percent foreign-born, about 20 percent second-generation. Ninety percent were college graduates, many of whom held graduate degrees and 20 percent of whom had attended one or another of ten large, prestigious universities. The fathers of most of them were skilled workers or laborers. But in terms of the distribution of such work in the population as a whole, these more modest family backgrounds were relatively under-represented; people whose fathers were businessmen or professionals (though they accounted for no more than 15 percent of this total) were overrepresented.[5] Breakdowns by agency also reveal interesting distribution curves. It is difficult, however, to conclude anything more precise than that there is reason to believe the civil service systems of this nation are on the whole reasonably representative of the various socio-economic groups and moderately effective as a means of upward mobility at least for men. This tendency is certainly

**Government Recruiting Practices**

more pronounced in the administrative branch than in either the legislative or judicial branch.

In sum, the President is the head of a complex bureaucracy and one of his major problems is to stimulate and at the same time control it. He must rely on this bureaucracy to help originate policies and to ensure that presidential policies (no matter where originated) are carried out. This structure, then, must both yield ideas and respond to them. Because the executive department contains specialists, because it is marked by great continuity of personnel, and because it is headed by the President, it has logically become the center of the decision process. This center, however, is characterized by an unequal distribution of political resources. That is, expertise, money, and influence with clientele and Congress vary in quantity and quality across the bureaucratic spectrum. The way the administration uses these resources is the nub of our public policy system. How each agency deploys its troops, how it evaluates its political resources, how it sees itself and is in turn seen by others; how, in short, it manages its clientele groups and its congressional counterparts, its internal budgetary system and its relationships with surrounding and competing bureaucracies —these are the critical variables in the American political system. These variables must be analyzed and understood at each succeeding layer of government if the political system is to be understood. We must therefore try to comprehend the major conflicts and ambiguities that shape this bureaucracy and influence its style.

**STATE AND LOCAL ADMINIS-TRATION AND BUREAUC-RACIES**

The American governmental system cannot be understood at all if the states and local units are ignored. Yet it is extremely difficult to do justice to these layers of government. We shall certainly sacrifice great richness of detail and many areas of subtle differentiation in the broad and brief survey of administrative life presented here.

Of the eight million civilians who work for state and local governments, about 25 percent are at the state level. (It is interesting to note that 75 percent of all government employees work below the federal level, and that if defense employees are subtracted from the total, so that only those involved in domestic concerns are considered, the figure rises to 84 percent.)[6]

On the whole, the public bureaucracies of American states and localities are far less integrated and far less susceptible to executive control and direction than the federal bureaucracy. Every state and local unit has a certain number of executive-led functional departments—generally too many. (Most states have anywhere from nine to seventy-eight, but a number of states have close to a hundred administrative agencies, and the larger numbers are the more typical. New York City, for example, has more than sixty-four units, which Mayor Lindsay has tried to consolidate into ten "superagencies.") The complexity of this array, moreover, is compounded by the prevalence of "independent" boards and commissions. Indeed, the variety of agencies at state and local levels defies imagination. Some of the variety, it is true, is more a matter of nomenclature than of operations. But the spectrum includes the full spectrum of independent commissions, corporations, services, agencies, boards, administrative offices, and so forth. Many of the key administrative functions of state and local governments may be in the hands of executives elected independently of the governor (or the mayor), such as New York State's separately elected attorney general, lieutenant governor, and auditor. In all but five states the chief education officer is either independently elected or appointed by some group not under the governor's control. In all, governors appoint only about half of their cabinet-level administrative posts. Many mayors also share their powers with executive groups and other specific officers. New York City's Board of Estimate and its five borough presidents are a case in point. In most towns and counties the administrative structure is a commission-style operation with, again, many pockets of independence and all the weaknesses of a plural executive. About 250 cities are governed by commissions too, although their use is declining.

The chief executives of state and local governments also have great problems with bureaucratic control because of a lack of adequate staffing. As a general rule they do not have sophisticated budget specialists. Most budgets even in the forty states that have executive-style budgets are simply prepared by some multipurpose unit of the gubernatorial staff. Governors rarely have personal legal advisers or special advisers for education or other functional areas. A typical governor is lucky if he has an executive secretary and perhaps one other professional assistant along with a handful of clerks. In the large industrial states, the governor's office might possibly employ as many as four dozen persons. It is only recently that New York City, the second largest government operation in the United States, could boast a deputy mayor. It now has two. These officials are supposed to relieve the mayor of some of his administrative and political responsibilities. New York's deputy mayor—city administrator, for example, has a small staff that tries to cope with the administrative problems of a city of eight million people, serviced by a bureaucracy of 320,000, or a quarter of a million employees if teachers are excluded. Finally, local control over administration is also

**Bureaucratic Control in State and Local Governments**

loosened by the shortness of typical terms of office. There are still seventeen states with two-year governors.

Only thirty-two states have what is called "generally extensive civil service coverage," and only cities with populations of ten to fifty thousand have any degree of general civil service merit coverage. Nonetheless, the coverage that does exist, coupled with the growing power of civil service unions and the generally lesser removal power permitted to governors and mayors, greatly reduce the ability of these local executives to control the bureaucracies.

The functional areas covered by some state and local administrations duplicate areas of federal concern. While there are a few areas that remain exclusively in the national domain (defense and foreign affairs), and others that are concurrently covered by both nation and state, certain areas can be said to be *primarily* reserved to states and localities: education, hospitals, sanitation and sewage, corrections and prisons, justice, public safety (police and fire protection), highways, welfare, and recreation. The states also do considerable work in the regulatory fields (banks, insurance companies, and public utilities).

**Local Civil Service Reform**

Although occasionally a state initiates a new trend in civil service reform, in general the states and localities have closely followed federal trends in this area. The executive branch studies made under Presidents Taft, Franklin D. Roosevelt, Truman, and Eisenhower were quickly followed by a rash of similar state and local studies. Twenty states, for example, have had "Little Hoover Commissions" since World War II, in imitation of the national executive investigations made in 1949 and 1955 by a special team of management experts headed by former President Hoover. The recommendations of these groups have remained strangely similar over the years and from place to place: centralize authority and responsibility; group similar functions into integrated departments; eliminate irresponsible islands of policy-making; eliminate multiheaded groups; coordinate staffwork; improve executive budgeting; provide independent budgets; and improve and increase the executive's staffing.

In essence, of course, few seem to appreciate that each procedural reform sows the seeds of the disease that requires the next cycle of reform. Thus procedures to eliminate corruption breed institutional rigidity, which then must be loosened up by a return to the old-style procedures. These in turn inevitably breed charges of diffusion of responsibility and favoritism (i.e., corruption), which again require centralization, and so on.

We must now account for the fact that although the public bureaucracies are our political heartland, they still do not appear to be sufficiently powerful to break through our policy stalemate. They might, however, be far more effective than they are now if we could find some means of providing them with clear, unambiguous, and legitimized sets of rank-ordered goals. This we shall discuss in the final chapter. But even before such reform is explored, our bureaucracy can be made to work more effectively by resolving some of the internal conflicts that beset their operations. More specifically, the public should resolve its own thinking about what a bureaucracy truly is and what it should be. This would itself improve matters. As things stand now, we permit ourselves the costly and shortsighted luxury of making bureaucrats our whipping boys. The bureaucracies are damned if they do and damned if they don't. Let us therefore examine some of our ambivalent attitudes in more detail, so that we can see the vise in which we often put our public servants.

It is commonly thought that the United States is obsessed with size. We believe in big business, big expenditures, big splashes. Jokes, novels, movies, and psychologies revolve around this theme. Yet in the arena of government we have assiduously held to quite opposite beliefs: "The least government, the best." There is a continuing nostalgia for small-town America. Our economic enterprises are based on concepts of maximum production and maximum efficiency, goals for which considerable size is usually necessary. We normally conceive of General Motors as a hard-hitting, profit-making enterprise, and when one of its former presidents was brought in to head the national Defense Department, it was generally regarded as a smart move. Somehow big business and its practitioners are folk heroes. But big government bureaus and their toilers are likely to be regarded as drones, as feeders at the public trough. These big enterprises are pointed to as examples of the working of Parkinson's previously quoted law: "Work expands to fill the time available for its completion." It is empire-building at its worst. The clamor against big government is quite naturally directed at the administrative sector. The legislatures, the executives, and even the judiciaries have remained relatively stable and certainly relatively small, and they have retained whatever prestige is left to American public officials. So while it is sound enterprise for A & P to expand, it is wanton for HEW to do so. There is here a kernel of confusion and prejudice. This particular American ambivalence can be illustrated by the recent public demand for the government to be an "employer of last resort" (which in many instances it already is). Yet the public simultaneously calls for the government to cut out all unnecessary and inefficient personnel.

**THE BASIC CONFLICTS OF PUBLIC BUREAUCRACIES IN THE UNITED STATES**

**Bigness versus Containment**

INDIVIDUAL-
ISM VERSUS
GROUPTHINK

William H. Whyte describes the organization man as a man "who most urgently wants to belong."[7] To accelerate his belonging and the benefits that presumably accompany it, many large bureaucracies indulge in all sorts of practices, from brainstorming sessions to sensitivity training and weekend retreats—anything to ensure that their people will function well in groups and that the best ideas will be generated by group interaction. Contrast this with the traditional ideology of this nation, the so-called Protestant ethic, with its emphasis on individual salvation through individual conscience and individual work. It is a spirit eloquently expressed by Emerson, Walt Whitman, and many other American literary apostles, and it is still very much alive. These conflicting themes compete for the hearts and minds of bureaucrats and taxpayers alike. Yet these attitudes reflect two quite different styles, and any organization that must contend with both of them is inevitably subject to strain.

POLITICS
VERSUS
ADMINISTRA-
TION

Among sophisticated political scientists it is no longer fashionable to argue about whether or not politics can be separated from administration. It is presumed that the issue has been forever resolved—negatively. But this supposed resolution is neither well known nor necessarily well received in the outside world. Woodrow Wilson's belief that "administration lies outside the proper sphere of politics"[8] has had many advocates, and still does. It is the theme of most local elections. "Administration" remains for many people the opposite of "politics."

Yet to the more sophisticated, the notion seems both absurd and mischievous. Most administrative scholars hasten to point out that politics is the allocation of power and resources, and where are they allocated if not in bureaucratic corridors? They point out further that the substance of every decision is supplied by the administrators, or bureaucrats, who inevitably flesh out the details of broad policies as well as carry them out. Thus there is more policy (and politics) in the hands of the immigration officers who decide whether or not to issue a passport than in the Congress, which supplied the guidelines that supposedly control this issue.

Where one stands in a controversy of this sort has very real and grave consequences for our public bureaucracies and our public policies. Certain agencies, for example, may be consciously organized along lines precisely designed to ensure independence from politics. This has been true of the so-called independent regulatory agencies described earlier. But as we have seen, these agencies are not out of politics at all, and their independence is a rather sorry joke on the public, which has been blinded by its own aphorisms. Indeed, there is a growing spate of books illustrating the fact that independent regulatory agencies do not have to be corrupt in order to be estranged from their original tasks and hopes. They are virtually programmed that way by their so-called independence, which strangles competition of viewpoints, evades ordinary standards of due process, and even prevents efficiency.[9] All of this happens because we fail to recognize that they *are* political and must be organized as political bodies. Similarly, the typical city charter provisions and state constitutional arrangements that are based on the philosophy of separation produce severe problems for mayors and governors, who as political officers have to wrestle with police and education departments that have been fashioned as though they were really outside the realm of politics.

Yet to succumb completely to the opposite notion that *all* is inevitably politics is perhaps to fall into other grave errors. Clearly administration should not be equated with politics in the partisan sense. It is also an error to assume that there is no action at all that can be decided on purely administrative (i.e., expert) criteria. Herbert Simon and many other organizational theorists firmly believe that there *is* a reasonable way to sort out questions of value from questions of fact. Such a sorting is nothing more than another attempt to find the dividing line between politics and administration. So the argument is alive and well and increasingly important. But the ambiguities and myths that surround it do the practice of administration a grave injustice.

## ADMINISTRATORS ON TOP VERSUS ADMINISTRATORS ON TAP

The heading here is virtually a cliché in the profession of public administration. But the profession generally states it in reverse, and again does not view it as an arguable point, but rather as a professional commitment. That is, according to the principles of this profession, the administrator should *not* be on top. Yet once again the point is not always so clear to the public. There are many people who see administrators not only as a separate breed from politicians, but as a *superior* breed. These are the city manager cultists, the science cultists, the believers in a higher math capable of conjuring up answers to the gravest and most complex problems. The case to be made on each side of this argument is probably not contingent on any abstract and universally applicable wisdom, but rather on a tenuous, case-oriented wisdom. That is, there are surely instances in which the administrator should be on top (perhaps if he is an engineer in a bridge-building situation). But in most situations, as in an allocation of funds between schools and hospitals, perhaps the popularly elected politician, or better still, the public itself, is properly at the apex. This controversy too beclouds the making of policy and the bureaucratic apparatus set up to carry it out.

**EFFICIENCY VERSUS SATISFAC-TION**

Efficiency is so closely associated with bureaucracy and public administration that it is often a part of the very definition of the terms; for example, "The type of organization designed to accomplish large-scale administrative tasks by systematically coordinating the work of many individuals is called bureaucracy. This concept, then, applies to organizing principles that are intended to improve administrative efficiency. . . ."[10] and "The immediate objective of the art of public administration is the most efficient utilization of resources at the disposal of officials and employees." Efficiency is certainly the traditional and continuing yardstick used in most business bureaucracies. Indeed, it seems particularly well suited to profit-making institutions in a competitive market situation. But public bureaucracies are not in business for a profit. Their major purposes are often ill defined and certainly multiple. For example, in addition to providing a given social service, a city welfare department may also be charged with absorbing marginal workers who might otherwise be unemployable because of age, health, poor training, or some other disability. How, then, can efficiency control its operations? In many situations, therefore, some general measure of public satisfaction with an agency's role might be more meaningful than efficiency. What, for instance, is an accurate measure of police efficiency? Or hospital efficiency? The usual time and motion studies, cost-product analyses, and the like all hang on agreed measures of output that are largely lacking in the public arena. Even library efficiency is not measurable by agreed-upon units of output. In addition to the difficulties that surround the usual measures, there is a growing feeling among some scholars, and some part of the general public too, that in an environment of relative abundance and high mechanization, efficiency may be less important than it used to be. "Satisfaction" could actually come to include the degree of efficiency that *is* measurable and relevant to the public.

For all of these reasons, therefore, the notion of satisfaction —satisfaction of both clientele and employee groups—is emerging as a contending calculus for gauging bureaucratic performance. The notion that employees' satisfaction must be part of the equation stems from a considerable array of psychological research that notes that a man's work is one of the more important parts of his social identity. Needs that are fulfilled in work situations, therefore, are less likely to be displaced into other channels, where they may erupt into antisocial behavior at high public cost. The concept of clientele satisfaction implies nothing more complicated than the use of some instrument that can properly sample and record the intensities of favorable versus unfavorable opinions about public institutions among people who use them. Since the social scientists have succeeded in destroying our early simplistic faith in measures of output such as uniform crime statistics, arrest rates, infant mortality, library books checked out, and so forth, the notion of turning to satisfaction scales as possible output measures is not too farfetched. Such usage, however, is far from common. Indeed, the continued use of efficiency output measures probably has many more advocates than adversaries. The American public is still ambivalent about these contending measures.

The spoils system made famous by Andrew Jackson did more damage to American civil service through its subsequent cure than through its supposed ravages. At least, that is the less heeded side of a deeply divisive argument about our civil service. For most people, both in and out of the public service, the so-called spoils system is anathema. And on the face of it, this seems plausible. Surely a complex important public service agency deserves the very best personnel possible, not an ill-fitting assortment of some politician's friends and relatives. It is this view that has been the moral underpinning of all the hard-won battles for the merit systems in our civil service. The war is still being waged, since, as we saw earlier, there are many pockets of state and local public service that continue to escape the cleansing and uplifting effects of competitive exams and rigorous job requirements. But what started as a clear and simple mandate to throw the rascals out has become a dense jungle of rigid specifications, questionable exams, and fiefdoms of often inappropriate standards.

**MERIT VERSUS SPOILS**

One wonders, for example, whether a New York City welfare worker whose daily job is (or could be) nothing more than routine paperwork needs a college degree. One also wonders whether every position earmarked for registered nurses only really requires them, and if the labyrinthine exams constructed for patrolmen really correlate with any subsequent success on the job. Do the typical promotional exams serve as accurate guides to leadership potential? The antagonists of present merit systems would by no means line up behind a return to the old-fashioned, mindless spoils system, nor do they attack head-on the basic principle of merit. They do attack the present methods of ascertaining and measuring merit, and mindless escalations of conventional qualifications. But as soon as one abandons standard credentials such as professional licenses and college diplomas, or a rank ordering determined by objective tests evenly administered to faceless contestants, one is back on the shifting sands of subjective evaluations, which are notoriously subject to prejudice and favoritism. This is one of the bitterest conflicts now surrounding civil service systems throughout the nation. It is often a black-and-white affair, with the blacks on the side of a relaxation of the old merit rules, which ironically were introduced to ensure earlier under-privileged minorities a fair shake. But today's merit, in the minds of many blacks, Puerto Ricans, and others, is merely meritricious. In their view, merit systems are part of a con-spiracy among the middle-class white civil servants to keep their particular preserves free of encroachment by the newer minorities. This is clearly a tense situation and one that re-quires resolution. My own view is that a system of merit must be preserved—but not the specious "meritocracy" that is often camouflaged by the present proliferation of qualifications and credentials.

Minority sensitivity also underlies another conflict in current bureaucratic operations: the tension between hiring policies that reflect a presumably neutral attempt to gain expertise (however this may be evaluated) and hiring policies that re-flect a concerted effort to keep the members of minority groups employed by public agencies roughly proportionate to their numbers in the population at large. The trend toward propor-tional representation is another reversal of earlier "reforms." A previous generation fought hard to eliminate any hint of racial, religious, color, or ethnic identification from public service applications. Representativeness was not thought to be appropriate to public agencies. In the national govern-ment, as in New York State and many other state and local civil service establishments, it was against the law to inquire into any religious or ethnic matter. Photographs of applicants were not permitted.

Within the last ten years, however, one jurisdiction after another has sought an "ethnic census" among it employees in order to ensure some degree of representativeness. The civil service is no longer color blind; it is no longer a neutral expert-seeking agency. It is a popular arena in which the citizen at large is presumed to have a right to certain forms of identity representation. That is, if a school system serves a population that is 60 percent black, some think that 60 percent of its teachers and principals should be black. How far this type of quota system will go, and for how long, is of course uncertain. And the propriety and wisdom of this newer course of action is even more uncertain. But it is being actively debated in government circles. It is my view that expertise should take clear priority over representation where both cannot be ob-tained (see Chapter 3).

**IMPARTI-
ALITY VS.
RESPON-
SIVENESS**

All bureaucracies, private as well as public, are condemned as being "cold, impersonal, unfeeling machines." It would seem that most people seek individual treatment, warmth, and responses. But each client and each employee in a large organization is actually somewhat ambivalent about what he demands of public administrators. In many life situations, and often in rhetorical ones, people want nothing more than "even-handed justice." They want to be sure that no favoritism is shown. They want the bureaucracies no less than the courts to be symbolized by a woman wearing a blindfold and balancing a pair of scales. On the other hand, they do not want to be treated like a number, nor will they be punched, stamped, and coded. They want the rules to be flexible, subject to human bending here and there to fit each particular situation. It's the other guy who should be treated "fairly"; I need special attention. The patrolman should not simply write out his parking tickets automatically. If one of the cars is yours, he should be mindful of your emergency, your special disability. Indeed, most police agencies are victimized by this ambivalence among the public. More than most agencies, the police can and do engage in selective law enforcement. Yet the other side of this coin would be a playout of the "letter of the law"—every pushcart pushed away, every numbers player booked. Until we come to some agreement about which of these two contradictory styles we wish to enjoy, we can expect only confusion and the worst of each method from our various public agencies. Contradictory signals cannot be honored; invariably they result in erratic behavior. Resolution in either direction would be preferable to continued ambivalence.

The conflict between productivity and participation can be most clearly seen on college campuses. Students, particularly those in the large public universities, cry out against the "bureaucracy." They label it remote, rigid, stupid, and most of all endlessly slow in responding to reasonable demands. Almost all the remedies they propose hang heavily on "student participation." But more committees, and committees enlarged with student membership, are hardly an answer to the already cumbersome procedures of academia. These changes may indeed produce participation (which is perhaps a desirable end in itself), but they are hardly designed to promote speed, efficiency, and productivity.

**PRODUCTION VERSUS PARTICIPATION**

The same problem reveals itself in the required participation of the poor under the Model Cities Act. No funds could be made available for planning a project without appropriate designs for bringing the poor into active participation. But in many instances, getting the poor to participate became an end in itself, and it absorbed the lion's share of the available funding. Whatever "models" the planners might have wanted to project, whatever improvements people had in mind, got mired in the complexities of participation. Again, it is a matter for choice, not for continued evasion. And it is the public that must choose.

**BUREAU-CRATIC CONTROL THROUGH MANAGE-MENT OR MARKET-PLACE**

The problem of how to control bureaucracy is one of the cardinal issues in the United States. All three branches of government have been traditionally involved with it. The legislatures try to "check and balance" through investigating procedures, public exposure, appointment confirmations, control of civil service laws, and ultimately budgetary manipulation and informal pressures. The courts work mainly through procedural restraints and through the adjudication of suits brought against individual bureaucrats for alleged illegal acts or improper use of discretion. But it is primarily the President, in whose branch most bureaucrats work, who is ultimately saddled with the control problem. And his tools seem to be the most limited of all.

The usual procedural cure for the problems of bureaucracy has been the institution of more bureaucracy. Problems of control and accountability are often diagnosed as requiring further centralization, new layers of management, and occasionally new wrinkles in procedure. If a city school is floundering, the conventional wisdom says that a statewide tightening of administrative procedures will help. If the sixty-four operating agencies of New York City are running off in different directions, then a set of ten "superagencies" will put things right. If a function of an old line department is foundering, remove it and give it to an independent agency. If it is foundering as an independent agency, put it into an old line department. And sometimes each or any of these conventional cures actually works. Certainly they work well enough to keep most administrative reformers (if not the public) happy. It is of such stuff that the administrative reforms of the Taft Commission on Economy and Efficiency, Franklin D. Roosevelt's Commission on Administrative Management, and the two Hoover Commissions of Truman and Eisenhower were made.

But there is another wisdom. Actually the second Hoover Commission dabbled with it lightly. Men like Anthony Downs and Christopher Jencks seem smitten with it.[11] For men such as these the answer to bureaucratic bungling is the marketplace. If you want better schools, don't try to *manage* them into excellence—just allow the taxpayers to retain their school taxes as spendable income and thus permit them to "buy" the schools they want, unfettered by boundaries or bankruptcy. If you build a better mousetrap . . . In many ways, this second style of bureaucratic control is essentially democratic, since the coin of the realm is singularly neutral and as intrinsically "equal" as any device we have. Conventional controls always have large elements of "interpretation" of citizen desires read into them by nonelected bureaucrats. The high school that shifts from permissiveness to punishment *interprets* local demands that it "do something" about student unruliness as a mandate for stern measures and assumes that it has hit the right note. But under a market system the citizen speaks directly with his feet and with his money, and his desires are thus made loud and clear. Moreover, if each student were provided with a sum of money, a sort of rough equivalency in the distribution of resources could be ensured. Such pure marketplace control is the subject of a recent, and very limited, but possibly revealing experiment in Massachusetts.

The squabbling over community control of public schools in New York City illustrates a facet of this conflict. Here it might be more aptly billed as a pull between decentralization and devolution of power. The proposals for New York City schools have not gone directly to the marketplace as the potential arbiter of bureaucratic problems. Instead, New York City has tried to get the various neighborhood committees to do this. Parent groups have demanded that each local school district be allowed to run its own school bureaucracy (a devolution of power) on the theory that those closest to home can provide more flexible and effective supervision than some remote central board. In the past, small areas of decision were farmed out to individual schools, but the ultimate supervision and the basic ground rules were left in the hands of "Livingston Street" (that is, the central authority). The idea of community schools is just beginning to flex its muscles. The central board has not yet disappeared and this experiment is also too new and too incomplete to justify any conclusions.

## BUREAUCRACY: BENEFACTOR OR BEHEMOTH

The controversies surrounding American bureaucracies are often more one-sided and less reflective than I have indicated. Often there is virtual unanimity among ordinary citizens in their appraisal of bureaucracy. The word "bureaucracy" is most frequently used as a term of opprobrium. It has become a virtual synonym for waste, red tape, confused authority, rigidity, meanness of spirit, sloth, inefficiency, irrelevance. It is only among social scientists who specialize in the study of bureaucracy that the word is occasionally used neutrally, and even here there is often little love lost on the subject. Most scholars have strayed far from Max Weber's unabashed enthusiasm for an "ideal bureaucracy," in which the necessary characteristics of such an organization—hierarchy, specialization, professionalism, fixed rules, routinization of authority, and even secrecy—were seen as strengths and virtues.[12] The contemporary student of bureaucratic agencies is more likely to be seeking some panacea for what he often portrays as inherent (and perhaps even incurable) pathologies. From William Foote Whyte to C. N. Parkinson, from Peter Blau to Chris Argyris and Warren Bennis,[13] diagnosticians and prescribers are assiduously trying to achieve twentieth-century goods and services without the patently essential bureaucracies and without their essential characteristics. Bureaucracy has become a pejorative term even in academia.

**Benevolent Bureaucracy**

I would like to suggest a different possibility: that despite what have been called the "bureaupathologies," *for most people* bureaucracy may be benevolent. More than any other institutional format it creates a psychologically satisfying homeland for its participants. That is, there is considerable evidence that man craves not freedom but certainty.[14] Big Brother may not always be a bogeyman; for many he may be a benefactor. The privacy, eccentricity, and individualism so ardently sought by the upper classes may be a series of unwanted luxuries for far larger numbers of persons. The "big office," after all, breaks down into little face-to-face work groups, many of whose members spin off in joint leisure activities: the office bowling club, the firemen's poker games. Knowing one's prescribed place and one's eventual rewards, moreover, may be more satisfying than an endlessly open, highly competitive, unstructured marketplace. Finally, bureaucracy properly used may be the best hope for achieving the fundamental goals of the average citizen. I am not sure of this analysis, of course, but it is at least worth more argument and attention than it gets. It deserves at least to be part of the controversy.

# CHAPTER 9

# CITIZEN PARTICIPATION IN THE AMERICAN SYSTEM

Every political system requires some form of citizen participation. Political participation runs the gamut from coercive to voluntary, from grudging to enthusiastic. While coerced behavior may often be paired with grudging attitudes, this is not always so; nor is voluntarism a necessary and sufficient cause of enthusiasm in political behavior. The critical variable here is citizens' perception of their role. The more direct the relationship they see between their political participation and some desired policy output, the greater their enthusiasm. Thus even a conscripted army will fight with vigor if its members believe in their cause and sense a possible victory. So too with a conscripted labor force. Even the purely symbolic gesture of voting in a totalitarian system can sometimes elicit a degree of enthusiasm. Conversely, freedom and ease of participation do not invariably bring enthusiastic compliance. The United States, for example, today offers truly free access to many avenues of political activity, yet few choose to rise to the occasion. Even people who have previously known force and intimidation, and who have been effectively barred from political participation, like black Americans, are showing far less enthusiasm than had been expected. This attitude is sometimes explained as a reaction of bitterness. But then how do we explain the widespread disaffection of those citizens who have never known any such negative coercion? They too are dragging their feet.

In the United States, politically relevant behavior can run from mere talk to the holding of public office. In between there are such things as letter writing, group action, passive and active membership in political parties, campaign work, and regular or sporadic voting. All of these are available, and nothing is coerced. But relatively little is chosen by relatively few. Why? I believe it has to do with our ambivalence about certain key ingredients in our participatory system; ambivalence in our attitudes toward politicians, about the propriety of pressure groups, about campaign methods. But most important is our quite general conviction that whatever we might do, it is unlikely to matter.

**Forms of Political Activity**

PRESSURE
GROUPS:
Special Interests
versus Public
Interest

Most Americans are joiners, and this gregarious instinct is an important factor in our political decision-making apparatus. For some citizens, political activity is likely to center on interest groups of one sort or another. We should not, however, exaggerate the role of pressure groups as a widespread political action vehicle, since they are still the preserve of a relatively small percentage of Americans. But for those who do join and use such groups, they have considerable impact. Since the entire governmental process is a method for distributing resources and values, there are always prizes for some and losses for others. The fundamental controversy here is whether group politics (as it is sometimes called) can arrive at anything like a public interest, or whether it is inherently weighted against such an interest.

Pluralism and
Its Critics

The argument between the protagonists and adversaries of group politics goes beyond criticism over particular pressure groups or blatant forms of corruption; it is a quarrel over the basic thesis that there is a kind of automatic and invisible hand directing this type of pluralism which inevitably produces the greatest good for the greatest number. The antagonists challenge this assumption, and the further assumption on which it is based: that group membership assures broad and overlapping coverage of interests. They wonder if group politics actually produces an automatic brake against the emergence of a single dominating elite whose special interests seem always more equal than others. They wonder if it can distribute prizes to everyone, with truly neutral ground rules and truly open access to the game.

The prizes under discussion here are of varying types and importance. Clearly there is a time and a place where every individual is affected by the distribution. For example, the government is the distribution agency for a vast array of jobs, for profitable contracts, for licenses and permits necessary to the pursuit of many occupations, for monopoly franchises, zoning regulations, sanitary regulations, health and hospital services, veterans' benefits, children's benefits, welfare payments, disability pensions, educational services, scholarships, tax rebates, and many other tangible benefits. In the formulation, regulation, and enforcement of every one of these matters (whether it is the setting up of a new post in a merit system, the creation of a new judgeship, a change in a government retirement plan, the adoption of a new parking regulation, or the promulgation and enforcement of a factory inspection law), a vested interest is closely affected. It is this direct effect upon certain individuals that generally stimulates the rise of a pressure group. Depending on the action involved, the pressure group may impinge primarily on legislatures or on the executive branch. Some pressure groups, of course, arise from continuous, recurring interests; others are ad hoc pressure groups responding to an intermittent or unique situation. Thus we have teachers' organizations, PTAs, conservation groups, veterans' clubs, labor unions, chambers of commerce, civil service employee organizations, welfare mothers' groups, and on and on. Many such groups have interests so closely tied to government policy actions that they function as year-round lobbyists. That is, they maintain special professional units at the seat of government at each level that might possibly influence any policy in which they are interested. Such lobbying units attempt to keep informed about the policies within their range of interests which are being formulated by the government, and at the same time they try to influence such policies. The lobby educates its own group members, keeping them abreast of decisions in administrative and lawmaking circles. More important, it educates (or propagandizes) the administrators and legislators concerning their own group interests. Thus conservation groups present the facts necessary to convince legislators of the near extinction of the bald eagle in the hope of obtaining certain game regulations to conserve the species. Temperance groups have careful statistics on alcoholism; doctors have educational data on the benefits of private medical care; hospital administrators have data on hospital deficits. Occasionally a group forms spontaneously for a special event such as a demonstration against a particular nuclear bomb test or a "mothers' march" to protest the destruction of a neighborhood playground. These too are pressure groups and serve as the foci of the particular plans, ideas, and interests of a heterogeneous population.

Thus there are many publics, each with its own interests. How should we evaluate the adequacy of these groups in promoting their interests? Do the cross-pressures they generate result in policies that we are willing to believe are the "public interest"?

Educational policy, for example, probably comes closer than liquor policy to being a bedrock issue in this nation, even if the people organized to influence liquor policies appear to be more numerous (or more vociferous) than the members of education groups; but our system provides no litmus test for a legitimate "public interest." The fact that many Americans are dissatisfied with the present results of this scramble of special interests is manifest in many ways. First there are recurring attempts to regulate pressure groups and lobbies. Then there is a burgeoning of very broad-based new pressure groups, such as Common Cause. This is a "people's" lobbying group that tries to represent its public on a broad array of issues, such as peace and

**Pressure Groups and Lobbies**

pollution control, which it defines as the public interest. These groups, of course, compete with our traditional vehicle for representing the broadest spectrum of national problems, our political party system, which we shall discuss later. There is no restriction on participation in any of these groups as such. Participation in a group, whether it is a short-term local committee or a three-hundred-year-old organization, it is a constitutionally protected right of all Americans, and it is heavily used. And so it should be. We could not enjoin the formation of interest groups without violating our First Amendment freedom to speak, write, and assemble, and the companion protection of the right to petition the government. The restrictive laws that have been passed in this area are confined to certain state requirements that lobbyists must register and disclose their sources of financial support.

Yet there is fundamental dissatisfaction with pressure politics as it now operates. This is manifested also by the growing alienation of youth and other segments of society with their growing use of violence and violent rhetoric. Is there, then, some way to ensure that group politics becomes *public* politics? Critics like Theodore Lowi do not suggest either violence or the total replacement of pressure groups.[1] The protagonists of reform simply want a frank recognition of the dangers inherent in this system, a willingness to recognize that group politics and existing tactics do not automatically result in the greatest good for the greatest number, or even automatically represent substantial pockets of the public. Commitment to liberty and majoritarianism, on the other hand, will not permit us to accept a "public interest" ordained by some agency and presented to us by government fiat. We must therefore settle for ground rules that will at least ensure the existence of genuine creative conflict among special interests. We must guard against institutionalizing certain special interests, as we now often do (as when we set up supposedly independent regulating commissions that swiftly and almost invariably become the pawns of the special interests they are supposed to police). We must be ready to provide sufficient basic resources (skills, access, self-esteem, along with subsistence) to the disadvantaged segments of our society so that they too can become effective agents of group politics. Finally, we might encourage the so-called public lobbies such as Common Cause, which address the broadest areas of public policy and try to represent very large and hitherto amorphous and unheard segments of the public.

**ELECTIONS:**
**Decisions versus**
**Distractions**
The most obvious avenue for Americans to take to reach the citadel of politics is, of course, the election process. Elections are sometimes the tools of pressure groups and they are always

the prize of political parties. For some Americans they are a habit, for others a bore, and for a dangerously increasing number a sham. What indeed do American elections mean? There are short ballots, long ballots, propositions, referenda, constitutional amendments, and special recall elections scattered all over the calendar and all over the land. In the village in which I live, for example, I am entitled to vote in school district elections for members of the school board and for the school budget and for contingent bond issues. I may also vote for village trustees, members of a town board of supervisors, members of a county board, and the county executive, sheriff, and county clerk; for a state assemblyman, the governor, lieutenant governor, state senator, comptroller, and state attorney general; for a United States congressman, two United States senators, the President of the United States; and for a long list of judges, from local justice of the peace through county judges, state supreme court judges, and members of the court of appeals. In addition there are biennial primary elections within each party, and I may vote in the primaries of the party of my choice for party officers who serve me both locally and statewide and for the persons nominated for those public offices that are contended for by candidates selected in party primaries (and that covers most of the offices mentioned). On top of all this, the New York constitution requires that any amendment to it (and its need for amendment is all too frequent because of its inappropriate length and complexity) be approved by the people at a general election. It also requires that certain forms of debt and tax policy be put before the people as propositions for their approval; and finally it requires that every twenty years the people face a general "question," asking them whether or not they wish to call a constitutional convention to revise the document. All of this is simply par for the course.

There is no city, village, county, or state that offers much less. Indeed, there are many that offer more. All but one state require popular ratification of a state constitutional amendment, and thirteen of them permit the initiation of such an amendment directly by the people. All states but three require or permit some referenda on local matters to be approved (or vetoed) directly by the people. Twenty-two states use such direct action for state and local matters like those described above, and twenty states permit the people (following certain prescribed procedures) actually to initiate policy as well.

So far I have merely demonstrated that there are many elections. There are also many candidates for the offices at stake; but not always. The question that remains, however, is: What do they all mean? As they are presently constituted, they mean very little. No matter what test may be applied, it is distress-

**Referendum**

ingly apparent that *policy changes cannot be traced to electoral changes*. Vietnam policy has remained substantially unchanged despite four presidential elections and two switches in party. The history of most of our congressional legislation and our state executive and legislative policy-making also yields little substantive support for the idea that policy change occurs through elections. The changes that do occur seem to come either as a result of external or domestic crises or as incremental responses to broad circular sweeps in demographic factors such as population growth, technological innovations, and economic swings. Various analyses of poll data, including one based on material from 1935 to 1946, indicate that public opinion on such matters as birth control, divorce, taxes, labor relations, socialized medicine, government ownership, and race relations have not particularly governed the course of public policy.[2] And of course this is true in relation to Vietnam policy too.

**Voting Studies**     There appears to be a missing link somewhere between the voter and the politician. The election is supposed to provide the linkage, but it apparently does not do the trick. In fact, a study done in 1971 shows that the voting record of the House leaders of both parties did not reflect their constituents' views on such key issues as Vietnam, the draft, and the supersonic transport plane. This study also shows that between 80 and 100 percent of the voters were unaware of the way their congressmen had voted.[3] This conclusion might also be supported by the sort of data that show that 65 percent of eligible American voters do not vote regularly; half of them cannot name their congressmen and 65 percent cannot name both of their U.S. senators; 86 percent are not able to identify anything that their congressmen have done; and 96 percent cannot identify any policy their congressmen stand for.[4] Even among those who do vote, the operative force is more often habit than conviction. Some degree of cynicism about the procedure seems widespread.

There are two ways of interpreting findings of this sort. The usual way, the way that prevails in both the scholarly journals and the popular media, is to make the public out to be an idiot. It certainly does seem difficult to avoid a harsh judgment of people who said in 1970 that "ending the war in Vietnam" was the most important issue facing the nation, and then went on to say that they would vote for James L. Buckley of the conservative party in preference to Charles E. Goodell, liberal Republican, for U.S. senator. Yet over one-third of the respondents in a *New York Times* poll said precisely that during a campaign in which Buckley advocated continuation of the war until it was "won," in contrast to Goodell's insistence that it should be ended quickly.[5]

Most of the scholarly voting studies also paint the electorate as ill informed, irrational, and considerably alienated. We are seen as having reasonably strong attachment to one or the other major political party, but little if no ideological understanding, little or no information on issues, and a highly inconsistent and illogical set of voting or nonvoting responses. These findings are usually pinned on judgments concerning the psychological and social factors that appear to influence voting; that is, the limitations of intelligence, attention span, motivational apparatus, and general psyche of most people. Any blame that does not fall in these quarters is placed on the complexities of the problems themselves. But other interpretations are possible. I choose to put the blame on the election system itself and on certain other institutional devices that stack the game, from the outset, against rationality.

Even the voting studies themselves can be pruned for evidence against the prevailing theory of electoral incompetence. Indeed, the posthumous work of one of the most famous American political analysts, V. O. Key, is called *The Responsible Electorate*. Its theme is the necessity for reevaluating some of the conventional wisdom of our time concerning voter foolishness. His analysis reinstates the average voter as quite capable of self-interested common sense. "The mass electorate is a good deal less irrational, ill-informed or sheep-like than is fashionable to suppose."[6] The voter is indeed concerned about the central and relevant questions of public policy. Angus Campbell concludes that the reason for low turnout is the people's conviction that their votes will not count,[7] while still other scholars conclude that voting choices are rational when seen in terms of the voters' perceptions and information.

Why, then, should so many voters turn their backs on this hard-won privilege? Why is it that those who complain the most about our society are the least likely to vote? Persistent effort was required on campuses in 1970 even to register eighteen-year-old voters after they had battled vigorously to win the vote. Why? I suggest it is an understandable alienation. It stems from the seemingly unbridgeable gulf between the opinion polls and the public policy.[8] There seem to be at least five major explanations for this phenomenon, and all of them are institutional rather than personal.

The first is lack of issue crystallization. Very few candidates, from the President on down, bother to educate their publics. Although millions of dollars are spent each year to run for public office, the size of the expenditure often appears to be in inverse ratio to the intelligence of the campaign. The very largest sums go to pay for television spot announcements. These are image builders, not idea builders. In fact, the business of

**Electoral
Incompetence**

imagery is so great that people wonder whether TV will not prove to be a soporific rather than a stimulant to the nation's intelligence. I shall say more about this later. There is also a self-fulfilling prophesy involved here: the more the elite office-seekers believe the voters to be idiots, the more their campaigns will be geared to idiots, and the greater the possibility that the voters will respond as idiots.

Second, there is a great deal of ambiguity in the election-issue transmission belt because of the multiplicity of issues in every campaign and the failure of anything within or without the system to demand a rational ordering of these issues. In other words, after an election is won, how should the victor interpret the victory? Which position taken on which issue in which place brought him his office? And the reverse of this transmission system is equally obscure. After a man is in public office, whether legislative or executive, for what can he be held responsible? It is often difficult even to know where a legislator stands on any issue. Viva-voce votes evaporate and roll-call records can be seriously misunderstood. Legislators are frequently faced with the need for desperate compromises in a system of legislative voting that itself does not permit any conscientious, rational ordering of preferences.

The next two systematic faults lie in institutions and processes already reviewed: our legislative process and own lack of intergovernmental and intragovernmental cohesion. The story of American legislative abdication, deviousness, and delays has already been recorded here. The committee system, the rules, the voting processes, the chairmanships, the pull between the houses, all obfuscate or actually eliminate any possible resemblance between broad policy mandates by the electorate and any product of our legislative assemblies. The operation of federalism and of checks and balances also stacks the cards against the achievement of a visible and viable connection between the electorate and its executive officers in our 80,000 governments.

The final two deterrents to responsible and responsive voting can be laid at the feet of our party system. There is little real competition among parties and little internal party cohesiveness. In sum, the election system does not go very far toward realizing the people's fondest hopes. They know from experience—and experience correctly understood—that elections as they are currently contrived have little to do with policy outcomes.

**POLITICAL PARTIES**    Although in some ways a political party may be viewed as a large interest group open to public membership, it has certain unique characteristics that require separate comment. Political parties alone are legally empowered to nominate our public officers and run our elections. Although political parties were originally regarded as strictly private bodies, today their procedures are generally deeply embedded in the laws of each state. Each state has its own ground rules as to what constitutes a legally recognized political party with rights to present candidates on election ballots. Once a party is legally recognized, it must conform to state directives on such things as when and how to elect its officers, when to hold its meetings, and how it must proceed to nominate candidates for public office on the state's ballots.

Parties arise from certain obvious characteristics of human behavior. If a public office is offered as a prize but no set procedure is established for nomination to that office, at the time of election a large number of candidates will compete for it. In a system of elections based on a plurality vote, operation of the laws of chance would dictate a random scatter of votes. It quickly becomes obvious that any clique that preplans its voting pattern can elect its own choices. This simple calculation is the seed bed of a political party. Once the observation is made and acted upon, others will inevitably adopt the same tactic. Thus, an opposition party develops. Certain of the mechanisms and characteristics of our elections, such as the electoral college method of electing the President and the use of single-member districts for most legislative seats, together with the pull of tradition, help cement the system into a two-party affair on the national level, and something more or less than that on the state and local levels.

**Origin of Parties**

The structure of the party organization itself provides broad though often inchoate opportunities for citizen participation. The organization is invariably a rough pyramid of power. At the bottom are the county committeemen and -women, generally elected by the enrolled voters of the party at a primary from among names submitted by petition. Quite typically half of these posts have no incumbents. Village, town, and county committeemen meet annually to elect a chairman and executive board and perhaps other officers. The actual initiative and direction of party affairs is in the hands of these elected chairmen and executive committees. The county level is the heartland of party affairs. The county leaders (who in urban areas are often called district leaders, since they are elected on the basis of election districts) are generally the real power centers within each state. It is this hard core of truly active and often full-time personnel that actually selects the public candidates for the various elected offices at each level of government, as well as the nominees for the party offices themselves. The organization of political parties varies from state to state, from party

**Structure of Local Parties**

to party, and even within any state from county to county; but the overall picture generally follows this outline. At the state level it is customary to have another set of committeemen, chosen again at a primary by the enrolled voters, or occasionally at a convention. These persons choose the state chairman and executive committee. This leadership also decides on platforms, campaigning, funding, and other policies of the state party. The state chairmen, however, are often only figureheads; the actual power of the statewide organization may be wielded by the governor or a senator.

The United States has managed to develop a political party system that is remarkable for its breadth of opportunity for general citizen participation and equally remarkable for its lack of firm ideological commitment. Both of these characteristics stem from certain features of our constitutions and from our ambivalence about the values we hold.

**Party Functions**     The official purpose of the party organization, of course, is to choose candidates, run campaigns, raise money, help voters register and get to the polls, perform a community political education function, and do all the odds and ends necessary to comply with the states' cumbersome election laws and machinery—and also necessary to winning elections. In addition, American political parties have fed their own strength by filling many of the gaps in our complex system of divided, separated, and limited government. In the days before the government accepted any social service role, the party performed this function too. This was the era of the Christmas turkey, the kettle of coal, and the occasional handout. Today the party's service are in the form of legal and administrative help in understanding and obtaining the rights and privileges extended by a more paternalistic government. The parties, in other words, often help citizens break through the bureaucratic barriers that surround most government benefits and obligations. The new political clubs provide housing clinics (while the government provides public housing, rent-control laws, public health services, and building regulations). Those clinics provide guidelines to the government's complicated procedures. Political parties in urban centers also have civil rights sections. At the turn of the century the parties serviced immigrants, today they service non-English-speaking citizens and impoverished nonliterate ones. In the early nineteenth century the party was the steppingstone to virtually all civil service jobs; today, with a fairly broad merit system covering about half our state and local services and almost 85 percent of our national service, this patronage pot is much smaller, but there are still some juicy jobs available, particularly in the judiciary, to keep the party organization supplied with negotiable coin.

It is the contradictory attitudes about party life, however, that set its style and perhaps its future.

In no political institution are the unresolved conflicts of American values better illustrated than in its political parties. Here, in bold relief, one sees the inner turmoil of large numbers of Americans who have never faced up to some of their own mutually irreconcilable goals. The conflicts to which I refer are not those among the various partisan groups themselves (Republicans versus Democrats, Socialists versus Conservatives), but deep cleavages within the attitudes of a single individual toward the role of a political party. Americans tend to view all politicians and politics with distaste, yet at the same time make increasing demands for politically contrived decisions and problem-solving. To most Americans, to be a politician is to be a conniver, a mean-minded grafter, a hypocrite. Yet the same American who conjures up these images generally holds an exaggeratedly exalted opinion of his President, his U.S. senator, his state supreme court judges, and so forth. Apparently the equation between high public offices and low party offices is never made. Moreover, the typical citizen does not ponder how we can possibly demand more and more government services without generating more and more politicians.

Nor is the equation between the attributes of a successful businessman and a successful politician ever analyzed. Our typical citizen fails to see the dilemma involved in believing in a profit system for business on the one hand and a system of pure altruism for politics on the other. Nobody would dream of demanding that Henry Ford II spend his days and nights at hard work without pay or profit, nor would anyone demand it of one of his machine-tool operators. But citizens do demand it of their political party officers and their party committeemen. The national chairman and the ward leader both serve long and hard often without salary. Until recently the United States came close to demanding this selflessness of certain high public officials as well. It is only within the last decade that the salaries of most of our high public officers were made somewhat competitive with those of the business world. But if one's basic assumption about human motivation includes an impulse for self-preservation, why should any one group be expected to be exempt from it? Most party workers piece out a living by getting a public sinecure. Although it is our own shortsightedness that forces this situation, we take every opportunity to complain about it.

The question of taste arises very clearly when one tries to figure out what Americans want in the matter of party style. There is an unresolved conflict between that part of the American character which is "Puritan," moralistic, elitist, and reform-oriented, and the part that is pragmatic, egalitarian, uncommitted, and easygoing. The two sides occasionally jell into two different factions: an early-twentieth-century Tammany type and a Lincoln Steffens mugwump. But often they are combined in the same individual. The New Yorker who considered Jimmy Walker a fine fellow and easily forgave him his pecadillos (including his all too obvious connections with blatant public stealing) may be the same man who later hitched his wagon to Fiorello La Guardia's fusionist reform movement. It is really hard to know with certainty just which strain is ascendant at any moment; but if I had to guess, I would say the pragmatic "live and let live" style usually prevails. More people seem to respond to the pungent but at least warm and lively style of George Washington Plunkitt, who explained so clearly the difference between "clean and dirty graft,"[9] than to the multisyllabic, antiseptic, and often bloodless appeal of a typical reformer. Perhaps these tensions can be seen most clearly in the perennial battles traditionally fought against "bossism" in our states and cities.

## THE MACHINE VERSUS THE ORGANIZATION

From a logical viewpoint, it is hard to account for the anti-boss, antimachine crusades that persistently crop up. For one thing, the very people who make up the crusades are likely to be organization men in their business and social lives. The political reformer usually has an upper-class or at least an upper-middle-class background and is seldom at all critical about the need for organization in business, or about the inevitable hand-maidens of the organizational style—compromise, bargaining, hierarchies, territoriality, monetary rewards, and other individual incentives. But for one reason or another, he holds these truths to be suspended when he enters the political arena. Here organization and its tactics become suspect. The leader of a political party, if he is particularly and repeatedly successful, becomes a "boss" in the most pejorative sense. His loyal workers become "henchmen"; his array of incentives becomes dirty "patronage" and "spoils"; his tactics become "back-room wheeling and dealing." In short, his very success becomes the proof of his deviltry. Yet the only alternative to winning elections (and that is the goal of party life) is losing them; and a successful boss understands this. Moreover, he knows full well that elections are won only by hard-working, well-motivated organizations. When we stop to realize that more than half the county committee posts throughout the United States go begging, we begin to understand the basic ingredient in the power allocation system. Most citizens do not want the burdens that active party membership entails. Many a caucus among the "organization boys" is as open to the public as the corner cinema, but few citizens leave home and television to attend. Then come the fall balloting and the complaints about the "boys in the back room." The most unfortunate machine practices are likely to continue until it occurs to the American public that party officers ought to be paid openly, directly, and appropriately for the work they perform for the community. Salary will then replace sinecure. Until then, those reformers who are successful will prove to have staying power only to the degree that they themselves form and maintain organizations. And once any such organization becomes so highly efficient that its profitable results become reasonably predictable, then the moment has arrived to label it a "machine," and the cycle of reform begins once more.

This particular conflict, however, may well be one that we can afford to leave unresolved. The notion of "kicking the rascals out" may be the better part of wisdom. The only serious danger here is the tendency to confuse a housecleaning operation with a basic goal achievement. The history of most political party reform is the history of "outs" becoming "ins" through some manipulation of or change in a technical procedure. More often than not, the reformers themselves have concentrated on a change in procedure as *the* goal. I wish neither to speak against procedural reforms nor to minimize the possible (though not inevitable) connections between a procedure and a later substantive change. I do wish to point out the tenuous nature of such reforms, the uncertainty of their future direction, and the wisdom of keeping continuous watch over results rather than viewing any such procedural change as a victory in itself. I can think of no large substantive goal that has been won or reversed by the party reforms so far introduced.

Take, for example, the history of our nominating procedures. Even before the Constitution was adopted, the caucus was viewed as the acceptable, even respectable method of naming candidates for public office. Meeting with the boys in the back room to put together a slate of acceptable nominees was viewed as patent common sense. By the time King Caucus ran afoul of Andrew Jackson, procedural change was in the offing. Reform in this period was represented by a democratizing method called a convention. The floodgates were opened and the rank and file of the party were invited to a huge forum to select candidates. To this day the convention remains the final method of selecting presidential nominees, and in many states it continues to be used for state offices as well. But it did not take reformers long to see the fly in this ointment. After all, who selected the delegates at the convention? The old bosses. Moreover, when any gathering gets too large, it is easily led by a small, previously organized group (a caucus).

The next democratic reform invention was, therefore, the pri-

**Primaries, Conventions and Caucuses**

mary. Here the voter himself was asked to take part in an election of nominees for various public offices. Today most states use the primary system for nominating the largest number of their public officers. And fourteen states plus the District of Columbia use primaries indicating presidential preferences as a basis for the selection of delegates to the quadrenniel national nominating convention. An astute student of politics, however, would be quick to ask, "How do the names appear on the *primary* ballots?" The answer again, as one might suspect, is those boys in the back room, the caucus. Indeed, a former mayor of the city of Bridgeport, Connecticut, Jasper McLevy (a socialist and a self-styled slayer of political machines), warned Connecticut in 1955 that its then newly proposed primary law might actually increase the power of the bosses. And one can note wryly that in Hartford, where nonpartisan primaries were part of the scene even earlier, the Democratic regulars seem to have had little trouble in continuing their control of candidacies. There are also other straws in the wind. In the early sixties, Massachusetts reverted to a preprimary convention, and just before that, California finally became convinced that its reformers' dream, a "cross-filing" primary in which candidates could appear under any or all party labels, had turned into a nightmare. It had been introduced by Governor Hiram Johnson in 1915 in a crusade to defeat entrenched machines, but time did not deal kindly with it. It was finally abandoned.

Other forms of procedural legalism are equally uncertain. Fifty detailed election reforms in Chicago during the 1950s do not seem to have strangled Richard Daley's machine yet. And New York's similarly reformer-designed laws concerning designating petitions, originally introduced to prevent wholesale machine-made forgeries, swiftly became the bulwark of the machine. Indeed, many of the reforms attempted in New York City in the early and middle 1960s were made difficult or impossible by requirements such as these: petitions must appear on sheets of the prescribed shade of green; only black ink (no ballpoint pens) may be used; no abbreviations are permitted in date or address; no titles such as Mr. or Dr. may be used; married women must use their given first names; signatures must be identical with those on registration lists. It has taken the reformers quite some time to catch on; and it is only as they begin to settle down and take on many of the characteristics of the machine that they are themselves able to "use" these reforms.

Even such a massive procedural victory as the substitution of a merit system for an outright spoils system has lent itself to party manipulation. The very personnel procedures of merit often become spoils. For example, classifying a certain position

**The Power of the Bosses**

in a certain "grade," arranging the date of an examination so that it does or does not coincide with particular training school graduations, defining certain posts as competitive or noncompetitive—all these decisions carry patronage with them. That is, they benefit some at the expense of others; and they have been used to do so.

Clearly procedural reform must be examined with care. To the degree that it is effective, it is so only when citizens are continually ready to adapt and try again. It is very much like good housekeeping: it may very well improve a house's appearance and help pave the way for a better home life, but it is no guarantee in itself of a sound and healthful family. It is an endless and continuing task.

The pols (that is, the professional politicians), whether they are Republicans, Democrats, Liberals, or Socialists, share a bond of brotherhood, a likelihood of assessing the basic needs of the nation in the same way, and a deep appreciation of the fun and drama of political party life. To these people the central business of a polity is managing conflict, and the best vehicle for doing so is a political party. Shifting coalitions, bargaining, compromise are time-honored methods of managing conflict. To the reform-minded, however, all of these procedures smack of illegitimacy, the machine, corruption, the lowest level of self-regarding opportunism. They have a naive faith in anything that promises them an escape from "politics." The name of the game is not compromise, but goal achievement. Reformers generally feel secure with goals *they* interpret as attuned to the public good or the public interest, and they are more than willing to ride roughshod over any opposition in their efforts to achieve these goals. But of course the goals they set are their own, not necessarily anyone else's, and they are often short-sighted. There is thus a deep social and psychological divide between the pols and the public benefactors, and it is manifest in many ways large and small, from speech and dress style to voting behavior and issue orientation. This is, I believe, a creative controversy as long as the public understands what is involved and becomes willing to withdraw its own contradictory demands.

**DOGMA VERSUS DEALS**

The essence of American parties is their nonideological nature. The fact that the national scene is dominated quite exclusively by two very broad parties, while many states and local arenas are dominated by only one party, testifies to the rather loose, non-issue-oriented base of our party life. Most foreigners are loath to believe that we can operate our system through parties that not only mean all things to all people, but frequently attract people whose views are directly opposed to those expressed by the party slogans. Thus while the Democratic party is generally viewed as being to the left of the Republicans, its membership includes many southerners whose views are at least as conservative as any to be found within the Republican party. A recent remark of a Democratic senator with presidential aspirations is in point here. In referring to the war in Vietnam, he told an audience of West Coast workers, "Our party has room for the hawks and room for the doves." If so, one might wonder what purpose the party could possibly serve. This ideological schizophrenia has drawn comment from many observers. Typical are the remarks of two public opinion experts, Free and Cantril:

> The paradox of a large majority of Americans qualifying as operational liberals while at the same time a majority hold to a conservative ideology has been repeatedly emphasized. . . . We have described this state of affairs as mildly schizoid, with people believing in one set of principles while acting according to another. . . . As already indicated, it is only because the American system has demonstrated such flexibility and such a capacity to accommodate to new situations that this schizoid state has not more seriously impeded operation and direction of the Government.[10]

**The Two-Party System**

Our system of two decentralized and undisciplined parties is seen by some as the major vehicle for bridging these gaps between and among conflicting beliefs. Yet the desire to tighten up the parties and make them more coherent and cohesive is a recurrent theme. There are many who agree that

> there is little doubt that the time has come for a restatement of American ideology to bring it in line with what the great majority of people want and approve . . . to enable the American people to implement their political desires in a more intellegent, direct and consistent manner.[11]

Party realignment, electoral reforms such as proportional representation, and internal stick-and-carrot methods to require party cohesiveness are among the suggestions that are often made.

**Party Characteristics**

But two-party roots are deep in America. The theories advanced to explain this phenomenon are extensive.[12] Our election system, including the use of single-member districts in which the winner takes the entire prize with a mere plurality vote, lends itself to two-party organization. The electoral college does the same, only more so, since it virtually rules out a third party for the only existing national offices (President and Vice-President). As we have noted before, the electoral college system gives the entire state delegation of votes—perhaps as many as forty-five—to the winner, even if he has won by only one popular vote. This arithmetic adds up to a two-party system. But today, the two-party system rests just as heavily, if not more so, on tradition. Even if we were to change the electoral college (as well we may), I doubt that the two-party tradition would fade away very quickly. Third parties, of course, will continue to appear. They serve as policy path-finders for the other two, and as any issue becomes acceptable to middle America, it is made a plank in the platform of each of the major parties.

As long as we remain a two-party nation, we will have to deal in compromises rather than consistencies. The federated nature of our polity assures that national politics must reflect the parochial interests of fifty states with somewhat different economic and geographic interests. This means platforms that are platitudes, not policy statements. The check-and-balance principle of the Constitution also favors deals over dogmas. Since coordinate branches of government are often in the hands of rival parties, the policies of each must be compromised if anything is to be accomplished at all. And since each party realizes that it may soon be in the other's shoes, the spirit of compromise is highly valued among professional politicians. It is this type of situation that gives American party life the quality of a game. The chief characteristic of a game is that enjoyment stems as much from continued playing as from winning. One does not kill off the other team in a game; one wants it to survive to play again.

Gamesmanship, humor, and compromise in American party life are also outgrowths of the amazing sloppiness of rank-and-file party membership. There are no card-carrying Democrats, as there are card-carrying Communists. In the American party system there are privileges but no obligations. The average citizen's concept of his party membership is likely to be vague. If you ask a typical American whether he is a Democrat or a Republican, you may get a quick and definite response, but if you try to probe what this means, you will get diverse and fuzzy replies. To some persons, belonging to a party means only that in the last presidential election they voted for that party's candidate. To others it may connote voting a straight party ticket regularly and for many years. To a few more sophisticated persons it means (as it technically should) their ability to vote in that party's nominating procedures for public candidates, as well as for the officers of the party organization itself; that is, to vote in the primaries.

But even among sophisticated voters, party membership entails no services on their part. They rarely pay any dues, nor do they attend meetings, perform chores, or accept any discipline from the party leaders. They even insist on the right to oppose, both in and after election, the very candidates that they may have originally helped select in a primary. In fact, this aura of independence is very attractive to a considerable

**Compromise versus Consistency**

segment of voters. They not only like to believe that they themselves are independent; they apparently value this streak in the
people they elect. Far from being convinced that the best legislator is the one who votes the party line (when there is one),
Americans are often enthusiastic about the renegades, the people who stand "above party." But it is quite clear by now that
this is another of the major ambivalences in the American
breast. Which way do you want it? The party made consistent,
clear, and cohesive, or the individual made a so-called statesman who knows no authority other than his own conscience?
The party as a policy protagonist or as a machine to oil the
gears of other policy-makers? My own view is that the time has
come to shape political parties in at least a somewhat more
ideological, issue-oriented mold. Along with other suggestions
that I shall propose in the final chapter, such an innovation
would help the rank-and-file American resolve some of his
own basic value ambivalences. And I would argue that some
such resolution is occasionally necessary. The parties, I believe,
are appropriate mechanisms to help in setting out certain basic
directions for our society. If we do not know where we want to
go, how can we get there?

**MADISON
AVENUE
VERSUS
MAIN
STREET**
The matter of style is becoming so important that from time
to time it threatens to snuff out substance. It is the question
of the role of the communications media in American public
life, particularly television. Is Madison Avenue supposed to
reflect Main Street? Cater to Main Street? Educate Main
Street? Ignore Main Street? Indeed, would there even be a
Main Street without Madison Avenue? After all, the old idyll
of small-town America is waning. There is little of it left today
outside of the movies. Indeed, one often wonders if the only
remaining hick is one invented by a slick. One often wonders
too just what the qualities of the true Main Street are or were;
but clearly the American dream street is one where people
know each other and care; where the golden rule prevails;
where there is a deep-down honesty, and the few phonies are
as obvious as an elephant in the town square. And it is patently
true that most Americans would not buy a phony product or a
phony person if they knew that that was what they were getting. This is particularly true in politics. Historically, Americans
have always seemed quite ready to take their homespun politicians as they appeared to be, warts and all. If there were a few
Warren Harding types, all dignity and profile, there were more
Harry Trumans. In the days of the party clambake, the genuine
article had to be displayed along with the American flag on the
town bandstand. There were homespun speeches along with
the home-baked cakes. There were conversations rather than
commercials, real time instead of prime time.

Neither style has yet obliterated the other, and neither style has a monopoly on virtue. While Madison Avenue is a long way from home for most Americans, it is still a tribute to America's highly prized professionalism. It is technology, salesmanship, speed, bigness, superstars. It is many things we obviously hold dear. And if not all of Main Street can be shown to be pure, so not all of Madison Avenue can be shown to be phony. The tension between the two styles in political life should be managed by using the techniques of Madison Avenue to reach the highest, not the lowest, common denominator on Main Street. The mass media can present a man, rather than package him. Television can lend itself to great debates quite as well as it does to simplistic slogans. It can be a wedge against provincialism and parochialism, and it can be a bulwark against any single power citadel as well. But all of this requires not only resolution on the part of media managers, but also regulation on the part of the citizenry. That is, we have to establish ground rules that will ensure that the products sold on television—particularly the political products—are fit to sell. We have to be sure that warning labels are attached where necessary. We cannot, in short, substitute the media for the message; we must demand that the media *deliver* the message, loud and clear, far and wide, in black and white and all the colors necessary to make clear the inevitable complexities of modern politics.

I have reserved a final word for a trend that is becoming more pronounced with each passing year. It is the shunning of traditional politics—elections, pressure groups, parties, letter-writing, petitions—in favor of certain less conventional methods: sit-ins, lie-downs, marches, burnings, lootings, demonstrations, street gangs, demagogues. It is the politics of the desperate, the alienated, the thoroughly confused. This is often called the "new politics." And it is understandable.

**THE NEW POLITICS**

If one stops to consider the traditional smorgasbord of solutions and action styles available for dealing with a particular problem, the special skill and opportunities necessary to take advantage of these approaches become evident. And the special frustrations and roadblocks encountered by certain groups of people will also stand in clear relief.

Consider, then, a quite simple and common community problem: a grade-school intersection with considerable morning traffic and no arrangement to help get children safely across the street. Now there are many possible solutions and many possible styles of action. The possible solutions for middle-class America come quickly to mind: a traffic light, a stop sign, the assignment of a paid traffic guard, the assignment of older student guards, the use of volunteer parents, the rerouting of traffic during certain hours. Each alternative can also be clearly seen as contingent on a different type of action and a different focal point of help. Thus a traffic light is known to require not only police action, but in most communities approval by the village board or city council as well. Some solutions are known to require changes in state law.

**Problem-solving: The Middle Class**

In any event, among the affected residents of a middle-class community there is an array of skills, experiences, connections, time, money, and sophistication. Here the people quickly sense the important variables involved: the legal complications; the various intensities of concern with the problem; the variety of interests involved, including adversary interests (pedestrian, motorist, police); the strengths and weaknesses of the political and administrative access points. There is sufficient time available for some mothers to meet and talk the matter over. There is sure to be somebody with a room large enough for such a meeting. There is someone who knows the principal, the police chief, the traffic engineer. The PTA, the typewriter, the telephone, the city council are all household words or household items. Somebody has a sister in the school system and somebody else a brother who is a lawyer, and somebody there works for the local newspaper. These people have the knowledge and experience to make an intelligent plan of action and to set it in motion; they probably also have some reasonably approximate understanding of the potential costs, liabilities, and time involved in the various alternatives before them.

**Problem-solving: The Poor**

None of these things is likely to be true in the world of extreme poverty. Here people are often so distracted by severe personal problems, so overwhelmed by too many children in too few rooms with too little food and too many diseases, that they cannot begin to concentrate on a situation such as this. They are likely to lack leadership, experience, specialized skills, free time, typewriters, even telephones. They are often severely restricted by a tradition of legal and illegal disenfranchisement, community intimidation, and encouraged passivity. Here nobody's father is the district judge or the county clerk. Often nobody even knows the teachers in the local school, and they see the principal only when their children are accused of serious misbehavior. The police are to be avoided like the plague. Any experiences they may have had with government agencies are likely to have embittered them. In such a setting, there is every chance that a dangerous school crossing would remain a nonissue until blood had been spilled. Then there would be rage. If some few remarkable residents did try with their inadequate resources to do something, they might well underestimate the time that would be needed, or fail to distinguish between appropriate and inappropriate access points. They would merely raise their own hopes, and if the tragedy were to occur then, rage would be escalated to outrage. Lack of information, technique, and experience not only minimizes the ability of the poor to cope with a problem situation, but often maximizes their expectations; and this gap becomes the measure of their frustration and despair. Very often, moreover, the poorer areas of our cities and towns get far less service coverage, and far less news coverage than more affluent sections. Garbage is not collected so often or so well, street lights are not repaired so swiftly. A mugging in the high-rent district is a front-page story; a mugging in a slum is not. Thus in many ways, large and small, help always seems to come in inverse ratio to the need for it.

This is the fuel and fodder of the "new politics." The part of the style that is merely unconventional—a peaceful march to a bureaucratic office— should be accepted by the community. The part of the style that is sheer violence—sniping at firemen from tenement rooftops—must be rejected and punished. If, however, the community at large wishes to see a return to the politics of elections, pressure groups, and parties, then these traditional agencies of democracy must show a greater capacity for "outreach." They must take the initiative in educating the people who are not now their current clientele in the techniques of joining, organizing, voting, and campaigning. More than that, they must address themselves to the issues and needs of these often hidden people. They must see that policies reflect *their* demands, anticipate the demands they *should* be making. If they do not, our entire society is likely to be victimized by a style of politics that moves all to swiftly from vehemence to violence.

**"Outreach"**

# CHAPTER 10

# THE MANY GOVERNMENTS OF THE UNITED STATES

**Federalism**

The United States is an amalgam of a large number of governmental units varying in degree of autonomy and in size, power, and style of operation. There was a time when it was fashionable to picture this governmental system as a layer cake; more recently it has been described as a marble cake.[1] The first characterization emphasizes that there are at least two distinct sovereign units in the United States: nation and state. Some people might add the not so sovereign local governments as a third layer. The second emphasizes that there are really no distinctive and pure functional areas, but rather a blend of all units in all programs. In each case, however, the analogy is somewhat misleading. Any cake has a definite form and texture, no matter how it may crumble; our Federal system is an expanding and contracting conglomerate of units, subject to internal and relational changes along a broad series of variables. Yet some understanding of this complex situation is crucial to an understanding of politics—of who gets what, when, how, and why. Recognition of American ambivalence concerning these units is also necessary to that understanding.

On the basis of legal definitions and census reports, our many governments include a central government, and the governments of 50 states, 3,049 counties, 18,048 municipalities, 17,105 townships, 21,783 school districts, and 21,264 special districts. This makes a total of 81,300 and an average of 1,626 local units per state. But of course no state is average. There are ten states that include more than three thousand units. Illinois has more than six thousand. One state, Hawaii, has twenty. The same disparity of distribution exists for each separate type of governmental unit. Thus a few states have only a score or so of special districts, but eleven states have more than seven hundred special districts each. One-third of our counties have fewer than ten local governments each, but 3 percent of our counties have more than one hundred units. As for trends, the total number of governments has dropped by about ten thousand since the 1962 census report. But the drop was not spread evenly among units or among regions. Counties remained static, townships showed a small decrease, but special districts increased by 16 percent. The largest drop was among independent school districts. Towns and cities still remain more abundant in the Northeast and townships prevail in the Midwest.[2]

In general, this rather sterile classification of who's who among American governments must yield to quite a number of other ways of looking over the terrain. To begin with, we might note one rather broad divide that greatly influences the entire range of functions and powers of all these units. It is a difference that separates the men from the boys, one might say, in the business of power distribution. This is the distinction between the federal relationship among states and between states and nation, on the one hand, and the unitary relationship between the states and all their internal subdivisions, on the other. We have come to regard the state as the original locus of popular sovereignty, but the manner in which power has radiated up and down has been distinctively and consistently different in the two cases. The federal relationship is specified in the U.S. Constitution and has been subject to broad interpretation by the U.S. Supreme Court. The Court's favorite vehicle for such interpretation is the doctrine of "implied powers." This doctrine has proved sufficiently flexible to permit the central government a large array of powers that are not explicitly delegated to it by the Constitution itself, but which are inferred by the Court from such specified powers as the power to tax and spend, the power to regulate interstate commerce, and the power to wage war. Over the years this doctrine has produced a decided trend toward centralization (despite occasional and temporary lapses). Even though many important functions are still reserved to the states, most observers view Washington as the pivot of today's government action. The relationship between the states and their local governments, on the other hand, is quite different. This is a unitary system. Despite the colonial roots of many towns and villages, power in this arena rests with the states and very little has been delegated downward. Moreover, the states' courts have almost universally honored a strict form of interpretation encapsulated in what is known as "Dillon's law."[3] This ruling by an Iowa state supreme court judge has prevailed through most of the nineteenth and twentieth centuries. It certifies the state as the creator, destroyer, abridger, and controller of all its subsidiary units. It resolves any doubt about muncipal power vis-à-vis state power. Indeed, the popular expression "home rule" has little actual meaning. It is certainly rarely honored in any court and it is perhaps best understood as an expression of hope.

Despite this general limitation of all local units, there are nonetheless many ways in which the units are distinguishable from one another. To begin with, there is a rather clear divide

**Implied Powers and Dillon's Law**

between what I call the natural governing arenas from the unnatural ones. The former almost universally bear the characteristics of a corporation. Indeed, they are usually referred to as municipal corporations. They include villages, cities, and towns of all sizes. This typology is based on the fact that the natural units are self-conscious groupings of people. There is a sense of community, and the units are invariably multifunctional. The unit itself is a magnet for its population. The unnatural units, by contrast, are rarely thought of as home by their inhabitants. They are quasi corporations, and serve primarily as administrative units for the state government. They have been arbitrarily designed to serve as arenas for the necessary decentralization of operations for one or more state functions.

**Local Government Powers and Characteristics**

All the units listed, however, share certain political attributes: they all have certain formal powers, certain methods of allocating resources and values. The methods run the traditional gamut of government coerciveness: inspections, warnings, registration, licensing, franchising, zoning, code enforcement, taxation, property condemnation, fines, suits, contracts, and other milder and harsher forms of direction and enterprise. Each unit has some finite geographic boundary and some degree of autonomy—some way of being distinguished from the other units, despite territorial and functional overlapping. Among all units, moreover, there is a salient political variable best described by Robert Dahl[4]—an uneven distribution of political resources; and this brings us again to distinctions. Different states and local governments possess quantitative and qualitative differences in leadership, expertise, time, and money. Aristotle said that the true constitution of a political state is embodied in its ruling class.[5] Let us then look at the class divisions among our units of government, and at the attributes of the ruling class in particular.

Here the literature presents many models. The major ones have been formulated by those who see local governments in terms of a single ruling elite,[6] those who see competing elites emerging for different problems,[7] and those who build more complex matrices involving different nuances that concern elites as well as masses and government structures.[8] Depending on which model is used, state and local units may be located anywhere on a continuum from unadulterated oligarchy to reasonably participatory democracy. There are cities, towns, counties, and villages that are run (according to one estimate or another) by political bosses, by dominant economic interests, by church groups, by insurance companies, banks, and utilities, by labor unions, and by various racial and ethnic organizations. The underworld often figures in these portraits, as do big agricultural organizations, universities, and a variety of other institutions and groups.

And there are still other variables that distinguish the various local governments from one another: the various kinds of community life style as they are rather impressionistically perceived by ordinary citizens. These perceptions may be influenced by an unequal mix of social, economic, geographic, climatic, and other environmental factors, along with the inhabitants' interior landscape (nostalgia, dreams, insecurities, prejudices, and the like). All of these elements in varying degrees may combine to produce the big-city style, the satellite-city style, the autonomous-city style, the neighborhood style, the rural style, the small-town style, and various suburban styles. There are, of course, hybrids and transient styles that probably completely escape this classification. The hippie communes might be a case in point.

The big-city style is the dream of Lewis Mumford.[9] He sees the megalopolis as the expression and stronghold of civilization. The big city is the focus of culture, religion, politics, education, ceremony, and all the trappings of a full life. It offers its people anonymity, excitement, the heights of achievement, glamour, fashion, variety, escape from convention, and many other formidable attractions. For many people, both here and abroad, to be alive is to be in the big city. Others want some portion of this style, but bigness is less blessed to them. For them a satellite city might do, or might have to do. A satellite city shares some characteristics of the big city—some heterogeneity of population, some degree of density, and some degree of diversity of enterprise—but it revolves about the nearby core big city, on which it depends for its cultural life and possibly a good part of its industrial life too. Its style is less distinctive than many others. The small autonomous city is similar to the satellite city, but it has no core city about which to revolve and therefore is more likely to make its own independent moves toward cultural autonomy.

The neighborhood style is embedded in large cities, and it has a number of functions. It seeks to reconcile the ubiquitous clannishness of people—many of them newly arrived from diverse and often far-off lands and seeking recognition and support—with the necessities and choices of big-city life. More recently it has become a rallying point for black separatists. But whether historic or recent, distinct and distinctive neighborhoods have always been a fact of big-city life. Most neighborhood enthusiasts want some of the attributes of the big city —its employment opportunities, its variety of foodstuffs, its free and varied recreational and cultural facilities, its cheap transportation—but at the same time they want to recapture a bit of

**Cities and Their Satellites; Neighborhoods**

the village, perhaps the very village from which they came. Until recently neighborhoods had no real political autonomy. Their trappings were largely symbolic: festivals, titular "mayors," tacit acceptance of certain cultural customs, selective law enforcement (no Sunday-closing enforcement in Jewish neighborhoods, no gambling-code enforcement in the Mah-Jongg parlors of Chinatown), and some recognition by the "nationality" clubs of the two major political parties. The most recent variant, however, is asking for actual power—power to run schools, hospitals, police, and so forth. The results of these demands are not yet in.

The rural style is, of course, the lifeblood of American individualist mythology. Its symbol is the isolated, embattled farmer-rancher-miner struggling against a hostile environment and winning. It is today a minute part of the actual American landscape and it is increasingly on the wane. Transportation and the mass media have made all Americans part of some community or other. But some of the underlying values of rural America probably still dominate small-town America.

Small towns, of course, introduce new elements, such as the constant face-to-face communication that is part of their lifestyle but not part of the older rural isolate style. The small-town style is America's favorite, to judge by a large portion of our literature. Its chief characteristics are friendliness, egalitarianism, and the protection of consensual conventions. It cannot boast the diversity of population, enterprise, or culture of the cities, and its values are dramatically different. In the city, individuals are anonymous. Not here. In small towns everybody knows everybody else, and everybody in some mysterious egalitarian sense is "as good as everybody else," except for a few agreed-upon outcasts. Here status is more likely to be ascribed than achieved. The small town covets stability, security, involvement, morality, friendliness, egalitarianism, and rules over mobility, freedom, noninvolvement, efficiency, and pragmatism. Where the city emphasizes secondary groups, the small town emphasizes primary ones. Where the city wants professionalism, the small town wants loyalty. Where the city wants variety, the small town wants at least the façade of homogeneity.

**The Suburbs**

Suburbia is still another variant. In fact, it includes more than one variant. This point is made clear in a number of recent works,[10] but it can be readily observed by anyone driving a short distance from any city. Some suburbs are entirely residential; others cluster around an industry. Some are upper class; others are middle or lower-middle class. The distinguishing characteristics that differentiate most of them from small towns and cities are a lack of historic roots, more mobile populations, frequently only a partial range of economic and public services, large numbers of commuters, and large numbers of people who are fleeing from something rather than continuing a stable existence.

To those who like their politics neat and clear, all this is dizzying. More than that, it is demonstrably problem-prone. Overlap, waste, uncertainty, delay, confusion, unevenness of goals and goal achievement, and many other factors inherent in this multiplicity of styles make it difficult to arrive at and deliver public policy. Both an urban developer from the business world and an urban planner from the public sector face miles and years of forms, regulations, visits, and conferences between the time a basic decision is made in Washington to do slum clearance, let us say, and the actual day of ground-breaking on any slum street. In the face of these difficulties, is there any justification for continuing our allegiance to the use of all of these governments? I believe there is. On one level the traditional arguments are often philosophical. They deal with sovereignty, natural rights, and fundamental values. On another level the arguments are severely practical. They deal with corruption, tax bases, talent, and personal ambitions. In general, however, arguments for the superiority of any single format among local units as well as for the centralization of the entire system both fall apart.

Both the federal system of "united states," each with its own areas of sovereignty, and the variety of local units are among the most firmly entrenched principles of American government. They are rooted in our laws and our Constitution. They are cemented by our decentralized political party systems. This means that heavily vested interests that would control the avenues of change in this area are opposed to any change. There is also the glue of existing public finance and public employment. The fact is that state and local governments spend twice as much as the federal government for most domestic functions. And this arithmetic does not include federal grants to the state and local units.[11] State and local governments, not Washington, play the major role in administering justice, highways, police, education, recreation, and many other functions. They also figure far more heavily in controlling (or attempting to control) public utilities. Whereas federal public service employees number about two and a half million, those in state and local civil services total more than eight million. These figures represent firmly entrenched vested interests. There is also the less tangible but nonetheless vital sentiment for some of these units of government. Despite the fact that loyalty toward and interest in the national scene far outweighs localism of any sort, any attempt to abolish the governmental functions of states,

"United States" and Local Units

cities, and villages obviously would be vigorously challenged by an aroused citizenry.

There is also a persuasive argument in the inevitability of some form of decentralization. There is no unitary state of any size that has failed to come to grips with this reality. Whether it is a question of enlarging the scope of the prefectures in Italy or France, or of decentralizing factory management in the USSR or China, governments everywhere bow to some amount of local decision-making. Indeed, the literature of American administrative reform illustrates that the defects of too much decentralization are identical with those of overcentralization. Both breed waste, duplication, confusion, red tape, delay, loss of purpose, and goal confusion.

Further, the idea of retaining some form of stability in a highly mobile society is psychologically sound. Almost all social psychologists agree that people crave a certain feeling of rootedness. The tradition of states, cities, and villages that either have or pretend to have historic roots therefore has some social meaning. Perhaps it can help in some measure to mitigate the effects of the "future shock" that concerns certain social commentators, without sacrificing too many other values.[12] Americans appear to change their residences quite frequently. In 1971, 18.4 percent of our population moved. Most of these moves appear to represent changes of life style within one region, rather than changes of residence from one region to another or even across county lines. It would appear that more people move between city and suburb or among nearby cities or suburbs than in other possible directions.[13] A large majority of Americans are born within the loose outlines of our so-called metropolitan areas. Yet it is not clear that they have a fixed focus on any preferred life style. The social taste of many Americans changes across time, region, and class. For others, taste in life style remains static, yet circumstances—employment opportunities, family crises, and so on—force a change of residence. One of the ways of supplying a necessary ingredient of at least psychological rootedness, then, is to offer a variety of life styles, so that one or another of them is always at hand to supply the needs of those who want to recapture what they had in childhood (or thought they had) or who wish to escape from a mode of life to which they now feel alien. This element of choice is always important to those who crave freedom. Freedom is clearly increased as choices increase. Indeed, it appears to me that the chief difference among political systems of the world lies in the variation of scope and quality of individual and group choices. The primary difference between the life styles of totalitarian and nontotalitarian nations lies in the degree of control that the individual has over his own daily routines. How much control does he have over the schooling he gets, the work he will do, the part of the country he will live in, the way he will dress, eat, and entertain himself, the books he will read, the places and people he will visit? How many decision centers can he try to influence? I concede the irrelevance of many such choices for a starving peasantry—or for an entrenched urban ghettoite. But for about 80 percent of America, the idea of choice *is* relevant. For the remainder, the task is to bring them into the mainstream of choice, not to eliminate choice itself. And a system of multiple governments clearly expands choice.

Local governments, or at least certain variants of them, have also appealed to those who see "democracy" (popular control) as basically a grass-roots operation. And it does appear that those who argue for centralization are more often than not elitists. Government centralizers are frequently enthusiasts of expertise and professionalism, of knowing the "public interest" and delivering it as swiftly and efficiently as possible. Such persons often have a profound distrust of the common man. Those who like to keep politics as close to the individual as possible, on the other hand, are likely to have a more Jacksonian faith in the common man. Or they may look to Thomas Jefferson as their patron saint. They also tend to feel, as Tocqueville did, that "town meetings are to liberty what primary schools are to science. They bring it within the people's reach, they teach men how to use and how to enjoy it."[14] This sentiment for grass-roots democracy is burgeoning again both in the hippi-style communes and in the ghetto-style decentralization experiments. There is a persistent feeling that control is easier when a function rests close to home than when its center is far away. The truth about the realities of such control is often less relevant than its persistence as a perception.

Indeed, this matter of perception is equally important in the argument that a continuation of multiple governments can help in the achievement of individual self-actualization and other ego needs. These, as you may recall, are among Maslow's "hierarchy of needs." They are at the bottom of the hierarchy, but they are nonetheless signally important. The demands for basic creature comforts, for fundamental safety, and for simple primary group affection are, of course, priority problems; but it is still essential to individual and group mental health that people have ample opportunity for social contacts, group achievement, ego development, and creativity. In an era that promises increasing leisure time and technological accomplishment, the work place may no longer fulfill as many of these needs as it once did. Opportunities for public service and community discussion, which are implicit in many styles of local government

**The Perception
of Control**

and even state government, may well serve as substitutes for the traditional informal functions of the workplace. Citizenship as a participant sport may become a national pastime, with many fruitful consequences. Clearly, it is feasible only through a system of multiple governments. Indeed, the sense of political community and efficacy which many small villages bestow on some of their citizens is a major source of their continuing attractiveness. While it is sometimes real and sometimes spurious, local government often appears to offer more in the way of participation, political equality, and political responsiveness.

Finally, those who argue for our system of multiple governments points to evidence of success in the historical achievements of New England town meetings, and the later achievements (though temporary and partial) of local innovations in direct democracy. Many other actual programs for education, penal reform, and welfare have also been conducted successfully at the grass roots. It was at the state and local levels of government, after all, that we first achieved any type of social legislation (wage and hour reform, factory inspections, welfare and public assistance), and it was here that movements for pollution control and civil rights were initiated. The record is not all bad.

**Arguments for Centralization**
The advocates of one or another variant of centralization, on the other hand, stress the interdependence of all people, the sameness of modern problems, the existence of a community good that transcends individualistic self-interest, and, of course, efficiency. They too have their public philosophers and their practical triumphs. Many of the New Deal experiments, including national wage and hour standards and social security, are now stable ingredients of American life. Of course, we can never second-guess history. We cannot know whether undertakings at one level might have fared equally well at another. We must also be aware that history is always a repository of examples on all sides of any question. Like legal precedent, it often seems to run in equal and opposite directions.

Yet this is still a critical issue today in America. We must resolve the conflict, at least operationally—and in fact we do. Every day, issue by issue, both in Washington and in our state capitals, we decide just who will do what. But is the settlement as favorable as it might be? Are the right factors being reviewed when these determinations are made? The usual twentieth-century machinery for achieving programmatic goals within the maze of state and local governments has been the federal grant-in-aid. It has been used as a prodding device and as a way around constitutional barriers to federal action. It has had a long and checkered history. Both the narrow categorical grants (made to specific state agencies for specified programs and subject to a jungle of federal rules) and the somewhat broader grants that attempt to skip at least certain jurisdictional lines and somewhat lighten the federal administrative grip have been subject to great criticism. Too much fragmentation, too much review, too many delays—the catalog of criticism is long and monotonous. Today major hope is being focused on a new type of thrust: revenue sharing. But even this thrust must still at some point come to grips with the question of how and where we want to operate and control our various programs. While the nation may supply money and devolve authority to the states for all sorts of unspecified purposes, the states must still decide how, where, and to what degree to devolve its own authority for the implementation of its programs.

I think that the answer to the problem of what to do about the multiplicity of governmental units and how to rationalize our decision lies in improving the allocation of functions among existing units rather than in any large-scale reordering of the units themselves. Clearly a certain amount of judicious pruning is in order. The consolidation of special districts—or perhaps their merger with contiguous local multipurpose government units—would be a step in the right direction. More often than not, the existence of these proliferating special districts (for fire and police protection, sewage disposal, highway construction and maintenance, and almost every other government function) merely testifies to the failure of the community to devise a more general and appropriate scheme for allocating functions. The special district appears to be a practical expedient for holding the question in abeyance a little longer. But the time may have come for more appropriate and long-range solutions. These special districts have none of the traditional, sentimental, political, legal, or constitutional staying powers of the other units of local government. Nevertheless, "federation" of this or that unit, "annexation," "consolidation," "special authorities," and "nationalization" through compacts, grants, and other devices seem to arouse less enthusiasm than projects aimed at better allocation of the functions of existing units and more rational funding of their operations. Basic reform in poverty programs, pollution programs, education programs, and so forth is more likely to be achieved through rethinking our monetary commitments than through changes in jurisdiction.

Perhaps, however, we can grope toward Aristotle's idea of "ethical self-sufficiency" (which was the proper basis for a city-state, in his view) by reconsidering which functions are best allocated to which level. Since any state, whether or not it is nominally centralized, is actually a community of communities, we must consider this problem no matter how we name or con-

**Special Districts**

struct the communities. The forms, instrumentalities, and goals of subcommunities should ideally be congruent with each other and with the state, not at cross-purposes with them. With this in mind, let me offer for consideration an obviously untested paradigm that might help rationalize the assignment of government programs among our various units. The determination of the functions to be programmed at each level should rest, I believe, on the following considerations: (1) the degree to which expertise is available concerning the particular function: (2) the degree to which uncertainty about matters of both science and high principle has been absorbed; (3) the degree to which a program permits a collective cancellation of individual choices; (4) the degree to which individual choice seriously impinges on community life style; (5) the availability or lack of a reasonably free competitive marketplace for the function under consideration; and (6) the relative presence or absence of perceived scarcity in relation to the elements involved in the program. These factors, in turn, help us to assess the relative need for either variety or uniformity in program delivery. The greater the need for uniformity, the higher the decision level, and vice versa.

The Founding Fathers, evidenced a general preference for leaving as many matters as possible to the individual citizen or to the local communities and states. Religion, for example, was left completely to the individual, as was choice of vocation, place of residence, style of food and dress, recreation, and other customs. Some of these decisions still remain with us as individuals, although others have become, at least in part, functions of the local, state, or federal government. This is because a growing number of items seem to impinge so directly on community life style (in a land where more and more people live on fewer and fewer acres of land) that we have had to move the functions up the ladder of control. But certainties have a way of disappearing as regularly as they appear.

**Individual Decisions versus Societal Restraints**

Consider, for example, policies concerning sexual morality. We might be persuaded that individual adults should be permitted to make their own decisions in this realm. Perhaps we do not need any unit of government to tell us with whom, when, and how we should have sexual relations. There is, after all, virtually no generally accepted expertise on this matter. The history of societal restraints and requirements covers every possible combination—heterosexual, homosexual, and asexual. Uncertainty seems rampant even in areas that were previously resolved. There is little scarcity and a quite extensive and competitive marketplace for this activity. Moreover, there is little evidence that community interests are necessarily or inevitably affected by any particular practice in any preordained direction.

There are stable families in both monogomous and polygamous situations, matriarchal as well as patriarchal households. Finally, there is some evidence that individual determination in this area would lead to a type of mutually self-cancelling series of decisions; the number of people who decide to marry may be randomly balanced by the number who decide to remain single. This, then, appears to be a matter we might well leave in individual hands. But clearly we do not now do so. We do not even keep these decisions at the level of local communities. In fact, we have given the states the right to legislate on all sorts of sexual matters: we have laws to control the type of sex relations permitted to consenting adults, laws that penalize "unsanctified" unions, and so forth; until quite recently some states had laws forbidding interracial marriages. We thus clog our courts and burden our bureaucracies with contradictory and often irrational decision-making that could well be avoided.

But what about more complex functions such as education? Which level of society should make policy here? For many decades in our early history, schooling decisions were left entirely to the parents of minors. Education was at the bottom of the decision ladder. As available expertise increased, as uncertainties consequently became absorbed, as the educational choices made began to impinge more and more directly on communities' life styles, and as scarcities in the educational market appeared to increase, state policy-making in this area began to blossom. Schooling became compulsory, not optional; curriculum and teaching qualifications were scrutinized and certified by local or state authorities; and an entire bureaucratic educational apparatus arose. All of this was quite in keeping, by the way, with the formula for rational allocations described above. Indeed, as these trends burgeoned, the level of decision-making moved slowly upward. Local policy-makers ceded some functions to the state, and the state ceded some to the nation. But today, as these trends reverse—expertise becoming confused, uncertainty more pronounced, the marketplace more extensive and competitive, scarcity relatively relieved—we are beginning to reconsider the proper placement of educational policy-making. We are properly considering a return to community control, to a greater individual choice through "external degrees," "voucher systems," "open classrooms," and even "nonschools." There is no need here to describe and argue the merits and demerits of each of these educational styles. Their very proliferation seems to indicate a growing need for variety and a shift to lower levels of decision-making.

Oddly enough, the delivery of health care, despite the dependence on doctors and other highly qualified professionals,

**Educational Policy**

has over the years become less and less an arena of certainty. The professionals are at odds with one another. Hospital management seems more a mystique than a formula. We are increasingly uncertain about priorities in improving American health. Should improvement in hospital care be at the top of the list? Or an increase in the number and availability of doctors? Or improvement in the management of nutrition? Or something else altogether? Coincident with this uncertainty is the enlargement of the marketplace through various insurance programs that pay benefits directly to individual policyholders. While the weightings on all the criteria are not uniformly clear, the balance seems to tip in favor of considerable localism in matters of health. So too in such areas as housing programs, renewal programs, recreational facilities and planning (except for national parks), and even transportation systems.

**Policy Areas: Upward Mobility**

Are there any policy areas that might rationally be moved upward? Again I would rely on the suggested criterion that as uniformity becomes more valued than variety in any area, its programs should become more centralized. First, therefore, I would argue for the centralization of "rules of the game." That is, matters of fundamental constitutional values should be centralized in their scope and application. These are, after all, matters in which uncertainty has been legally and perhaps even morally absorbed (or should have been), and in which uniformity of application is the *sine qua non* of the effectiveness of their programs. Indeed, the ultimate goal of our nation —liberty and justice for all—requires uniformity. This means that programs designed to carry out our fundamental principles —our election system and our court system—could well be centralized. There seems to be little value in variety in these procedures. They are monopoly enterprises (there is no true marketplace); they are highly connected to community rather than individualistic life styles; and uncertainty regarding these functions has been largely absorbed. They seem clearly earmarked for nationalization. Any variety that is required would be automatically produced by the very nature of judicial activity. Each individual judge has great independence of action, even—or especially—in a unitary system. The humanistic balance that many Americans find desirable in judicial decision-making should stem from the meticulous application of constitutional "due process," and from the continued use of judicial review.

Programs involving fiscal management, utility regulation, income maintenance, and insurance schemes (particularly as the marketplace for insurance disappears), certain programs of environmental conservation and control, and the maintenance of foreign policy—all these probably fit the centralizing criteria rather better than they do those of local or individualistic decision-making. More surprising, however, might be the suggestion that all forms of public safety work be centralized at least at the state level. Analysis of police, fire, and other civilian defense programs might show that there is no real marketplace for these functions, that they impinge to a high degree on community life style, that considerable agreed-upon expertise is available in these areas—in sum, that they call for uniformity rather than variety. Many of the values that supposedly flow from local government delivery of these programs are demonstrably not attached to localism at all. America's traditional and well-placed fear of military control, of police-state intrusiveness, of brutality and other police excesses, are fears that have not been banished by localism in the centuries of our experience. The proper antidotes here are nationally and vigorously applied standards of civil liberty and the development of a civic culture in which certain norms for the conduct of police work and defense missions are internalized by effective socialization programs. These services might be centralized with no loss of civil liberties by the use of national service volunteers (sixteen-, seventeen-, or eighteen-year-olds of both sexes) who might be trained and deployed for one year's service in these and perhaps a few conservation programs. Such service would provide a broadening work experience for youngsters at a natural breaking point in their educational careers, and the use of average American youngsters for the nontechnical aspects of this type of work might produce exactly the sort of leavening that these programs need. We might also note in passing that the British system of central police control has not produced a police state, while the nominally federated system of Brazil often has. In essence, the characteristics of police and fire programs conform to our "upward" indicators, while the anticipated dysfunctions appear to be ones that can and should be coped with by solutions other than devolution of power.

**Civil Liberty and Civic Culture**

In all events, I find little evidence that merging states into regions, consolidating counties, erasing villages, annexing cities, or creating new special districts, metro areas, or special authorities produce any magical solutions. These procedures in themselves rarely solve any of the substantive problems connected with education, pollution, or police programs. Although, as noted before, some special district consolidation seems in order, any gains produced by jurisdictional changes are usually short-run and ephemeral. Brooklyn annexed itself to Manhattan at the turn of the century to the applause of all the reformers of that era; now, seventy-five years later, similar-minded reformers are suggesting its return to independence as a separate city. Some historical villages hang on and thrive. Others annex and fail. The critical problems—poverty, ill health, pollution,

**Resource
Allocation
versus
Boundary
Adjustment**

congestion, racial prejudice, crime—rarely yield to governmental boundary relocations. If New York City were made into a state, as is being urged in some quarters, its financial situation would in no way be improved. Indeed, it might be worsened. And money is at least part of the key to solving the extraordinary problems of our time. Solutions are more often a variant of resource allocation than of boundary adjustment.

# CHAPTER 11

# WHO GETS WHAT?

Since the days of Aristotle, many political scientists have argued that an important measure of any political system is the justice with which it distributes its basic privileges and resources.[1] That is, who gets what? Who receives the income and commodity subsidies, health services, insurance, recreational facilities, work and status opportunities, political access, and the other chances for self-fulfillment that lie largely in the hands of the polity? And who pays for all these benefits? And why?

The idea of a "just" distribution is as elusive as it is ubiquitous. On this matter America is understandably ambivalent, and evidence is often ambiguous. There seems no limit to the range of rationalizations. Some Communist governments, for example, have been willing to use extreme coercion toward the goal of "equality." So far, however, equality does not appear to have resulted. Indeed, there is less equality in many Communist nations than in certain capitalist ones. On the other hand, those who dream the capitalist dream of an automatic distribution system based on a totally free marketplace, in which returns represent individual efforts, must suffer equal disappointment. Here, too, fact has moved far from fantasy. There are no such free markets, no "invisible hands" evenly and automatically distributing the nation's wealth. Individual effort is often incompatible with results. There are always nonmarket benefits like "defense" which require conscious (not automatic) public distribution, and there are always nonmarket restraints like taxes and monopolies which require conscious manipulation. The result is invariably some mixture of market and management by political decision-makers; but by recognizing certain commitments, assigning certain priorities, and using certain procedures, we might be able to achieve more rational (if not just) distributions.

The commitments and priorities that I urge, of course, conform to the scale of values previously explored in Chapter 3. That is, we must make a primary commitment to a totally free exchange of ideas, and a concomitant commitment to an apparatus by which the majority decides subsequent fundamentals

"Just"
Distribution

of policy. The majority must decide who should get what from the public domain. Should there, for example, be a base-level life style for all members of society, supported by the more productive members of society? Should we aim at equalizing opportunity, or at least enjoining artificial and prejudicial barriers to opportunity? These are among the questions that the majority should decide; and these are indeed the goals that are decided by our various political institutions. Equality, for example, has been recently interpreted by the Supreme Court as meaning an equal expenditure of funds for each child's public education. But despite the fact that concrete data are clearly necessary for rational decisions concerning equality or any other public goal, our decision-makers and the American public are seldom exposed to any explicit or systematic presentation of relevant facts. A procedure for doing just this has, however, been developed: Planning-Programming-Budgeting Systems (PPBS). It is a method of cost-benefit analysis, and it promises to provide immeasurable help in answering the question: Who gets what and why? The widespread adoption of PPBS would, I believe, help Americans to understand ambiguities of policy and perhaps reduce ambivalence about our goals.

**Cost-Benefit Analysis**

This cost-benefit style of political analysis is nothing more than the collection and reporting of data in such a way as to make possible an analysis of all the consequences of our public decisions, immediate and future, hidden and apparent, direct and indirect. It requires a systematic comparative analysis of each set of costs and benefits as against alternative costs and benefits that would flow from different decisions.

Although President Johnson announced the national debut of PPBS in 1965, the national Office of Management and Budget has only recently begun some partial and tentative moves toward implementing it. At state and local levels, talk such as this is in the realm of science fiction. Even in academic circles it is just nascent.[2] Moreover, though it is virtually untested, strong voices are already raising grave doubts about the viability of this approach.[3] It has been so little used, however, that a balanced judgment requires more concrete evidence, which can come only from putting its basic tenets into practice.

Perhaps a look at the decision process at a typical public university would throw this matter into clear relief. Suppose, for example, a state legislature reduces the budget of a public university (we need not go into the strange and inappropriate methods used to reach decisions of this sort). Consider what happens at the university. It might be thought that inside the ivy-covered walls, the incumbent experts and logicians with their computers would carefully and systematically calculate just how to go about cutting down programs in order to cope with this unpleasant reality. Nothing could be further from the truth. Instead, faculties will be emotionally rallied to save their own programs, no matter what. From the presidents of the colleges on down to instructors, there will be no genuine assessment of the relative merits of programs; no review of the basic goals of the university and the relative congruence of the various programs to these goals; no attempt to assess the costs and benefits of the various programs. No, there will be only near-hysterical pleas to save this or that program or institution, in order that each professor's life style may suffer as little disruption as possible. That is, after all, very human and understandable. Whatever expertise a professor or dean may possess is no match for his wish for survival and aggrandizement. Left to pursue these goals, all professors will need secretaries, all secretaries will need assistants, all assistants will need secretaries, and there will soon be a remarkable pressure group ready to insist that more professors are needed. Nor should we expect that anyone is going to ask the crucial questions: "Could my program be cut? Could *I* be eliminated?" Yet such questions—questions that cut to the bone of program analysis—are required.

Two things seem necessary to bring these questions to the fore: (1) an outside agent who is responsible for the ultimate decisions on basic values, when such values are beyond any rational cost calculations (this problem will be discussed in the final chapter); (2) the automatic, habitual usage of PPBS so that the situation may be clearly assessed. Each public institution should require the collection and presentation of all relevant data. While PPBS may not ensure intelligent and rational decision-making, it certainly improves the chances.

Very occasionally the public is treated to a glimpse of this style of thinking and reporting. Reports like those of Nader's Raiders[4] and the recently instituted Council for Policy Evaluation are cases in point. These self-appointed protagonists of the cost-benefit school of thought try to alert the American public to who *is* getting what, at whose cost. Does the Pure Food and Drug Administration ensure pure food and drugs? Is the licensing of nursing homes benefiting the clientele of those homes? Who pays the cost of America's highway system and who uses it? Who gets the use out of California's land-use laws? Who benefits from local zoning ordinances, and who is victimized by them? This is the sort of thinking upon which American political decisions must be based. We cannot leave the questions and answers to a hit-or-miss approach that depends on the charity of foundation support. We should be asking our public agencies to deliver estimates on these matters regularly to official decision-making bodies like our national,

**Alerting the American Public**

state, and local legislatures, and to the public at large. When the "what" of "Who gets what?" is analyzed, revenues as well as expenditures must be taken into consideration. This question should be answered for programs that are not explicitly fiscal as well as for those that are.

Consider first typical public expenditure programs. Here we must include everything from the village playground up to the supersonic transport. We must determine who benefits, in terms of income and income-related items, from direct subsidy programs, from programs that manipulate fiscal policy, and from programs that presumably control monopolistic industries. When a village decides to put in sidewalks, for example, it should know not only how much the sidewalks will cost immediately (they always do know that); it should also know the future costs (the necessary upkeep) and the number of people that will benefit—and which people, and to what degree. Will everyone in the village really enjoy substantial benefits, or will the advantages be minimal to many people? Will shopkeepers be the major beneficiaries? Commuters? Schoolchildren? What are the benefits to the contractors who will install the sidewalks? The laborers who build them and who in the future will repair them? The village should also try to ascertain the resources that will pay for this improvement and the main contributors to the particular tax funds or borrowings that will be used. Finally, the village should compare the costs and benefits of this particular project with those of other projects that would have to be foregone or minimized to carry out this one. These alternative projects must be analyzed in the same style.

**Analyzing Expenditure Programs**

Expenditure programs of far greater complexity need this same touch. Take defense programs, for example. Even though one would have to concede at the outset the impossibility of assessing the value to individuals and to society of lives lost in past or future "defensive" postures by ordinary cost-accounting methods, one can try at least to figure the economic costs of explicit government defense expenditures. Murray Weidenbaum, for one, has tried to do this. He sets for himself the questions: Does spending by the Department of Defense contribute to a more equal spread of personal income through the country, or does it concentrate money in certain specific places? And how does the pattern of defense spending compare, for example, with aid to education and farm price supports? Among his many interesting conclusions is that

> Defense and space programs are regressive—they tend to give a larger than proportional share of expenditures to high-income states. In contrast, non-defense programs are progressive—on a simple per-capita basis, low-income states generally tend to receive a larger than proportional share of non-defense programs. . . . Hence any shifts in the federal budget from defense

to non-defense activities—assuming no fundamental change in the geographical patterns of individual public programs—will tend to narrow income inequality among the various regions.[5]

Bruce Russett looks at another side of the picture.[6] He concludes that the payments for defense benefits also fall unequally on different groups. His analysis hangs primarily on estimates of the sacrifices of alternative uses for these funds. All such studies are, of course, fraught with pitfalls, and I am not advocating reliance on any particular set of existing conclusions. I *am* advocating a commitment to this *style* of political thinking. We must insist on asking this sort of question and on gathering these sort of data in the manner best calculated to reach the core of the problems that beset us. And more and more analyses of this kind are being made.[7]

We must know, to start with, who does get what. Take direct subsidies as another case in point. Neither Congress nor the states nor the people at large enjoy a full and complete idea of the extent of our subsidies—to say nothing of their more subtle implications. Such data are not supplied routinely anywhere. Just a partial list includes welfare subsidies to certain groups of aged, veterans, dependent children, unemployed, disabled, and other poor people. These are probably reasonably well publicized. But what about the welfare payments to the business and well-to-do communities: the $200 million contingency fund for Lockheed Aircraft, the $125 million loan to the Penn-Central Railroad, the government-controlled $150 million insurance corporation for security brokerage houses, the $85 million programs of federal loans for middle-income housing, the $3.8 billion price support for farmers, the $2.7 billion subsidy to shipyards? Are the costs and benefits here clearly recognized? And this is only the beginning. Within each of these categories there are also some very surprising distributions. Farm subsidies, for example, give an average farmer just a few hundred dollars a year; but a farmer like Senator James Eastland of Mississippi received almost $147,000 in 1970.

**Direct Subsidies and Revenue Bills**

Revenue bills also contain hidden prizes for certain persons and groups at the expense of others: oil depletion allowances, business expense write-offs, religious and private charitable foundation exemptions. No income tax at all was paid in 1968 by 381 Americans whose income exceeded $100,000, or by 21 persons who had income of $1 million each. Are facts such as these widely and clearly understood?[8]

**Hidden Prizes**

We must do better than merely continue our casual, unexamined, hit-or-miss approach to these grave questions. From top to bottom we need systematic PPBS-style analysis, and not only for programs involving direct expenditures, subsidies, and revenue matters. This style is equally relevant, for example, to

the analysis of such things as bail-bond procedures, parole systems, and selective service. Who gets selected to serve? A PPBS
study has been made of this particular policy by James Davis
and Kenneth Dolbeare, and it sheds some much-needed light
on the question of whether our manifest purposes are being
met by certain conscription practices, and on the possible latent
purposes that may be served by our present system.[9] The same
style is also being used vis-à-vis some other selected public
policy areas.

Let us mount a campaign to build into every jurisdictional
level and into every public institution a routine capacity to do
systematic alternative cost-benefit analysis, and let us also build
up the public's desire to know who gets what. Without widespread demand for the answers to questions of this sort, we are
unlikely to get the changes our society needs. The style of
thinking being advocated here is not in itself an advocacy of
any particular set of answers. I urge only that we ask the questions, so that we can get a wide range of alternative answers
and determine whether our publicly announced goals are indeed being met.

**Who Gets What?— Possible Categories**

Posing the basic question of who gets what, however, requires a preliminary decision that has so far remained unexamined here. There is an almost endless list of possible categories
that could be inspected in determining who it is that gets what.
We could, after all, look at the relative fulfillment of basic living needs for redheads as against blondes and brunettes. (We
are led to believe, after all, that blondes have more fun.) Or
we could play out the question by scrutinizing the distribution
of resources among short versus tall adults. In short, there are
many categorizations of "who." Yet serious scholars do not
seem to have had so much trouble with this problem as might
be assumed. They have turned away quite readily from patently
trivial categories and have moved as though by instinct to certain categories that seem universally meaningful. These categories include race, religion, sex, occupation, income, education,
age, place of birth or domicile, and perhaps a few others. The
rationale for the selection of the most frequently researched
categories seems to be a spoken or unspoken suspicion that the
distribution of resources among certain of these categorical
units is not entirely random. There is a hint here that there
may be prejudicial treatment of certain groups—treatment that
violates either the explicit laws of our nation or some implicit
norms of "equal opportunity." Let us then give particular attention to certain fundamental socioeconomic and jurisdictional
groupings as we go about the task of ascertaining who gets
what in the American polity.

The cost-benefit style can help us analyze jurisdictional distributions, for example. We can use this tool to note the gross amounts of fiscal aid from Washington to the states and from the states to the localities. We can also learn if relatively greater or lesser efforts toward achieving public goals are being exerted by different units. Does Mississippi try harder than New York to educate its children in terms of available measures of effort as against resources? Here too studies are beginning to become available.[10] In the same vein we should be analyzing the impacts of various forms of taxation and borrowing among jurisdictions. Who is paying the lion's share of our expenses? Is New York City carrying New York State or vice versa? Systematic analysis might disclose the way the contribution of an individual taxpayer moves differentially across the various jurisdictions in which he lives. Thus a $20,000-a-year commuter (head of a family of four) who lives in New Jersey or Connecticut but works in New York City pays $45 in income taxes to New York City and $804 in income taxes to New York State. It does not require extensive analysis to conclude that the city provides him with more services than the state. But whatever the relative outlays and benefits, they should be generally and specifically made known to public officials and citizens alike.

Cost-benefit analysis will also throw a clearer light on public policies of differential distribution according to race, sex, age, and income. Both scholars and laymen already appear particularly sensitive to the racial category. American racial concern may be partially due to well-earned guilt feelings over our history of slavery and Indian extermination. Having forceably brought blacks to this continent and having kept them in bondage for over two centuries, and having less than heroically driven the indigenous Indians from their lands, we are highly sensitive to these two racial categories; more so than we are, say, about ethnic groups such as Lithuanians, Poles, and Irish, or about religious categories. These latter groups, after all, represent persons who came here voluntarily and were not *legally* separated from the mainstream of society.

**Differential Distribution**

What, then, do the records show about blacks and Indians? A 1964 report of the President's Council of Economic Advisers shows that while only 22 percent of the nation as a whole is "poor" (a subject we shall pursue in more detail shortly), over half of the black population is poor.[11] Even when educational attainment is held constant, blacks are twice as likely to be poor as whites. The average black family income was $1,300 below the poverty level, as the government defines it, in 1970.[12] A 1968 report of the National Advisory Commission on Civil Disorders shows that black unemployment in 1967 was double that for whites (in 1970 the Urban League reported a slight improvement) and that the employment level of blacks was at the "lowest end of the occupation scale."[13] In fact, John Kenneth Galbraith reported in 1971 that women and blacks divided only 4 percent of jobs paying salaries above $15,000 a year.[14] The Bureau of the Census reported that in 1966 only 12 percent of nonwhite families had incomes over $10,000, as against 30 percent for whites. In fact, the median income for whites was $7,517, while that for blacks was $4,481. Nonwhites, moreover, held only 6 percent of professional and technical jobs.[15] The 1968 Civil Disorder Report also tells us that the mortality for nonwhite babies under one month old was 58 percent higher than for whites and three times higher in the one-to-three-month range. Of the estimated 14,000 rat bites in the United States in 1965, most occurred in ghetto neighborhoods. Indeed, this report shows that "between two and two and a half million Negroes, 16 to 20 percent of the total population, live in squalor and deprivation in ghetto neighborhoods."[16]

**Ghetto Conditions**

The quality of these ghettoes is even more graphically described by Ramsey Clark, former U.S. Attorney General. He calls attention to the fact that four-fifths of all crime takes place in these ghettoes, "yet most who live in poverty never commit a serious crime." The life expectancy here is lower than for the city as a whole. The ghetto death rate is about 25 percent above the overall rate for cities. Ghettoes have a 50 percent higher incidence of mumps and measles—a disease notable for causing subsequent birth defects. Other diseases check in at a 25 percent higher rate. There is 100 percent more food poisoning and venereal disease. These are the areas with the greatest incidence of narcotics addiction and pushing, alcoholism, and prostitution. Mental retardation may be five times higher in ghettoes than in cities in general, and accidental injuries are also considerably higher. Ghetto schools are the oldest, the dropout rate is highest, the ratio of students to teachers is lowest, and illiteracy hovers around 15 percent. Three-fourths of ghetto residents do not finish high school and their overall educational attainment is four years less than that of the rest of the city population. Home ownership in ghettoes is one-half to one-tenth the rate of cities as a whole, and half the homes of residents are more than fifty years old and in bad repair. Population density here is four to ten times the city's average. Sanitation and other services are less frequent and less thorough here than elsewhere.[17] Another study, made by the Federal Trade Commission, also shows that ghetto neighborhoods have the highest food prices and the greatest credit-gouging practices. It is, in sum, not a pretty picture. I do not argue that public policy intentionally structured ghettoes in this way; but public policy, if it is clearly informed, may make the facts known.

The picture is bleaker still for Indians, both on and off reservations. In 1967 the income of the average American Indian family was $1,500. Unemployment on reservations ranges from 45 to 80 percent.[18] The various studies available try to dramatize the short life expectancy of Indians, the high infant mortality, the huge school dropout rate (50 percent, as against the overall average of 29 percent), the amazing record of time spent in jail for drinking, the dismal employment record, the crude quality of life on Indian reservations.[19] This too is a totally depressing picture.

Data such as these substantiate our need to scrutinize public decision-making, program commitments, and fiscal assessments in the light of probable costs and benefits vis-à-vis racial categories. The picture does not seem to indicate that purely random forces are at work.

Our preoccupation with age and sex is somewhat less intense than our concern with race, and somewhat more recent. We are only now beginning to question whether we are quite so benevolent to women and the aged and quite so kindly to young people as we might like to think. We must again face a record that shows that women too are systematically underpaid and underpromoted.[20] It is commonly estimated that women earn about $60 for every $100 earned by a man. Women with college degrees earn what men with eighth-grade educations receive. Women account for only 9 percent of full professors, 7 percent of physicians, and 3 percent of lawyers.[21] Even the federal government, which might be thought to be a pacesetter in these matters, has hired women for only 1.6 percent of its major appointive posts.[22] Women are also on the short end of elected government positions. In 1972, only eleven members of the House of Representatives, for example, were women; there was only one woman in the United States Senate; and only three women held federal judgeships.

The incidence of families below the poverty line and of low-income families headed by women is also dramatically disproportionate: 50 percent of all families headed by women are poor.[23] Similar statistics apply to the aged. Nearly one-third of all "poor in metropolitan areas," for example, "are in households headed by employed men over sixty-five whose poverty results from low earnings rather than unemployment, disability and old age."[24] And so it goes. Cost-benefit analysis should be available to make quite clear to Americans at large just how it goes.

The prime target for our concern, however, might well be the common denominator of the previously listed categories: the "poor." This category subsumes all the others. Why should the poor so concern us? If equality of life style is neither attainable nor desirable (as I have earlier been at pains to establish), will

**Women,
the Old, and
the Young**

not the poor always be with us? And if, indeed, there always will be persons with more and persons with less, why this concern? The concern is not with differences per se. The operation of inequality in itself is not in my view destructive to our overall social fabric. What may be iniquitous and intolerable, however, are certain peculiarities about particular dimensions of American poverty: its scope and range, the quality of life at the very bottom, the overtones of its demographic profile, and finally its predictable recidivism.

**The Range of Poverty**

What is disquieting about the range of poverty is the enormous spread between the bottom and the *middle*. The spread between extremes, oddly enough, may be less significant. It is rather the way the people at the very bottom perceive the people they think are average that counts heavily in our social balance. It is doubtful that many people at the bottom level of poverty are embittered by comparing their lot with that of a few movie celebrities. For most of them the American dream is not extravagant riches. It is simply some quite reasonable hope that they will reach a middle range of affluence. The results of polls reported by Free and Cantril support this contention.[25] These analysts used a self-anchoring scale to assess, among other things, the personal aspirations and fears of Americans. They found that 40 percent of Americans do want an "improved or decent standard of living." They go on to explain:

> Mostly this aspiration took the form of a desire for a modest improvement, as in the case of a security guard in Michigan:
>
> "Everybody wants the best out of life. I wouldn't want to be a millionaire, but I would like enough money to stand in my own shoes. I want more than the way I live now. I'd like a little more comfort and security. I'd like a better job without having to worry when I might get laid off. I'd like to live in a nice flat. . . . I don't want to be like Liz Taylor, afraid to step outside because she's rich and popular. I just want enough money to live a little better without any worry."

This seems to me to indicate that what we must aim for is a system open to fulfillment of the aspirations of that security guard; and one that is so perceived by everybody. But this is hard to achieve if the income distribution pattern continues to make the rich get richer while the poor, at best, mark time.[26] Perhaps the science of econometrics can determine more precisely what is a safe spread between middle and bottom. But even without exact measures, one can use self-scaling devices to estimate this crucial matter of perception, in the manner of the opinion pollers. What we should be asking is: Do people at the economic bottom of our society feel as though they can make it to the middle? There is no point in trying to skirt this question by bringing in comforting data from other lands. International comparisons suggesting that the diet standards of Harlem would look magnificent in Pakistan are entirely beside the point. The people of Harlem compare their life styles with those they see on television, not with those of Pakistan.

Many analysts now agree that the least common denominator of poverty, wherever it occurs, is the recognition of it. If people *think* they are debased (whether they are the untouchables of India or the not-so-poor poor of America), then they are cancers in their own society. The image of poverty is an image that lacks self-respect. And it seems reasonable to suggest that in this matter, image is reality. If you think poor, you are poor. To be poor is to be recognized as such by yourself and others. This is a difficult hurdle for many to jump. To understand the qualitative difference between the poverty of a bankrupt businessman and a third-generation welfare recipient is to understand the nature of today's poverty. The poverty of the bankrupt businessman is viewed both by him and by society at large as accidental and temporary. It in no way affects a basic perception of potential opportunities: advances in work, income, education, and so forth. The second type of poverty is hopeless. It is not even introspective. Imagination generally dies here before the eighth grade—if it ever blossomed at all.

But after all of this has been said, we must still look at the reasonable aspects of this bottom level of poverty—the second dimension of my concern. I believe that most Americans are ready to make judgments about the concrete conditions below which they are unwilling to let fellow citizens fall. There is no harsh commitment in the United States to the inevitability of all human suffering. There is, on the contrary, a desire, however partially fulfilled, to help. We see this in our welfare laws, public assistance programs, disability pensions, tax laws, and many other public policies. No matter how we may wail about the limitations and inadequacies of these laws, they still mirror our basic concern. As a nation we *are* concerned with keeping people afloat. We differ, of course, as to what this means. I simply argue that Americans believe that even those at the bottom should receive food, clothing, and sanitary housing commensurate with good health. Most Americans would not deny basic health care to anyone, regardless of income. Our concern also includes access to free recreational facilities (at least of a simple sort) and access to extensive and free education commensurate with job skills in a technological society.

Are our concerns met by our fiscal commitments? What does the record here show? It shows, to begin with, that if we wanted to put a price tag on poverty, we would have a variety of options. A large number of scholars are already doing this arithmetic.[27] The estimates run from those of Michael Harring-

**Recognizing Poverty**

ton on the left through Robert Lampman, Mollie Orshansky, Leon Keyserling, the Social Security Administration, the Bureau of the Census, the Council of Economic Advisers, and Rose F. Friedman on the right. Each has a different cutoff point for "poverty" and offers some differing details. But even the sober figure put out by the Census Bureau in 1970 places the poverty level at an income of $3,968 for a family of four.[28] The official definition of poverty in actual use by the government is that of the Social Security Administration, which certifies any household as "poor" if its annual money income is less than three times the cost of a minimal diet for the persons of that household. Thus, in 1967, a family of four required by that count a minimal income of $3,335 per year.

**Life Style: The "Average" versus the Poor**

What these figures look like in terms of actual life style is naturally a matter of where you live and what you choose. But it takes little imagination to see that no matter where you live, this poverty income is likely to produce a style that is beyond the boundary lines of genuine hope. The "average" American family was shown to be moving along at $9,870 in 1970. The *New York Times* described the life style of the members of this average family.[29] They live in five rooms in a suburb, have two old cars, eat decently but not lavishly, and enjoy home entertainment almost exclusively. The couple interviewed for this modest portrait seemed happy and reasonably content. Surely there is nothing outrageous in what they have, or even in their aspirations for a little bit more. They hope that their two sons will go further than they, get better educations and better jobs. And such hopes seem rational enough. But what kind of life style and what kind of hope could anyone have while existing at the official poverty level with an income of substantially less than half of this?

By the very kindest count, there are nine million families in the United States below this poverty level, and many more are hovering all too close to the brink of it. And all of these data must be seen against the statement that "to increase the income of all poor families to the poverty minimum, the Census Bureau estimates would cost $11.4 billion."[30] We now spend more than $11 billion on the subsidies to the affluent that I outlined a few pages back. These disquieting quantitative aspects of poverty are the ones that perhaps deserve some reconsideration. It is not at all clear that if Americans understood how public resources were being distributed, they would approve.

My third concern with poverty as a category needing special attention has to do with its demographic profile, and with certain recidivist qualities. Who are the poor? I have already answered this question when I described the pattern of distribution of resources to nonwhites, women, and the aged; and I might have added minors. These turn out to be the people who are predominant among the poor. Anthony Downs calls them the "poverty-prone." This then suggests that we may be systematically (even if unintentionally) doing in certain groups. The poor by definition have low incomes. They are not by definition black, female, elderly, or young. While we have been at some pains to proclaim that irrational and prejudicial indices (like race, age, and sex) must no longer be used as determinants for the allocation of jobs, housing, and education, we must nonetheless face the fact that these very criteria continue to appear as nonrandom factors in our general income distribution system. We must somehow come to grips with this problem.

The recidivist nature of American poverty is part of this problem. It appears that certain Americans keep missing the success escalator that we thought we had built into our system. For most of America, perhaps more than 85 percent, the idea of a success escalator seems real enough. There seems to be a real possibility of getting on this conveyor belt and moving up; perhaps not as far as one might wish, but nonetheless up. But then there is a hard-core, unchanging, self-reproducing group that does not seem even to see this escalator. These are the third-generation poor, the hopeless hereditary poor. It is not known just how many of them there are, but clearly they exist. Indeed, the woeful lack of a generation gap may account for the continuing reappearance of certain of the foregoing categories of people in the ranks of the poor. It is their presence that requires us to look again at our system, to try to discover what is skewing the outcomes so badly. Why do not the current holders of the badge of poverty appear in random fashion, in the generational style of past eras? Anthony Downs analyzes the problem this way: "Their continuance in this deprived state is reinforced by many institutional arrangements in our society, including those supposedly designed to aid them."[31]

**The Success Escalator**

Our society may require a rather dramatic rethinking of all the determinants of our income distribution system. It may even have to reconsider some of the now acceptable determinants of income, such as college degrees. Intellectual differences, after all, may be as resistant to change and just as unearned as racial or sex differences. If so, these differences will also operate to produce a continuing elite that also will defy the conventions of "equal opportunity." That is, opportunity will always be rigged in favor of that group. We may find, therefore, that there is something inherently unfair in making college degrees into passports for an extra $100,000 in lifetime earnings—at least for men. This is the much-advertised figure that drives many people into college when they might properly prefer to be elsewhere. It may also be driving colleges into enterprises that might properly belong elsewhere. What may be needed, therefore, is some way to award status, income, dignity, and respect to all sorts of workers, not just to degree-bearing ones. Moreover, we may wish to toy with the possibility that not every attribute of status has to accrue to individuals in tandem with all of the others. If some forms of work are inherently more pleasant, or provably more healthful, then at least the money income for these jobs might be lessened in comparison with the fiscal rewards of jobs that are inherently dangerous or distasteful.

These considerations, in any event, are the concerns of a society that wishes to wrestle honestly with the question of who gets what and why. Cost-benefit analysis, the presentation of alternative solutions, attempts at measuring outputs—such procedures are hardly the end of the line, but perhaps they are a good beginning. Admittedly all of this is a difficult enterprise. More than that, many of these questions cannot be quantitatively answered. But it is my conviction that if we merely *try* to answer them, even if our answers are somewhat speculative and impressionistic and incomplete, we shall have a better basis for public decisions than we commonly have now. Most public jurisdictions and institutions, even the sophisticated and important ones, do not now use anything close to this style of thinking. In short, a cost-benefit (PPBS) style of analysis should help us to estimate the direction, size, and causes of the institutional skew to which Downs refers. Once armed with such knowledge and with arrays of alternative policy costs and benefits, we shall be in a better position to know who gets what, and to arrive at policies that will reduce the *avoidable* ravages of disease, crime, alienation, ignorance, and violence. Perhaps we may also arrive at policies that will reduce the avoidable ravages of our own consciences.

**Poverty Budgets versus "Defense" Budgets**

Consider, for example, Table 1. We can see that in the aggregate, the expenditures meant to accrue directly to the "poor" do not constitute the lion's share of our public budgets. When we lump together public welfare, old age and disability, and unemployment benefits (even though the latter two carry the well-to-do along with the poor), we do not reach even half the amount of money spent for "defense." We must also realize that only a part of these welfare expenditures—the items most directly targeted for the poor—actually ever reach them as benefits. Large proportions, after all, represent overhead, salaries for middle-class case workers, and indirect (and perhaps unintended) beneficiaries of the programs. A number of the studies previously cited suggest that most of the benefits popularly thought of as helping the poor actually end up in the middle-

| | Total | Per Capita | |
|---|---|---|---|
| | (in Millions of Dollars) | (in Dollars) | Table 1 |
| National defense and international relations | $74.6 | $377 | ALL GOVERN-MENT |
| Education | 40.2 | 203 | EXPENDI-TURES, 1967 |
| Old age and disability | 23.9 | . . . | |
| Interest on national debt | 13.4 | 68 | |
| Highways | 14.0 | 71 | |
| National resources | 10.1 | 51 | |
| Public welfare | 19.6 | 48 | |
| Hospitals | 7.0 | 35 | |
| Postal service | 6.2 | 31 | |
| Space research | 5.4 | 27 | |
| Employee retirement | 4.9 | . . . | |
| Veterans' benefits | 4.4 | 22 | |
| Police | 3.3 | 17 | |
| Sanitation | 2.5 | 13 | |
| Health | 2.5 | 13 | |
| Housing and urban renewal | 2.4 | 12 | |
| Financial administration | 2.4 | 12 | |
| General control | 2.1 | 11 | |
| Unemployment compensation | 2.0 | 11 | |
| Fire protection | 1.5 | 8 | |
| Parks and recreation | 1.3 | 7 | |

SOURCE: U.S. BUREAU OF THE CENSUS, *STATISTICAL ABSTRACT OF THE UNITED STATES: 1969* (WASHINGTON, D.C.: U.S. GOVERNMENT PRINTING OFFICE, 1969).

class orbit. This may be true of education programs, police programs, recreation programs, and housing programs. The recent New York City University open admissions program is a case in point. This was originally touted as a vehicle for bringing into the university system the most disadvantaged elements of New York's population—the very poor blacks and Puerto Ricans. In the first year of its operation, however, it became clear that while it was serving this purpose to some degree, it was even more effectively bringing in lower-middle-class white Italians and Irish (not the most disadvantaged of the city's people).

In addition, there are programs that, while not meant to help the poor directly, are clearly not publicly expected to *hurt* them. Yet once again unintentional hurts do appear to occur. A study of the selective service system, for example, concludes that "men from higher income families are less likely to see service than men from lower income families."[32] There are concomitant racial overtones here too.

Hurting the Poor

We should conclude, therefore, that it is important for us to know far more than we now do about the degree to which all public programs—even full employment—benefit the various significant categories of American citizens. We must know the costs and effects of Head Start, job training, legal aid, and all other policies, no matter how beguiling their names. We must also know which taxes are regressive, which proportionate, and which progressive in the way their burdens fall upon various population groups. We must know, in short, where all the chips fall. There are no panaceas. Choice is inevitable. But choice can be made more intelligent, and even more humane.

**The Moral Commitment**

This is the juncture at which the moral commitment mentioned earlier must enter. My hope is that when all the facts are widely available, as PPBS can make them available, and where they are made understandable by educators, politicians, and other leaders and responsible media, we will find that *most* people will express heightened concern. At a minimum, I hope they will at last put into practice their existing agreement to enjoin the use of race, religion, sex, and age as determinants of employment, education, income maintenance, health benefits, social security, and other public privileges and benefits. There is clear evidence in our existing legislation (social security, public assistance, medicare) that the public is equally committed to programs that in one way or another "take from the rich and give to the poor"; or at least to programs that take from everybody proportionately to give to everybody a minimum of food, health, and income security. There is also the idea of "equal services," from schools to sewers. These, then, represent our moral commitments today. And they may be implemented and enlarged as the facts become more clearly and widely known. The burden of PPBS is to get these facts to the people. When we finally clearly understand who gets what, it is very likely that we shall adjust our system so that the answer becomes more and more congruent with the aspiration of the greatest number of Americans and with the intelligent, long-range self-interest expressed in a viable and humane American dream.

# CHAPTER 12

# A NEW FUTURE FOR
# AMERICAN POLITICS

To close a general textbook on American political processes with a proposal for American politics is at least a novelty. Yet all texts do contain viewpoints, and it might therefore be the better part of honesty to make such views not only explicit (this I have tried to do throughout the book), but as complete and coherent as possible. I am less interested in convincing anyone of the soundness of the details of my proposals, however, than in provoking thought about our general philosophy and the usual style of American politics.

The fundamental element in my proposal is a marriage of two virtually untried but highly promising operational devices: majority rule and cost-benefit analysis. At first blush these may seem an odd couple because of their remarkably diverse characters and styles. But that is precisely the strength of the union. Each partner compensates for the major weaknesses of the other. Cost-benefit analysis relies heavily for its fullest application on computers, data banks, mathematical models, and expertise; majoritarianism relies heavily on broad participation, individual judgment, even sentiment. The majoritarian procedures can supply ingredients missing in PPBS, and PPBS can do the same for majority rule.

As we have seen, PPBS is in need of a device to clarify fundamental goals and to settle questions of goal priority in a way that avoids the otherwise inevitable clash between the individual survival needs of public decision-makers and the clearly perceived needs of the community at large. In other words, PPBS must be made "politically feasible." Ralph Huitt, in an admirable essay describing this problem,[1] says that our decision-makers cannot now afford to use the information that PPBS would provide; they must operate on judgments made by the "seat of the pants." Members of Congress are quoted as saying that even though they are convinced that a certain policy is necessary and wise, they cannot come out in favor of it because "it would be political suicide."[2] Huitt's analysis of the presidency itself shows that electoral politics as it now operates must also cloud the President's vision. He too must make final judgments in accordance with "political feasibility." This pro-

The
Odd Couple:
Majority Rule
and Cost-Benefit
Analysis

posed system therefore takes a number of very fundamental policy questions out of the hands of such decision-makers and places them squarely in the hands of the electorate. This means that certain basic directions are settled for both elected and appointed officials by a group of people who cannot be turned out of office at the next spin of the wheel. The buck will then stop where it cannot be passed and where it cannot be perverted.

On the other hand, majoritarianism is at its weakest when it forces people to make decisions about which they can have little information. Properly used, PPBS can remedy this grave deficiency. It can offer far more comprehensive and systematic information about basic policy matters than is now available, and it can institute a new style of thinking among decision-makers and the public at large. The proposal therefore requires a firm belief in neither saints nor sinners. It requires only the quite credible conviction that people are inclined to try to effect their own self-interest and that the interest of the American population as a whole can be reasonably well understood. The proposal simply tries to supply the missing link in the American political system—the link that would generate sufficient power to move us beyond stalemate, the link between felt and perceived needs and their reasonable fulfillment. In a way, the proposal is a device to realize the sentiments and values expressed by President Dwight D. Eisenhower when he said, "People want peace so much that one of these days governments had better get out of their way and let them have it."

**Getting Government Out of the Way**

Getting the government out of the way of our basic desires, whether for peace or health or whatever, is the key function of the majoritarian aspect of this proposal. The proposal aspires to do this by providing a relatively straightforward way for people to express themselves on fundamental policy values, followed by a mandatory mechanism for translating that expression into public policy activities and programs.

Let me now present the proposal in some detail before continuing with arguments that attempt to justify it or to rebut the more obvious rejoinders. The sketch that I now present is to be understood as only the most tentative of beginnings. The model-building experts would have to play with the ideas offered and with many alternatives. But here is the general thrust:

Congress would pass legislation (under its generous implied powers) which would provide for a national referendum every four years, at the time of our presidential elections. The voter would be given a ballot, adjusted for later computer compilation, which would offer two overall sets of choices. The first set would have to do with revenues, the second with expenditures. The revenue ballot would ask voters to indicate which of the following types of tax systems they prefer:

(1) Taxes and borrowing arranged so that all adult citizens share the burden as much as possible in proportion to their incomes. That is, revenue would be collected more evenly than it is now.

(2) Taxes and borrowing policies arranged so that all adult citizens share in them, but with those with higher total incomes bearing larger proportions of the burden. That is, the burden borne by the top groups would be increased and that of the bottom groups decreased.

(3) Taxes and borrowing policies arranged only in terms of collection convenience and without regard to the particular proportions of burden falling on various groups of citizens, so long as no citizen faces the loss of more than half his income.

As will be explained later, other proposals could be substituted here. The upper portion of this ballot would offer a brief recapitulation of the way the current system works, stating as succinctly as possible how existing tax and borrowing policies work out in terms of income. That is, it would show something like this: Our present taxation and debt system is arranged so that those persons whose incomes are in the top 10 percent of national income are supplying—percent of our revenues; those persons whose incomes are in the second 10 percent are paying —percent; and so forth.

The second part of this ballot would deal with expenditures, and would offer the voter a list of all ongoing major social policy areas:

Programs to deliver the mail

Programs to monitor private utilities (banks, media, transport systems, etc.)

Programs to ensure national safety (defense against outside aggression, foreign policy)

Programs to improve health quality (extend life, eliminate disease, control drug use)

Programs to ensure community safety (defense against personal and property damage)

Programs to educate the citizenry (grade school, high school, university, and other programs)

Programs to provide adequate housing

Programs for maintaining full employment (job training, public service corps, etc.)

Programs to subsidize special occupational groups (farmers, shipbuilders, small businessmen, etc.)

Programs for maintaining basic income patterns (social security, unemployment insurance, etc.)

Programs for supporting the disabled (veterans, blind, etc.)

Programs for improving transportation (highways, mass urban transport, etc.)

Programs for protecting the environment (conservation, air preservation, water pollution control)

Programs for recreation and culture

Programs for administering justice

These items form the substance of all public budgets in the United States—national, state, and local. The voter would be asked to number these categories in the order of his estimate of their importance. The voter would have been carefully instructed before entering the booth as to the mechanics of the ballot, and clearly informed that his choices would result in mandated priorities in the policy-making of all government units during the succeeding four years. That is, the ballots would be tallied so as to obtain an order of preference among these expenditure programs and revenue systems, and aggregated for the nation as a whole and for each individual state. The nation and the states would then be required to produce budgets that reflected these overall guidelines. Thus the preferences of North Dakotans would be used separately for the internal programming of revenues and expenditures in North Dakota, New York preferences for New York programming, and so forth. Each state, however, would have the option of tallying its votes according to locality if it decided to grant this type of home rule. The national program and budget would reflect the nationwide preferences.

**Preference Rating and Commitment**

What, then, would be mandated by this exercise in preference rating? A sense of commitment. That is, if housing, let us say, were to emerge at the top of the list of national priorities, then the goal of providing safe, clean, and adequate housing would receive first call on the national budget immediately after basic safety-valve limits (which I shall describe shortly) have been siphoned off. This does not mean that housing will actually absorb the greater number of dollars; it only means that the best cost-benefit alternative that the agency in charge of housing programs has to offer (through it PPBS system) will be fulfilled before the item of next priority is budgeted. Even if national defense emerged last on the list of national priorities, it might still command a larger number of actual dollars than some other program, simply because even minimal fulfillment here might be more expensive. An example on the village level makes this clear. If traffic safety appeared at the top of a list of local priorities and education at the bottom, it is easily conceivable that the best alternative emerging from a cost-benefit analysis of traffic safety might be a signal-light system that would cost far less than the operation of even the most minimal school system.

Moreover, in order to prevent any institutional suicides or insupportable disruptions of individual human lives, the system would provide for retention of basic safety levels. That is, the Office of Management and Budget would be charged with working out the lowest possible support level for every service consistent with the overall proviso concerning broad social disruptions. If higher education, for example, were to emerge as an item of low priority, an analysis would be available to show the amount of reduction that would occur through normal attrition, the amount that would occur by simply halting all new projects, and the amount that could be swallowed without adding too much to the costs of, let us say, maintaining full employment. This would then be the safety level, and the budget plans in this arena would have to stay close to that minimal figure. The point here is that just as expansiveness in a program breeds automatic aggrandizement without necessarily severe consequences, so does attrition breed further attrition. This system, however, would provide a far greater possibility for overall directional change than is now possible through unmitigated incrementalism.

The enabling legislation for this plan would also provide for money to be siphoned off the top of our revenues for a special fund for unforeseen emergencies and for the management of housekeeping and fiscal manipulation programs that are automatically generated by priority expenditures. All direct programs necessarily breed indirect costs for such matters as accounting, record-keeping, data collection, budget analysis, hiring and firing operations, and the like; these institutions and practices must remain sufficiently stabilized to carry out the programs they exist to serve. The role of decision-makers, from chief executives on down to village supervisors, would remain almost untouched. They would still be expected to advise the people at large on the broadest policy objectives they see as viable and to advise legislators on the necessities of the subprograms with which these legislators would still be charged. That is, the legislative role would also continue, but it would be circumscribed by a set of ready-made broad policy mandates. Within this range, however, they too would continue their traditional decision-making, though it is hoped they would now be forced to do so in a far more rational manner. It would still fall to them to approve or disapprove projects within each category. Which housing plan best fulfills the assigned priority? Which health project? The entire business of regulatory legislation would also continue. Laws would still be passed (or overturned) requiring people to put lids on their garbage cans, to comply with naturalization procedures, to register guns, and so forth. The administrative arm of the government would likewise continue its day-to-day operations: garbage would still be collected, teachers would go to their classrooms, nurses would care for the sick, and the police would patrol their beats. Specific taxes and specific rates would still have to be determined on the revenue side of the ledger—but here too the overall objectives would have been settled by the ballot.

**Consequences: Differences in Style**

Crucial differences in style would immediately be apparent. There should be a profound alteration in such institutions as campaign and party systems and in budgeting and planning systems. The foreknowledge that this type of referendum is part of the system would influence every incumbent and aspiring officeholder, both elected and appointed. Those who must campaign for public posts would now have to tell all the people a straight story. No more parceling out of inconsistent and irresponsible tidbits in the hope that they will do some electioneering good. A man would no longer be able to try to be all things to all people. He would have to tell these people precisely what he wants—and what he wants first. The people would know what questions to ask. On the one hand, this means a candidate would have the opportunity to influence the electorate rationally. This in itself would be a novel and salutary state of affairs. The slick slogans would be gone. Enter the thoughtful debates. Individuals and parties alike would be competing in providing sensible answers to questions they all knew would have to be answered, and answered responsibly. On the other hand, elected officials would no longer have so much to fear from the electorate: they could no longer be made scapegoats. The basic policies would have been set by the people themselves. The voters would therefore have only themselves to blame if the general tenor of public life seemed unrewarding, and they would also have themselves to rely on for at least partial correctives. The accountability of public officials would be tied to objectives over which they could more reasonably be expected to have some control. Moreover, a conscientious official would no longer have to grope around for the latest but possibly misread groupthink. He would not have to hold a finger in the air to feel which way the public winds were blowing. He would have clear answers about general directions. He would not have to pit his need to survive against a desire to work for the public good.

It is to be hoped that administrative personnel would be equally benefited by these clear signals. They would now be forced to put their efforts into carefully documented alternatives aimed at reasonably well-specified ends. This situation would fulfill a traditional part of the administrative dream: to have goals defined but means left flexible.

Certain technical arrangements remain to be considered. How, for example, to allow for new programs to appear on the ballot? How to decide on the wording and placement of these items? The enabling legislation for this referendum is envisioned as including a section making Congress responsible for outlining the substance of the revenue and expenditure items that are to be included on it. Safeguards would be provided to make it impossible for Congress to fail to list any current major program, and at the same time the law would provide sufficient flexibility so that legislative judgment might be applied to expand or contract the list as the future demands. There would be an original overall limit of, say, twenty items, to prevent the ballot from becoming too cumbersome. The details of the wording of these questions and instructions would be delegated to the appropriate division of the Office of Management and Budget, and it in turn might well accept advice from the media experts of the nation at large.

It is assumed, moreover, that once the system is initiated many trends would arise which would automatically combine to educate the people. The issues, for example, would be as newsworthy as the candidates. Television, radio, and other media would be at pains to discuss these matters in pointed and evaluatory terms. No longer would our serious journals be committed to the assessment of personalities rather than to the analysis of policy.

Experts could also be relied on to help in supplying the detailed plans for counting and aggregating the vote. A number of mathematical methods are now available for compiling a composite order of preferences from an array of individual ones.[3] Again, the Office of Management and Budget would be charged with this assignment; its goal would be the selection of the aggregation method that reflected the preferences of most Americans with the least amount of distortion. This too is well within the realm of the possible.

By now it is quite probable that readers are disconcerted by what they may perceive as critical weaknesses in the proposal. First, they may wish further evidence of our need for such a fundamental change as the one proposed here. Let me therefore present two lines of thought and data. One deals with the evidence that large numbers of people have lost confidence in our political institutions and our political leaders as they are now operating. This is often referred to as a "crisis of confidence" or a "crisis of legitimacy." The second line of reasoning concerns the existing evidence of the rationality of such popular perceptions. If indeed there is a crisis of confidence, is it only a phychological failing that might therefore be susceptible to psychological paliatives? Or do our institutions actually work the way many people have begun to perceive them as working? Do the institutions themselves cause the crises?

**The Loss of Legitimacy**

The first point, the loss of legitimacy (that is, the people's loss of faith in the fundamental myths and constitutional values of our society) can be illustrated by a national survey taken in the spring of 1971.[4] This study showed that there was a new and urgent concern over national unity, political stability, and "law and order." Almost one out of every two Americans sampled in this survey believed that the unrest was likely to lead to a "real breakdown in this country." The traditional optimism that pervaded the previous polls taken by these investigators was gone. People no longer demonstrated confidence that the nation was moving ahead and solving the problems most on their minds. And the problems perceived were more socially oriented than they had been earlier. People appeared less concerned with the material aspects of the American dream than they had been in the 1950s and 1960s. They appeared more concerned with subjects demanding joint political action: drugs, pollution, crime, and political instability. According to the authors of this survey, "This anxiety is general and widespread. The American people clearly feel their nation is in trouble." The leading reason given for this feeling was that "our traditional way of doing things is not working and some basic changes are needed." This same survey showed that there was decided sentiment in favor of greater national effort to solve domestic problems and less to solve international ones. The authors concluded that the data clearly showed "urgent and rapidly rising public concern about national leadership. And the possibility certainly exists that at some future point the public may make a *direct linkage* between their personal and national hopes and fears"[5] (italics mine).

Loss of confidence in the government is certainly exacerbated by abundant evidence of American officials' arrogant disregard of the public. That has repeatedly been made clear over recent years by the government's transparent lying when it claimed that Francis Gary Powers was collecting weather information when his U2 was shot down over Russia in 1960; that we had nothing to do with the Bay of Pigs invasion in 1961; that the U.S. Marines were sent to the Dominican Republic in 1965 only to protect American lives; that no H-bomb of ours had been lost over Spain in 1966; that American planes would never be sent into combat support missions in Cambodia; and that our Vietnam policy was a response only to treaty commitments. All of these items and more have produced our much-discussed "credibility gap." And this credibility gap threatens the very legitimacy of our ongoing institutions. The people no longer have faith in their own government, and they appear to have become cynical in the face of corruption. They are weary of their own powerlessness, yet fearful of facing the enormous complexity of forces they do not comprehend. Even the fabled military-industrial complex seems fragmented and confused, as do the publically elected officials. At other times the men at the helm seem to be steering their own course in arrogant disregard of the common will.

But are all these perceptions distortions? Is there any further evidence that our political institutions, as institutions, cannot reflect the people's views? Is it possible that the system itself produces these anomalies?

**System versus People**

Take, for example, our current election system. In 1968 the people replaced President Johnson with President Nixon, and six months later nobody, in or out of public office, seemed to understand exactly what this was to mean. In other words, the guidance provided to our political leaders by our twentieth-century election returns is more ambiguous than the entrails consulted by ancient Greeks. James Reston, one of the mainstays of the *New York Times* editorial establishment, assessed the 1970 elections this way: "They didn't give anybody a mandate to do anything in this election."[6] Daniel P. Moynihan, former counselor to President Nixon, voiced the same thought: "The silent majority, if you will accept this term, is silent not least because it finds it so difficult to say things in terms that will win a respectful hearing among those who judge such matters."[7] Evidently the voice of the people as revealed through our current election procedures is anything but loud and clear.

Even with outside devices to aid it, our system still seems to evade clear mandates. We saw the SST (supersonic transport) jammed through Congress despite very clear demonstration through public opinion polls and other devices that "the people" did not want it. It was just one of many remarkable demonstrations of how right Woodrow Wilson was when he observed that it was a matter of "great difficulty to let the people's voice be heard in the halls of Congress." A President who campaigned against the Vietnam war, and who subsequently witnessed antiwar demonstrations and read the results of public opinion polls that revealed an overwhelming majority in favor of ending the conflict, nonetheless extended that war into Laos within two years. Our system itself seems to muddy the waters. The Supreme Court says that public schools must be desegregated by busing; the President states flatly that he is against it. We see fifty governors running off in as many directions, and we watch officials chosen from the same party (Nixon, Reagan, Rockefeller, Javits, Goldwater) pursue not only different, but contradictory and mutually exclusive goals. At the same time we see people elected from presumably adversary parties who are indistinguishable from one another. In sum, our checks and balances, marble-cake federalism, cumbersome committee systems, frustrating filibusters, two-thirds majorities, prolix procedures, and undisciplined parties combine to produce a political game played on so many fields with so many players and so many rules that even the participants cannot follow the plays. Clearly the operation of our current politics has not measured up to our needs or our highest value preferences. Indeed, the systematic operations themselves encourage the loss of confidence.

One final example will help establish the tenor of our current decision-making apparatus and help us to locate certain systematic sources of difficulty. Once again, James Reston reports on the anti–ballistic-missile (ABM) debate in 1969:

> Very few people in this country, or even in the world, have the scientific and technical competence to pass judgment on whether this missile would be effective. . . . The defense of the nation, Dr. James Killian [formerly Science Advisor to the President, and at the time of this quote, a member of the Arms Control and Disarmament Agency] suggested, is too serious and complicated to be left to soldiers and politicians alone. . . . Congress could use some special help from outside the government from time to time in reaching decisions on great strategic questions of the day. The comments out of Capitol Hill on the ABM question illustrate the point. Mendel Rivers, Chairman of the House Armed Services Committee, said he was for deploying the ABMs. "I want protection, and like everybody else, I want the latest in technology." Representative Gerald Ford of Michigan, the House Republican Leader, made an equally profound remark. "If you have to gamble and err, err on the side of strength, and not weakness."

> This is the kind of thing that passes all too often for analysis in the Congress, and it sounds fine only until you begin to think about it. . . . For the moment it [the decision] has got lost in politics and opinions and past commitments.[8]

**The Failure of the Experts**

Reston is saying, and I heartily concur, that our politicians are indeed failing us, but so are our experts. In fact, the time is more than ripe for Americans to face up to their ambivalence and confusion about these experts. There has been misplaced confidence in "apolitical" civil services, "independent" administrative agencies, and science and expertise in general as self-propelling answers to the problems of this nation. All too often American have found out too late that in the crunch science and technology too have disappeared. Dr. Edward Davis, Jr., science adviser to President Nixon and one of the foremost experts on the administration of science, has had this to say: "Some experts . . . are doubtful that rational decision-making and management practices can ever succeed in imposing order on the complexities of science policy." In other words, final decisions about science itself may have to come from outside the scientific community. Dr. Edward E. Davis, Jr., went on to say: "A strict scientific system is itself impossible because science is a tool, not a system."[9] Thus scientists, technicians, experts, administrators—all of the latter-day witch doctors—cannot by themselves rationally order our basic priorities. They cannot set the broad directions for our society.

These, then, are the arguments that might persuade a reader of the need for some kind of fundamental change in our political operations. But why PPBS? Why majority rule? In sum, the current merry-go-round of politics and experts is understandably fueled by a set of quite human ambitions. Indeed, the system actually relies on these ambitions. For the politicians it is election and reelection. For the administrators it is promotion and aggrandizement. These are the objectives that in our current system are better served by obscuring policy than by clarifying it; by preserving short-run clienteles rather than by courting long-run publics. Incrementalism is the safe and sure (and sometimes only) way. This, in turn, means there can be no fundamental change in directions, and there is mounting evidence that certain directions do need fundamental change. We are not making sufficient inroads against crime, violence, congestion, pollution, hunger, and disease. We are always running but never catching up. It is all too often a question of too little, too late. PPBS in tandem with a majoritarian goal-setting device would provide the opportunity to get off the merry-go-round. PPBS offers evidence against which long-range goals and alternative solutions can be assessed. It is a built-in counter to incrementalism. Admittedly it is a somewhat technical and obscure matter, but majority rule is not. Cost-benefit analysis enjoys some advantages from its anonymity. Majority rule, however, is in everybody's mouth. Perhaps, therefore, the idea of majority rule—particularly the application that is suggested here—needs closer inspection and more detailed justification.

On the one hand, as rhetoric, majority rule possesses an almost instant superficial legitimacy. Very few Americans will come right out and say they do not recognize it as a preferred value. We are all socialized early and often into a respect for its supposed virtues. But the veneer of this conviction is thin. Majority rule is suspect in the eyes of many rank-and-file Americans because they often see themselves as members of one or another minority and are therefore fearful that they are vulnerable to some possible majoritarian idiosyncrasy. But of course, this view might be dispelled by suggesting that the issues here presented for majoritarian decision are not matters of individ-

**Human Ambitions**

ual life, liberty, and opportunity. The enemies of majority rule among the elite, however, may be more difficult to assuage, most particularly the political science professorial elite. It is from their pens that we most often hear about the allure of elitism and the pitfalls of populism. Because these works and ideas are particularly influential, I wish to deal with them in somewhat more detail than I would with other possible areas of controversy.

Attacks on the competence of the American electorate have been grinding out of the scholarly mills for a long time. The public emerges from all too many of the voting studies as ill informed, irrational, and considerably alienated. We are usually painted in these works as having reasonably strong attachments to one or another major political party, but little or no ideological understanding, little or no information on issues, and a highly inconsistent and illogical set of voting or nonvoting responses.[10] These findings are pegged on social and psychological factors that seem to influence voting: the limitations of voter intelligence, attention span, motivational apparatus, and general psyche. Any blame that does not fall in these quarters is placed on the complexities of the problems themselves. Yet virtually every exploration that produces these unflattering profiles turns on elections in which the voter simply chooses between two or more persons, under conditions that are in no way conducive to any rational belief in the efficacy of such a vote—or indeed in the subsequent efficacy of the candidates one is electing. This harks back to my earlier remarks on the limitations of our current pressure-group, election, and party systems. In reality the political cards are stacked against the voter and the voter knows it. It is not strange, then, that he

**The Alienated Voter**

often shows his alienation by apathetic or even inconsistent voting behavior.

Moreover, as I hinted before, a growing number of studies urge us to look more closely at these voters, and to look particularly at their perceptions of the elections at hand. When we do this, we find a more pleasing picture. For example, a number of authorities now note that the reason for low turnout among voters is the people's conviction that their votes will not count.[11] Others, too, have found the voter quite rational in terms of their own information and perceptions.[12] There is also interest in the degree to which voters are now shown to be issue-oriented.[13] Indeed, a good summary statement of this newer view can be found in the posthumous work of one of our greatest political scientists, V. O. Key. The title itself expresses his views: *The Responsible Electorate*. "The mass electorate is a good deal less irrational, ill-informed or sheep-like than is fashionable to suppose,"[14] says Key, and I heartily agree.

Let us now return to my remark that voting studies, favorable and unfavorable alike, invariably short-change the voter by testing him only in the crucible of nonissue, personality-oriented, often noncompetitive elections. What happens when we do put him up directly against an issue (and on occasion this does happen)? We have some studies that are in point, but of course they inevitably deal with existing referenda situations that do not look at all like the proposal made here. In general, American referenda are used (either by mandate or by option) in only twenty-two states. They occur at either statewide or local levels. When they are used, they suffer from obscurity, irrelevance, legalistic formalism, and massive inattention from parties, candidates, media, and all other applications of political resources. Most important, all American referenda are conducted on a "yes-no" basis. They are therefore intrinsically unrealistic and irrational. On top of that, most referenda offer totally inappropriate questions. Typically, referenda items pose either highly technical questions that ought to yield to the bureaucratic calculus of expertise or highly emotional questions that ought to yield to the judicial calculus of constitutional morality.

**Referenda Studies**

On every count, therefore, the referenda conditions that are now operative also stack the cards against the voter. Yet even these referenda do not conclusively demonstrate voter incompetence. At the outset it should be noted that the whole subject of referenda is relatively unexplored. A survey of articles that have appeared in the *American Political Science Review* since 1954, for example, reveals only two pieces on this subject; and interestingly enough, both of these are of quite recent vintage. Data are therefore sketchy, incomplete, occasionally biased, and invariably irrelevant to the proposal offered here.

Let me illustrate first what I mean by bias. Take the work done for the U.S. Department of Health, Education, and Welfare by Richard Carter and William Savard.[15] In their opening remarks these authors boldly state that they want to learn if low turnout in school bond and tax elections is "good or bad for the schools." This immediately implies that there is a known right answer. If this were true, it would simply indicate that these are patently inappropriate matters to put to popular vote. When certainty can be reached or approached, we can and should use expertise. Majority rule belongs to the arena of confessed uncertainty. Most referenda research displays a similar bias in its failure to separate those issues that are highly charged emotionally from those that are not so loaded. Referenda should not deal with subjects where "good" and "bad" are already established.

It is particularly interesting, therefore, that existing research, encumbered as it is with these difficulties and biases, still does not prove the incompetence of American voters. Quite the contrary. It still appears that when the public is placed in genuinely meaningful situations, it behaves consistently, vigorously, and even sensibly. Even the school bond and tax study just cited produces corroborative evidence along these lines. Voter turnout, for example, is found to be dependent on the importance of the issue, as well as on the directness of the issue's impact on the voter. This survey of more than 1,500 voters showed that where the people paid most of the school costs locally (rather than via state or federal funding), there was greater turnout. From this I posit that any kind of direct impact —knowing that the shoe will clearly and inevitably pinch *you*— will increase both interest and participation. This, I would argue, is a plus for the type of referendum I have proposed here.

**Are Voters Irrational?**

John Mueller's study of California referenda voting offers another favorable straw in the wind for a proposal like mine.[16] This study helps put to rest a number of tales in the folklore of voter irrationality, including the one that says that position on the ballot is a determinant of voting behavior, and the one that posits certain "types" of voters who irresponsibly and indiscriminately vote against everything. Both of these tendencies, if they existed, would bolster the argument that voters are somewhat irrational. But both of them were negated here. The same study also produced evidence that party campaigning does help to structure public opinion; and since then other studies have indicated that parties rarely, if ever, do rally votes on referenda items. From this I again draw positive conclusions for the type of proposition I am here putting forth. The referendum suggestion that I am making is frankly and explicitly geared to party politics.

Finally, what about the studies with clearly negative evidence? Let me, in fairness, touch on some of the recent findings that appear to be strikingly contrary to my assumptions about the common man's competence and decency. An analysis of the 1968 fair housing amendment in California pointed a damning finger at California voters, who turned down any opportunity to enact nondiscriminatory housing legislation—and this in the face of a successful fair housing act passed the previous year by their own legislature and supported by the then governor.[17] The analysis does away with convenient and reasonable excuses, such as confusion or a "general wave of conservatism." No, it is presumably established that these people clearly knew just what they were doing. The authors therefore, lavish unstinting and generalized praise for legislative over plebiscitory democracy. In their words, "The former [legislative democracy] not only permits but also is characterized by compromises between the initial demands of groups of various size and intensity." And this is to them clearly preferable. I, on the other hand, cannot accept these conclusions as having any relevance to the plans proposed here. First of all, the conclusion about legislative superiority rests on the assumption of an automatic "liberal pluralism" that deals out fair compromises among all sorts of groups. I have been at pains to question this assumption earlier and to indicate that this is often just not true. Second, the authors, in their generalized praise of legislation as against referenda, do not distinguish between questions that might be appropriately asked of all voters and questions that do indeed belong elsewhere. In this instance a previously determined national constitutional right was put before an inappropriate segment of the nation. A matter for judicial decision-making was made the subject of a statewide popularity contest. The prohibition of irrational discrimination on the basis of race is a well-anchored value. It does not require a referendum—most particularly not a referendum submitted to the voters of one state. (I have tried to deal with this point in Chapter 3.) Finally, this referendum, inappropriate as it patently was, was put in the usual silly perspective. Even this issue could have been better and more fairly stated if it had been presented in the context of priorities rather than simplistic dichotomies. There were no alternatives offered here, no cost-benefit analysis, just an inappropriate question badly asked.[18] I therefore, feel justified in turning my back on any implications drawn from such an example.

On the other hand, there are polls that do ask the American public to respond to items that approximate the plan suggested here. The most extensive and recent one of which I am aware was done in 1971 by John F. Kraft under the auspices of the American Business Committee on National Priorities.[19] The committee offered its sample population the opportunity to say whether the federal government should spend more or less on a set of fifteen items (education, medical care, national defense, housing, social security, the war in Indochina, welfare, air and water pollution, economic aid to friendly nations, urban problems, roads and highways, drug control, military aid to friendly nations, transportation, parks and open spaces). The sample appeared able to respond, and the "voters exhibited a marked concern for domestic as opposed to foreign and military matters." The voters indicated they would like to see more money spent on drug control, pollution control, education, medical care, social security, and parks and open spaces. They

**Voting on National Priorities**

listed the war in Indochina, military and economic aid to friendly nations, welfare, and national defense as the top choices for decreased federal spending.

The system proposed here is an attempt to harness such responses to the machinery of government in a reasonable and moderate manner in order to arrive at genuine directional changes, where such changes are indicated; to restore faith and legitimacy to democratic government; and at the same time to maintain the stability of as many institutions as possible and to avoid massive human dislocations.

This entire volume has been dedicated to the goal of stimulating thought both by describing some conflicts, and by presenting certain ideas that ought to generate other conflicts. Let me offer the following incomplete list of some of the more critical areas in which disagreement ought to be cherished and vigorously debated:

**Critical Areas**

1. We should reexamine the unarticulated myths of our society with a view to analyzing their possible implications for public policy and for the political institutions that make policy.

2. We should debate the possible operation of the concept of the self-fulfilling prophecy in many areas of public policy. We should also reassess the possible importance of other psychological perceptions and responses in many political situations.

3. We might consider the implications of a "future" orientation in many political policy-making arenas.

4. We should assess the need for resolving ambivalence about our basic value structures and our policy priorities. Indeed, *is* there any need to resolve political ambivalence, despite the viewpoint presented here?

5. We should argue the possibilities inherent in the concept of creative conflict across the entire spectrum of political institutions and their policy outputs.

6. We might profitably play out the implications of cost-benefit analysis in as many areas as possible.

7. Finally, we should reconsider the contending implications of market solutions versus management solutions in all of our various political decision arenas.

# APPENDIX

# CONSTITUTION
# OF THE UNITED STATES

We the People of the United States, in Order to form a more perfect Union, establish Justice, insure domestic Tranquility, provide for the common defense, promote the general Welfare, and secure the Blessings of Liberty to ourselves and our Posterity, do ordain and establish this Constitution for the United States of America.

**PREAMBLE**

---

Section 1.  All legislative Powers herein granted shall be vested in a Congress of the United States, which shall consist of a Senate and House of Representatives.

**I**
**ARTICLE**

Section 2.  The House of Representatives shall be composed of Members chosen every second Year by the People of the several States, and the Electors in each State shall have the Qualifications requisite for Electors of the most numerous Branch of the State Legislature.

No Person shall be a Representative who shall not have attained to the age of twenty-five Years, and been seven Years a Citizen of the United States, and who shall not, when elected, be an Inhabitant of that State in which he shall be chosen.

[Representatives and direct Taxes shall be apportioned among the several States which may be included within this Union, according to their respective Numbers, which shall be determined by adding to the whole Number of free Persons, including those bound to Service for a Term of Years, and excluding Indians not taxed, three fifths of all other Persons.] The actual Enumeration shall be made within three Years after the first Meeting of the Congress of the United States, and within every subsequent Term of ten Years, in such Manner as they shall by Law direct. The Number of Representatives shall not exceed one for every thirty Thousand, but each State shall have at Least One Representative; and until such enumeration shall be made, the State of New Hampshire shall be entitled to chuse three, Massachusetts eight, Rhode-Island and Providence Plantations one, Connecticut five, New York six, New Jersey four, Pennsylvania eight, Delaware one, Maryland six, Virginia ten, North Carolina five, South Carolina five, and Georgia three.

When vacancies happen in the Representation from any State, the Executive Authority thereof shall issue Writs of Election to fill such Vacancies.

The House of Representatives shall chuse their Speaker and other Officers; and shall have the sole Power of Impeachment.

Section 3. [The Senate of the United States shall be composed of two Senators from each State, chosen by the Legislature thereof, for six Years; and each Senator shall have one Vote.]

Immediately after they shall be assembled in Consequence of the first Election, they shall be divided as equally as may be into three Classes. The Seats of the Senators of the first Class shall be vacated at the Expiration of the second Year, of the second Class at the Expiration of the fourth Year, and of the third Class at the Expiration of the sixth Year, so that one third may be chosen every second Year; [and if Vacancies happen by Resignation, or otherwise, during the Recess of the Legislature of any State, the Executive thereof may make temporary Appointments until the next Meeting of the Legislature, which shall then fill such Vacancies.]

No person shall be a Senator who shall not have attained to the Age of thirty Years, and been nine Years a Citizen of the United States, and who shall not, when elected, be an Inhabitant of that State for which he shall be chosen.

The Vice President of the United States shall be President of the Senate, but shall have no Vote, unless they be equally divided.

The Senate shall chuse their other Officers, and also a President pro tempore, in the Absence of the Vice President, or when he shall exercise the Office of President of the United States.

The Senate shall have the sole Power to try all Impeachments. When sitting for that Purpose, they shall be on Oath or Affirmation. When the President of the United States is tried, the Chief Justice shall preside: And no Person shall be convicted without the Concurrence of two thirds of the Members present.

Judgment in Cases of Impeachment shall not extend further than to removal from Office, and disqualification to hold and enjoy any Office of honor, Trust or Profit under the United States: but the Party convicted shall nevertheless be liable and subject to Indictment, Trial, Judgment and Punishment, according to Law.

Section 4. The Times, Places and Manner of holding Elections for Senators and Representatives, shall be prescribed in each State by The Legislature thereof; but the Congress may at any time by Law make or alter such Regulations, except as to the Places of chusing Senators.

[The Congress shall assemble at least once in every Year, and such Meeting shall be on the first Monday in December, unless they shall by Law appoint a different Day.]

Section 5. Each House shall be the Judge of the Elections, Returns and Qualifications of its own Members, and a Majority of each shall constitute a Quorum to do Business; but a smaller Number may adjourn from day to day, and may be authorized to compel the Attendance of absent Members, in such Manner, and under such Penalties as each House may provide.

Each house may determine the Rules of its Proceedings, punish its Members for disorderly Behaviour, and, with the Concurrence of two thirds, expel a Member.

Each House shall keep a Journal of its Proceedings, and from time to time publish the same, excepting such Parts as may in their Judgment require Secrecy; and the Yeas and Nays of the Members of either House on any question shall, at the Desire of one fifth of those Present, be entered on the Journal.

Neither House, during the Session of Congress, shall, without the Consent of the other, adjourn for more than three days, nor to any other Place than that in which the two Houses shall be sitting.

Section 6. The Senators and Representatives shall receive a Compensation for their Services, to be ascertained by Law, and paid out of the Treasury of the United States. They shall in all Cases, except Treason, Felony and Breach of the Peace, be privileged from Arrest during their Attendance at the Session of their respective Houses, and in going to and returning from the same; and for any Speech or Debate in either House, they shall not be questioned in any other Place.

No Senator or Representative shall, during the Time for which he was elected, be appointed to any civil Office under the Authority of the United States, which shall have been created, or the Emoluments whereof shall have been encreased during such time; and no Person holding any Office under the United States, shall be a Member of either House during his Continuance in Office.

Section 7. All Bills for raising Revenue shall originate in the House of Representatives; but the Senate may propose or concur with Amendments as on other Bills.

Every Bill which shall have passed the House of Representatives and the Senate, shall, before it become a Law, be presented to the President of the United States; If he approve he shall sign it, but if not he shall return it, with his Objections to that House in which it shall have originated, who shall enter the Objections at large on their Journal, and proceed to reconsider it. If after such Reconsideration two thirds of that House shall agree to pass the Bill, it shall be sent, together with the Objections, to the other House, by which it shall likewise be reconsidered, and if approved by two thirds of that House, it shall become a Law. But in all such Cases the Votes of both Houses shall be determined by yeas and Nays, and the Names of the Persons voting for and against the Bill shall be entered on the Journal of each House respectively. If any Bill shall not be returned by the President within ten Days (Sundays excepted) after it shall have been presented to him, the Same shall be a Law, in like Manner as if he had signed it, unless the Congress by their Adjournment prevent its Return, in which Case it shall not be a Law.

Every Order, Resolution, or Vote to which the Concurrence of the Senate and House of Representatives may be necessary (except on a question of Adjournment) shall be presented to the President of the United States; and before the Same shall take Effect, shall be approved by him, or being disapproved by him, shall be repassed by two thirds of the Senate and House of Representatives, according to the Rules and Limitations prescribed in the Case of a Bill.

Section 8. The Congress shall have Power To lay and collect Taxes, Duties, Imposts and Excises, to pay the Debts and provide

**I
ARTICLE
(cont.)**

for the common Defence and general Welfare of the United States; but all Duties, Imposts and Excises shall be uniform throughout the United States;

To borrow Money on the credit of the United States;

To regulate Commerce with foreign Nations, and among the several States and with the Indian Tribes;

To establish an uniform Rule of Naturalization, and uniform Laws on the subject of Bankruptcies throughout the United States;

To coin Money, regulate the Value thereof, and of foreign Coin, and fix the Standard of Weights and Measures;

To provide for the Punishment of counterfeiting the Securities and current Coin of the United States;

To establish Post Offices and post Roads;

To promote the Progress of Science and useful Arts, by securing for limited Times to Authors and Inventors the exclusive Right to their respective Writings and Discoveries;

To constitute Tribunals inferior to the supreme Court;

To define and punish Piracies and Felonies committed on the high Seas, and Offences against the Law of Nations;

To declare War, grant Letters of Marque and Reprisal, and make Rules concerning Captures on Land and Water;

To raise and support Armies, but no Appropriation of Money to that Use shall be for a longer Term than two Years;

To provide and maintain a Navy;

To make Rules for the Government and Regulation of the land and naval Forces;

To provide for calling forth the Militia to execute the Laws of the Union, suppress Insurrections and repel Invasions;

To provide for organizing, arming, and disciplining, the Militia, and for governing such Part of them as may be employed in the Service of the United States, reserving to the States respectively, the Appointment of the Officers, and the Authority of training the Militia according to the discipline prescribed by Congress;

To exercise exclusive Legislation in all Cases whatsoever, over such District (not exceeding ten Miles square) as may, by Cession of particular States, and the Acceptance of Congress, become the Seat of the Government of the United States, and to exercise like Authority over all Places purchased by the Consent of the Legislature of the State in which the Same shall be, for the Erection of Forts, Magazines, Arsenals, dock-Yards, and other needful Buildings; — And

To make all Laws which shall be necessary and proper for carrying into Execution the foregoing Powers, and all other Powers vested by this Constitution in the Government of the United States, or in any Department or Officer thereof.

Section 9. The Migration or Importation of such Persons as any of the States now existing shall think proper to admit, shall not be prohibited by the Congress prior to the Year one thousand eight hundred and eight, but a Tax or duty may be imposed on such Importation, not exceeding ten dollars for each Person.

The Privilege of the Writ of Habeas Corpus shall not be suspended, unless when in Cases of Rebellion or Invasion the public Safety may require it.

No Bill of Attainder or ex post facto Law shall be passed.

No Capitation, or other direct, Tax shall be laid, unless in Proportion to the Census or Enumeration herein before directed to be taken.

No Tax or Duty shall be laid on Articles exported from any State.

No Preference shall be given by any Regulation of Commerce or Revenue to the Ports of one State over those of another: nor shall Vessels bound to, or from, one State, be obliged to enter, clear or pay Duties in another.

No Money shall be drawn from the Treasury, but in Consequence of Appropriations made by Law; and a regular Statement and Account of the Receipts and Expenditures of all public Money shall be published from time to time.

No Title of Nobility shall be granted by the United States: And no Person holding any Office of Profit or Trust under them, shall, without the Consent of the Congress, accept of any present, Emolument, Office, or Title, of any kind whatever, from any King, Prince, or foreign State.

Section 10.   No State shall enter into any Treaty, Alliance, or Confederation; grant Letters of Marque and Reprisal; coin Money; emit Bills of Credit; make any Thing but gold and silver Coin a Tender in Payment of Debts; pass any Bill of Attainder, ex post facto Law, or Law impairing the Obligation of Contracts, or grant any Title of Nobility.

No State shall, without the Consent of the Congress, lay any Imposts or Duties on Imports or Exports, except what may be absolutely necessary for executing it's inspection Laws: and the net Produce of all Duties and Imposts, laid by any State on Imports or Exports, shall be for the Use of the Treasury of the United States; and all such Laws shall be subject to the Revision and Controul of the Congress.

No State shall, without the Consent of Congress, lay any Duty of Tonnage, keep Troops, or Ships of War in time of Peace, enter into any Agreement or Compact with another State, or with a foreign Power, or engage in War, unless actually invaded, or in such imminent Danger as will not admit of delay.

**I
ARTICLE
(cont.)**

---

Section 1.   The executive Power shall be vested in a President of the United States of America. He shall hold his Office during the Term of four Years, and, together with the Vice President, chosen for the same Term, be elected, as follows

Each State shall appoint, in such Manner as the Legislature thereof may direct, a Number of Electors, equal to the whole Number of Senators and Representatives to which the State may be entitled in the Congress: but no Senator or Representative, or Person holding an Office of Trust or Profit under the United States, shall be appointed an Elector.

[The Electors shall meet in their respective States, and vote by Ballot for two Persons, of whom one at least shall not be an Inhabitant of the same State with themselves. And they shall make a List of all the Persons voted for, and of the Number of Votes for

**II
ARTICLE**

each; which List they shall sign and certify, and transmit sealed to the Seat of the Government of the United States, directed to the President of the Senate. The President of the Senate shall, in the Presence of the Senate and House of Representatives, open all the Certificates, and the Votes shall then be counted. The Person having the greatest Number of Votes shall be the President, if such Number be a Majority of the whole Number of Electors appointed; and if there be more than one who have such Majority, and have an equal Number of Votes, then the House of Representatives shall immediately chuse by Ballot one of them for President; and if no Person have a Majority, then from the five highest on the List the said House shall in like Manner chuse the President. But in chusing the President, the Votes shall be taken by States, the Representation from each State having one Vote; A quorum for this Purpose shall consist of a Member or Members from two thirds of the States, and a Majority of all the States shall be necessary to a Choice. In every Case, after the Choice of the President, the Person having the greatest Number of Votes of the Electors shall be the Vice President. But if there should remain two or more who have equal Votes, the Senate shall chuse from them by Ballot the Vice President.]

The Congress may determine the Time of chusing the Electors, and the Day on which they shall give their Votes; which Day shall be the same throughout the United States.

No person except a natural born Citizen, or a Citizen of the United States, at the time of the Adoption of this Constitution, shall be eligible to the Office of President; neither shall any Person be eligible to that Office who shall not have attained to the Age of thirty five Years, and been fourteen Years a Resident within the United States.

In Case of the Removal of the President from Office, or of his Death, Resignation, or Inability to discharge the Powers and Duties of the said Office, the Same shall devolve on the Vice President, and the Congress may by Law provide for the Case of Removal, Death, Resignation or Inability, both of the President and Vice President, declaring what Officer shall then act as President, and such Officer shall act accordingly, until the Disability be removed, or a President shall be elected.

The President shall, at stated Times, receive for his Services, a Compensation, which shall neither be encreased nor diminished during the Period for which he shall have been elected, and he shall not receive within that Period any other Emolument from the United States, or any of them.

Before he enter on the Execution of his Office, he shall take the following Oath or Affirmation:—"I do solemnly swear (or affirm) that I will faithfully execute the Office of President of the United States, and will to the best of my Ability, preserve, protect and defend the Constitution of the United States."

Section 2. The President shall be Commander in Chief of the Army and Navy of the United States, and of the Militia of the several States, when called into the actual Service of the United States; he may require the Opinion, in writing, of the principal Officer in each of the executive Departments, upon any Subject relating to the Duties of their respective Offices, and he shall have Power to grant Reprieves and Pardons for Offences against the United States, except in Cases of Impeachment.

He shall have Power, by and with the Advice and Consent of the Senate, to make Treaties, provided two thirds of the Senators present concur; and he shall nominate, and by and with the Advice and Consent of the Senate, shall appoint Ambassadors, other public Ministers and Consuls, Judges of the supreme Court, and all other Officers of the United States, whose Appointments are not herein otherwise provided for, and which shall be established by Law: but the Congress may by Law vest the Appointment of such inferior Officers, as they think proper, in the President alone, in the Courts of Law, or in the Heads of Departments.

The President shall have Power to fill up all Vacancies that may happen during the Recess of the Senate, by granting Commissions which shall expire at the End of their next Session.

Section 3. He shall from time to time give to the Congress Information of the State of the Union, and recommend to their Consideration such Measures as he shall judge necessary and expedient; he may, on extraordinary Occasions, convene both Houses, or either of them, and in Case of Disagreement between them, with Respect to the Time of Adjournment, he may adjourn them to such Times as he shall think proper; he shall receive Ambassadors and other public Ministers; he shall take Care that the Laws be faithfully executed, and shall Commission all the Officers of the United States.

Section 4. The President, Vice President and all civil Officers of the United States, shall be removed from Office on Impeachment for, and Conviction of, Treason, Bribery, or other high Crimes and misdemeanors.

---

Section 1. The judicial Power of the United States, shall be vested in one supreme Court, and in such inferior Courts as the Congress may from time to time ordain and establish. The Judges, both of the supreme and inferior Courts, shall hold their Offices during good Behaviour, and shall, at stated Times, receive for their Services, a Compensation, which shall not be diminished during their Continuance in Office.

Section 2. The judicial Power shall extend to all Cases, in Law and Equity, arising under this Constitution, the Laws of the United States, and Treaties made, or which shall be made, under their Authority; — to all Cases affecting Ambassodors, other public Ministers and Consuls; — to all Cases of admiralty and maritime Jurisdiction; — to Controversies to which the United States shall be a Party; — to Controversies between two or more States; — between a State and Citizens of another State; — between citizens of different States; — between Citizens of the same State claiming Lands under Grants of different States, and between a State, or the Citizens thereof, and foreign States, Citizens or Subjects.

In all Cases affecting Ambassadors, other public Ministers and Consuls, and those in which a State shall be Party, the supreme Court shall have original Jurisdiction. In all the other Cases before

**III
ARTICLE
(cont.)**

mentioned, the supreme Court shall have appellate Jurisdiction, both as to Law and Fact, with such Exceptions, and under such Regulations as the Congress shall make.

The Trial of all Crimes, except in Cases of Impeachment, shall be by Jury; and such Trial shall be held in the State where the said Crimes shall have been committed; but when not committed within any State, the Trial shall be at such Place or Places as the Congress may by Law have directed.

Section 3. Treason against the United States, shall consist only in levying War against them, or in adhering to their Enemies, giving them Aid and Comfort. No Person shall be convicted of Treason unless on the Testimony of two Witnesses to the same overt Act, or on Confession in open Court.

The Congress shall have Power to declare the Punishment of Treason, but no Attainder of Treason shall work Corruption of Blood, or Forfeiture except during the Life of the Person attainted.

---

**IV
ARTICLE**

Section 1. Full Faith and Credit shall be given in each State to the public Acts, Records, and judicial Proceedings of every other State. And the Congress may by general Laws prescribe the Manner in which such Acts, Records and Proceedings shall be proved, and the Effect thereof.

Section 2. The Citizens of each State shall be entitled to all Privileges and Immunities of Citizens in the several States.

A Person charged in any State with Treason, Felony, or other Crime, who shall flee from Justice, and be found in another State, shall on Demand of the executive Authority of the State from which he fled, be delivered up, to be removed to the State having Jurisdiction of the Crime.

No Person held to Service or Labour in one State, under the Laws thereof, escaping into another, shall, in Consequence of any Law or Regulation therein, be discharged from such Service or Labour, but shall be delivered up on Claim of the Party to whom such Service or Labour may be due.

Section 3. New States may be admitted by the Congress into this Union; but no new State shall be formed or erected within the Jurisdiction of any other State; nor any State be formed by the Junction of two or more States, or Parts of States, without the Consent of the Legislatures of the States concerned as well as of the Congress.

The Congress shall have Power to dispose of and make all needful Rules and Regulations respecting the Territory or other Property belonging to the United States; and nothing in this Constitution shall be so construed as to Prejudice any Claims of the United States, or of any particular State.

Section 4. The United States shall guarantee to every State in this Union a Republican Form of Government, and shall protect each of them against Invasion; and on Application of the Legislature, or of the Executive (when the Legislature cannot be convened) against domestic Violence.

The Congress, whenever two thirds of both Houses shall deem it necessary, shall propose Amendments to this Constitution, or, on the Application of the Legislatures of two thirds of the several States, shall call a Convention for proposing Amendments, which, in either Case, shall be valid to all Intents and Purposes, as Part of this Constitution, when ratified by the Legislatures of three fourths of the several States, or by Conventions in three fourths thereof, as the one or the other Mode of Ratification may be proposed by the Congress; Provided that no Amendment which may be made prior to the Year One thousand eight hundred and eight shall in any Manner affect the first and fourth clauses in the Ninth Section of the first Article; and that no State, without its Consent, shall be deprived of it's equal Suffrage in the Senate.

**ARTICLE V**

---

All Debts contracted and Engagements entered into, before the Adoption of this Constitution, shall be as valid against the United States under this Constitution, as under the Confederation.

This Constitution, and the Laws of the United States which shall be made in Pursuance thereof; and all Treaties made, or which shall be made, under the Authority of the United States, shall be the supreme Law of the Land; and the Judges in every State shall be bound thereby, any Thing in the Constitution or Laws of any State to the Contrary notwithstanding.

The Senators and Representatives before mentioned, and the Members of the several State Legislatures, and all executive and judicial Officers, both of the United States and of the several States, shall be bound by Oath or Affirmation, to support this Constitution; but no religious Test shall ever be required as a Qualification to any Office or public Trust under the United States.

**ARTICLE VI**

---

The Ratification of the Conventions of nine States, shall be sufficient for the Establishment of this Constitution between the States so ratifying the Same.

done in Convention by the Unanimous Consent of the States present the Seventeenth Day of September in the Year of our Lord one thousand seven hundred and Eighty seven and of the Independance of the United States of America the Twelfth. In witness whereof We have hereunto subscribed our Names,

**ARTICLE VII**

Go: WASHINGTON, — Presidt.
and deputy from Virginia

| New Hampshire | JOHN LANGDON |
| | NICHOLAS GILMAN |

| Massachusetts | NATHANIEL GORHAM |
| | RUFUS KING |

| Connecticut | WM: SAML. JOHNSON |
| | ROGER SHERMAN |

| New York | ALEXANDER HAMILTON |

| | |
|---|---|
| New Jersey | WIL: LIVINGSTON<br>DAVID BREARLEY<br>WM. PATERSON.<br>JONA: DAYTON |
| Pennsylvania | B FRANKLIN<br>THOMAS MIFFLIN<br>ROBT MORRIS<br>GEO. CLYMER<br>THOS. FITZSIMONS<br>JARED INGERSOLL<br>JAMES WILSON<br>GOUV MORRIS |
| Delaware | GEO: READ<br>GUNNING BEDFORD jun<br>JOHN DICKINSON<br>RICHARD BASSETT<br>JACO: BROOM |
| Maryland | JAMES MCHENRY<br>DAN OF ST THOS. JENIFER<br>DANL CARROLL |
| Virginia | JOHN BLAIR—<br>JAMES MADISON, JR. |
| North Carolina | WM. BLOUNT<br>RICHD. DOBBS SPAIGHT<br>HU WILLIAMSON |
| South Carolina | J. RUTLEDGE<br>CHARLES COTESWORTH PINCKNEY<br>CHARLES PINCKNEY<br>PIERCE BUTLER |
| Georgia | WILLIAM FEW<br>ABR BALDWIN |

In Convention Monday, September 17th 1787.

Present

The States of

New Hampshire, Massachusetts, Connecticut, Mr. Hamilton from New York, New Jersey, Pennsylvania, Delaware, Maryland, Virginia, North Carolina, South Carolina and Georgia.
Resolved,

That the preceding Constitution be laid before the United States in Congress assembled, and that it is the Opinion of this Convention, that it should afterwards be submitted to a Convention of Delegates, chosen in each State by the People thereof, under the Recommendation of its Legislature, for their Assent and Ratification; and that each Convention assenting to, and ratifying the Same, should give Notice thereof to the United States in-Congress assembled. Resolved, That it is the Opinion of this Convention, that as soon as the Conventions of nine States shall have ratified this Constitution, the United States in Congress assembled should fix a Day on which Electors should be appointed by the States which shall have ratified the same, and a Day on which the Electors should assemble to vote for the President, and the Time and Place for commencing Proceedings under this Constitution. That after such Publication the Electors should be appointed, and the Senators and Representatives elected: That the Electors should meet on the Day fixed for the Election of the President, and should transmit their Votes certified, signed, sealed and directed, as the Constitution requires, to the Secretary of the United States in Congress assembled, that the Senators and Representatives should convene at the Time and Place assigned; that the Senators should appoint a President of the Senate, for the sole Purpose of receiving opening and counting the Votes for President; and, that after he shall be chosen, the Congress, together with the President, should, without Delay, proceed to execute this Constitution.

By the Unanimous Order of the Convention

Go: WASHINGTON Presidt.

W. JACKSON Secretary.

ARTICLES IN ADDITION TO, AND AMENDMENT OF, THE CONSTITUTION OF THE UNITED STATES OF AMERICA, PROPOSED BY CONGRESS, AND RATIFIED BY THE SEVERAL STATES, PURSUANT TO THE FIFTH ARTICLE OF THE ORIGINAL CONSTITUTION.

**I AMENDMENT**

Congress shall make no law respecting an establishment of religion, or prohibiting the free exercise thereof; or abridging the freedom of speech, or of the press; or the right of the people peaceably to assemble, and to petition the Government for a redress of grievances.

**II AMENDMENT**

A well regulated Militia, being necessary to the security of a free State, the right of the people to keep and bear Arms, shall not be infringed.

**III AMENDMENT**

No Soldier shall, in time of peace be quartered in any house, without the consent of the Owner, nor in time of war, but in a manner to be prescribed by law.

**IV AMENDMENT**

The right of the people to be secure in their persons, houses, papers, and effects, against unreasonable searches and seizures, shall not be violated, and no Warrants shall issue, but upon probable cause, supported by Oath or affirmation, and particularly describing the place to be searched, and the persons or things to be seized.

**V AMENDMENT**

No person shall be held to answer for a capital, or otherwise infamous crime, unless on a presentment or indictment of a Grand Jury, except in cases arising in the land or naval forces, or in the Militia, when in actual service in time of War or public danger; nor shall any person be subject for the same offence to be twice put in jeopardy of life or limb; nor shall be compelled in any criminal case to be a witness against himself, nor be deprived of life, liberty, or property, without due process of law; nor shall private property be taken for public use, without just compensation.

**VI AMENDMENT**

In all criminal prosecutions, the accused shall enjoy the right to a speedy and public trial, by an impartial jury of the State and district wherein the crime shall have been committed, which district shall have been previously ascertained by law, and to be informed of the nature and cause of the accusation; to be confronted with the witnesses against him; to have compulsory process for obtaining witnesses in his favor, and to have the Assistance of Counsel for his defence.

**VII AMENDMENT**

In Suits at common law, where the value in controversy shall exceed twenty dollars, the right of trial by jury shall be preserved, and no fact tried by a jury, shall be otherwise re-examined in any Court of the United States, than according to the rules of the common law.

Excessive bail shall not be required, nor excessive fines imposed, nor cruel and unusual punishments inflicted.

**VIII AMENDMENT**

The enumeration in the Constitution, of certain rights, shall not be construed to deny or disparage others retained by the people.

**IX AMENDMENT**

The powers not delegated to the United States by the Constitution, nor prohibited by it to the States, are reserved to the States respectively, or to the people.

**X AMENDMENT**

The Judicial power of the United States shall not be construed to extend to any suit in law or equity, commenced or prosecuted against one of the United States by Citizens of another State, or by Citizens or Subjects of any Foreign State.

**XI AMENDMENT**

The Electors shall meet in their respective states and vote by ballot for President and Vice-President, one of whom, at least, shall not be an inhabitant of the same state with themselves; they shall name in their ballots the person voted for as President, and in distinct ballots the person voted for as Vice-President, and they shall make distinct lists of all persons voted for as President, and of all persons voted for as Vice-President, and of the number of votes for each, which lists they shall sign and certify, and transmit sealed to the seat of the government of the United States, directed to the President of the Senate; — The President of the Senate shall, in the presence of the Senate and House of Representatives, open all the certificates and the votes shall then be counted; — The person having the greatest number of votes for President, shall be the President, if such number be a majority of the whole number of Electors appointed; and if no person have such majority, then from the persons having the highest numbers not exceeding three on the list of those voted for as President, the House of Representatives shall choose immediately, by ballot, the President. But in choosing the President, the votes shall be taken by states, the representation from each state having one vote; a quorum for this purpose shall consist of a member or members from two-thirds of the states, and a majority of all the states shall be necessary to a choice. And if the House of Representatives shall not choose a President whenever the right of choice shall devolve upon them, before the fourth day of March next following, then the Vice-President, shall act as president, as in the case of the death or other constitutional disability of the President. — The person having the greatest number of votes as Vice-President, shall be the Vice-President, if such number be a majority of the whole number of Electors appointed, and if no person have a majority, then from

**XII AMENDMENT**

the two highest numbers on the list, the Senate shall choose the Vice-President; a quorum for the purpose shall consist of two-thirds of the whole numbers of Senators, and a majority of the whole number shall be necessary to a choice. But no person constitutionally ineligible to the office of President shall be eligible to that of Vice-President of the United States.

XIII AMENDMENT

SECTION 1. Neither slavery nor involuntary servitude, except as a punishment for crime whereof the party shall have been duly convicted, shall exist within the United States, or any place subject to their jurisdiction.

SECTION 2. Congress shall have power to enforce this article by appropriate legislation.

XIV AMENDMENT

SECTION 1. All persons born or naturalized in the United States, and subject to the jurisdiction thereof, are citizens of the United States and of the State wherein they reside. No State shall make or enforce any law which shall abridge the privileges or immunities of citizens of the United States; nor shall any State deprive any person of life, liberty, or property, without due process of law; nor deny to any person within its jurisdiction the equal protection of the laws.

SECTION 2. Representatives shall be apportioned among the several States according to their respective numbers, counting the whole number of persons in each State, excluding Indians not taxed. But when the right to vote at any election for the choice of electors for President and Vice President of the United States, Representatives in Congress, the Executive and Judicial officers of a State, or the members of the Legislature thereof, is denied to any of the male inhabitants of such State, being twenty-one years of age, and citizens of the United States, or in any way abridged except for participation in rebellion, or other crime, the basis of representation therein shall be reduced in the proportion which the number of such male citizens shall bear to the whole number of male citizens twenty-one years of age in such State.

SECTION 3. No person shall be a Senator or Representative in Congress, or elector of President and Vice President, or hold any office, civil or military, under the United States, or under any State, who, having previously taken an oath, as a member of Congress, or as an officer of the United States, or as a member of any State legislature, or as an executive or judicial officer of any State, to support the Constitution of the United States, shall have engaged in insurrection or rebellion against the same, or given aid or comfort to the enemies thereof. But Congress may by a vote of two-thirds of each House, remove such disability.

SECTION 4. The validity of the public debt of the United States, authorized by law, including debts incurred for payment of pensions and bounties for services in suppressing insurrection or rebellion, shall not be questioned. But neither the United States nor any State shall assume or pay any debt or obligation incurred in aid of insurrection or rebellion against the United States, or any claim for the loss or emancipation of any slave; but all such debts, obligations and claims shall be held illegal and void.

SECTION 5.   The Congress shall have power to enforce, by appropriate legislation, the provisions of this article.

---

SECTION 1.   The right of citizens of the United States to vote shall not be denied or abridged by the United States or by any State on account of race, color, or previous condition of servitude.

SECTION 2.   The Congress shall have power to enforce this article by appropriate legislation.

**XV AMENDMENT**

---

The Congress shall have power to lay and collect taxes on incomes, from whatever source derived, without apportionment among the several States, and without regard to any census or enumeration.

**XVI AMENDMENT**

---

The Senate of the United States shall be composed of two Senators from each State, elected by the people thereof, for six years; and each Senator shall have one vote. The electors in each State shall have the qualifications requisite for electors of the most numerous branch of the State legislatures.

When vacancies happen in the representation of any State in the Senate, the executive authority of such State shall issue writs of election to fill such vacancies: *Provided*, That the legislature of any State may empower the executive thereof to make temporary appointments until the people fill the vacancies by election as the legislature may direct.

This amendment shall not be so construed as to affect the election or term of any Senator chosen before it becomes valid as part of the Constitution.

**XVII AMENDMENT**

---

Repealed. See Amendment XXI, post.

**XVIII AMENDMENT**

---

The right of citizens of the United States to vote shall not be denied or abridged by the United States or by any State on account of sex.

Congress shall have power to enforce this article by appropriate legislation.

**XIX AMENDMENT**

---

SECTION 1.   The terms of the President and Vice President shall end at noon on the 20th day of January, and the terms of Senators and Representatives at noon on the 3d day of January, of the years in which such terms would have ended if this article had not been ratified; and the terms of their successors shall then begin.

SECTION 2.   The Congress shall assemble at least once in every year, and such meeting shall begin at noon on the 3d day of January, unless they shall by law appoint a different day.

**XX AMENDMENT**

SECTION 3. If, at the time fixed for the beginning of the term of the President, the President elect shall have died, the Vice President elect shall become President. If a President shall not have been chosen before the time fixed for the beginning of his term, or if the President elect shall have failed to qualify, then the Vice President elect shall act as President until a President shall have qualified; and the Congress may by law provide for the case wherein neither a President elect nor a Vice President elect shall have qualified, declaring who shall then act as President, or the manner in which one who is to act shall be selected, and such person shall act accordingly until a President or Vice President shall have qualified.

SECTION 4. The Congress may by law provide for the case of the death of any of the persons from whom the House of Representatives may choose a President whenever the right of choice shall have devolved upon them, and for the case of the death of any of the persons from whom the Senate may choose a Vice President whenever the right of choice shall have devolved upon them.

SECTION 5. Sections 1 and 2 shall take effect on the 15th day of October following the ratification of this article.

SECTION 6. This article shall be inoperative unless it shall have been ratified as an amendment to the Constitution by the legislatures of three-fourths of the several States within seven years from the date of its submission.

---

**XXI AMENDMENT**

SECTION 1. The eighteenth article of amendment to the Constitution of the United States is hereby repealed.

SECTION 2. The transportation or importation into any State, Territory, or possession of the United States for delivery or use therein of intoxicating liquors, in violation of the laws thereof, is hereby prohibited.

SECTION 3. This article shall be inoperative unless it shall have been ratified as an amendment to the Constitution by conventions in the several States, as provided in the Constitution, within seven years from the date of the submission hereof to the States by the Congress.

---

**XXII AMENDMENT**

SECTION 1. No person shall be elected to the office of the President more than twice, and no person who has held the office of President, or acted as President, for more than two years of a term to which some other person was elected President shall be elected to the office of the President more than once. But this Article shall not apply to any person holding the office of President when this Article was proposed by the Congress, and shall not prevent any person who may be holding the office of President, or acting as President, during the term within which this Article becomes operative from holding the office of President or acting as President during the remainder of such term.

SECTION 2. This article shall be inoperative unless it shall have been ratified as an amendment to the Constitution by the legislatures of three-fourths of the several States within seven years from the date of its submission to the States by the Congress.

---

SECTION 1. The District constituting the seat of Government of the United States shall appoint in such manner as the Congress may direct:

A number of electors of President and Vice President equal to the whole number of Senators and Representatives in Congress to which the District would be entitled if it were a State, but in no event more than the least populous State; they shall be in addition to those appointed by the States, but they shall be considered, for the purposes of the election of President and Vice President, to be electors appointed by a State; and they shall meet in the District and perform such duties as provided by the twelfth article of amendment.

SECTION 2. The Congress shall have power to enforce this article by appropriate legislation.

**XXIII AMENDMENT**

---

SECTION 1. The right of citizens of the United States to vote in any primary or other election for President or Vice President, for electors for President or Vice President, or for Senator or Representative in Congress, shall not be denied or abridged by the United States or any State by reason of failure to pay any poll tax or other tax.

SECTION 2. The Congress shall have power to enforce this article by appropriate legislation.

**XXIV AMENDMENT**

---

SECTION 1. In case of the removal of the President from office or of his death or resignation, the Vice President shall become President.

SECTION 2. Whenever there is a vacancy in the office of the Vice President, the President shall nominate a Vice President who shall take office upon confirmation by a majority vote of both Houses of Congress.

SECTION 3. Whenever the President transmits to the President pro tempore of the Senate and the Speaker of the House of Representatives his written declaration that he is unable to discharge the powers and duties of his office, and until he transmits to them a written declaration to the contrary, such powers and duties shall be discharged by the Vice President as Acting President.

SECTION 4. Whenever the Vice President and a majority of either the principal officers of the executive departments or of such other body as Congress may by law provide, transmit to the President pro tempore of the Senate and the Speaker of the House of Representatives their written declaration that the President is unable to discharge the powers and duties of his office, the Vice President shall immediately assume the powers and duties of the office as Acting President.

Thereafter, when the President transmits to the President pro tempore of the Senate and the Speaker of the House of Represen-

**XXV AMENDMENT**

tatives his written declaration that no inability exists, he shall resume the powers and duties of his office unless the Vice President
and a majority of either the principal officers of the executive department or of such other body as Congress may by law provide,
transmit within four days to the President pro tempore of the Senate and the Speaker of the House of Representatives their written
declaration that the President is unable to discharge the powers
and duties of his office. Thereupon Congress shall decide the issue, assembling within forty-eight hours for that purpose if not in
session. If the Congress, within twenty-one days after receipt of
the latter written declaration, or, if Congress is not in session,
within twenty-one days after Congress is required to assemble,
determines by two-thirds vote of both Houses that the President is
unable to discharge the powers and duties of his office, the Vice
President shall continue to discharge the same as Acting President; otherwise, the President shall resume the powers and duties
of his office.

**XXVI AMENDMENT**

SECTION 1. The right of citizens of the United States, who
are eighteen years of age or older, to vote shall not be denied
or abridged by the United States or by any State on account of
age.

SECTION 2. The Congress shall have power to enforce this
article by appropriate legislation.

**PROPOSED AMEND-MENTS**

## PROPOSED AMENDMENTS TO THE CONSTITUTION OF THE UNITED STATES

### Article——

Section 1. The Congress shall have power to limit, regulate,
and prohibit the labor of persons under eighteen years of age.

Section 2. The power of the several States is unimpaired by
this article except that the operation of State laws shall be suspended to the extent necessary to give effect to legislation enacted
by the Congress.

Proposed by the Sixty-Eighth Congress on June 2, 1924.

### Article —

Section 1. Equality of rights under the law shall not be denied or abridged by the United States or by any State on account
of sex.

Section 2. The Congress shall have the power to enforce, by
appropriate legislation, the provisions of this article.

Section 3. This amendment shall take effect two years after
the date of ratification."

Proposed by the 92nd Congress March 22, 1972.

1. Harold Lasswell, *Who Gets What, When, and How?* (New York: McGraw-Hill, 1936).

2. See S. F. Nagel, *The Theory of Social Structures* (Glencoe, Ill.: Fress Press, 1957); Talcott Parsons, *The Social System* (New York: Free Press of Glencoe, Macmillan, 1959); Robert K. Merton, *Social Theory and Social Structures* (Glencoe, Ill.: Free Press, 1957); C. Wright Mills, *The Power Elite* (New York: Oxford University Press, 1957).

3. See Paul A. Samuelson, *Economics* (New York: McGraw-Hill, 1971); John Kenneth Galbraith, *The Affluent Society* (Boston: Houghton Mifflin, 1958).

4. See David Easton, *A Systems Analysis of Political Life* (New York: Wiley, 1965); Robert Dahl, *Who Governs?* (New Haven: Yale University Press, 1961); Norton Long, *The Polity* (Chicago: Rand McNally, 1962).

5. See Erving Goffman, *The Presentation of Self in Everyday Life* (New York: Doubleday, 1959); Karen Horney, *The Neurotic Personality of Our Time* (New York: Norton, 1937); Rollo May, *Man's Search for Himself* (New York: Norton, 1953).

6. Sigmund Freud, *New Introductory Lectures on Psychoanalysis* (New York: Norton, 1933).

7. Leon Festinger, *A Theory of Cognitive Dissonance* (Evanston, Ill.: Row, Peterson, 1957).

8. Bertram M. Gross, *The State of the Nation* (London: Travistock, 1966), p. 30.

**CHAPTER 1**

1. William P. Burch, *Daydreams and Nightmares* (New York: Harper & Row, 1971), p. 51 (italics mine).

2. John Q. Wilson and Edward C. Bonfield, "Public Regardingness as a Value Premise in Voting Behavior," *American Political Science Review*, 58 (December 1964): 871–77.

3. Paul A. Samuelson, *Economics*, 8th ed. (New York: McGraw-Hill, 1970), p. 17.

4. "War Tax Resistance," mimeographed (New York, 1971).

5. *New York Times*, August 4, 1970, p. 30.

6. Seymour Melman, "Cost of Militarism," *New York Times*, November 3, 1970, p. 35.

7. Roland A. Paul, "The $10 Billion Misunderstanding," *New York Times*, February 12, 1971, p. 37.

8. *New York Times*, August 26, 1971, p. 36.

9. Abraham H. Maslow, "A Dynamic Theory of Motivation," *Psychological Review*, 50 (1943): 370–96.

10. Edward Banks, *Endeavor Journal*, ed. John Beaglehole (London: Angus & Robertson, 1963), 2:130.

**CHAPTER 2**

11. Lewis Mumford, "Transportation I," *New York Times*, March 15, 1971, p. 37.

12. Such works include Chris Argyris, *Integrating the Individual and the Organization* (N.Y.: Wiley, 1964); Alvin Gouldner, *Patterns of Industrial Bureaucracy* (Glencoe, Ill.: Free Press, 1954); Warren Bennis, *Changing Organizations* (N.Y.: McGraw-Hill, 1966).

13. General Mark Clark, "No Retreat in South East Asia," *New York Times*, February 24, 1971, p. 41.

14. Samuelson, *Economics*, p. 669.

15. Ibid.

16. Ibid., p. 804.

17. Ralph K. White, *Nobody Wanted War* (New York: Doubleday, 1970).

18. T. W. Adorno et al., *The Authoritarian Personality* (New York: Harper, 1950).

19. White, *Nobody Wanted War*, p. 244.

20. Ibid., p. 249.

21. Robert Rosenthal and Lenore Jacobson, *Pygmalion in the Classroom* (N.Y.: Holt, Rinehart & Winston, 1968), pp. 61–71, 174–82.

22. David Binder, "Feeling of Neighbors on Germans Still Mixed," *New York Times*, May 12, 1971, p. 1.

23. Konrad Lorenz, *On Aggression* (New York: Harcourt, Brace & World, 1963).

24. John G. Stoessinger, "Toward Reality," *New York Times*, July 31, 1971, p. 23.

25. Stoessinger, *Nations in Darkness* (N.Y.: Random House, 1971)

26. Herman Kahn and G. R. Urban, "Most of Traditional Causes of War Have Disappeared," *New York Times Magazine*, June 20, 1971, p. 13.

27. Lewis Mumford, "Transportation and Human Enrichment," *New York Times*, March 16, 1971, p. 37.

**CHAPTER 3**

1. Alexander Hamilton, John Jay, and James Madison, *The Federalist* (New York: Modern Library, Random House, 1937).

2. *Baker* v. *Carr*, 396 U.S. 186 (1962).

3. Robert Dahl, *Who Governs?; Democracy and Power in an American City* (New Haven: Yale Univ. Press, 1961), pp. 276–325.

4. *New York Times Magazine*, August 3, 1969.

5. CBS News poll, "Public Attitudes Toward the Bill of Rights," March 20, 1970.

6. Ibid.

7. *Gitlow* v. *New York*, 268 U.S. 652 (1925).

8. *Thornhill* v. *Alabama*, 310 U.S. 88 (1940).

9. *Burstyn* v. *Wilson*, 343 U.S. 495 (1952).

10. *West Virginia State Board of Education* v. *Barnette*, 319 U.S. 624 (1943).

11. *Tinker* v. *Des Moines Independent Community School District*, 393 U.S. 503 (1961).

12. *Schenck* v. *United States*, 249 U.S. 47 (1919).

13. *Dennis* v. *New York*, 341 U.S. 494 (1951).

14. *Yates* v. *United States*, 354 U.S. 298 (1957).

15. A classified U.S. government publication formally entitled *History of United States Decision-Making Process on Viet Nam Policy*. The two cases dealing with the leak of these materials are *New York Times* v. *United States*, and *United States* v. *Washington Post Company et al.*, 29 L.Ed. 2nd 822 (1971).

16. *Roth* v. *United States,* 354 U.S. 476 (1957) and *Alberts* v. *California,* 354 U.S. 476 (1957).

17. *Burstyn* v. *Wilson,* 343 U.S. 495 (1952); *Palmer* v. *City of Euclid,* 402 U.S. 544 (1971); *Coates* v. *City of Cincinnati,* 402 U.S. 611 (1971).

18. Alexander M. Bickel, "Obscenity Cases," *New Republic,* May 27, 1967, pp. 15–17.

19. *Ramon* v. *U.S. Post Office Department,* 397 U.S. 728 (1970).

20. *New York Times,* December 9, 1969, p. 48.

21. *Blount* v. *Rizzi,* 400 U.S. 410 (1971).

22. *West Virginia State Board of Education* v. *Barnette,* 319 U.S. 624 (1943).

23. *United States* v. *Seeger,* 380 U.S. 163 (1965).

24. *United States* v. *Welsh,* 398 U.S. 333 (1970).

25. *United States* v. *Gillette,* 399 U.S. 925 (1971).

26. *Gitlow* v. *New York,* 268 U.S. 652 (1925).

27. *Powell* v. *Alabama,* 287 U.S. 45 (1932).

28. Ramsey Clark, *Crime in America* (New York: Pocket Books, 1971), p. 254.

29. This issue was taken up in *Wyanno* v. *James,* 400 U.S. 433 (1971). A welfare family protested periodic warrantless visits by caseworkers for purposes of determining welfare eligibility. The family lost the case.

30. *Griswold* v. *Connecticut,* 381 U.S. 479 (1965).

31. *Time* v. *Hill,* 87 U.S. 534 (1967).

32. *Ramon* v. *U.S. Post Office Department,* 397 U.S. 728 (1970).

33. Alexis de Tocqueville, *Democracy in America* (New York: Vintage Books, 1957), 2:270.

34. Daniel Patrick Moynihan, *The Negro Family: The Case for National Action* (Washington, D.C.: U.S. Government Printing Office, 1965).

35. Robert Lane, "The Fear of Equality," *American Political Science Review,* 53 (1959):35–51.

36. *Missouri* v. *Holland,* 252 U.S. 416 (1920).

37. U.S. Constitution, Article 1, sec. 2.

38. *Guinn* v. *United States,* 238 U.S. 347 (1915).

39. *Smith* v. *Albright,* 321 U.S. 649 (1944).

40. The Twenty-fourth Amendment forbids the denial of voting rights in any national election to any citizen "by reason of failure to pay any poll tax or other tax," and the 1965 Voting Rights Act directs the Justice Department to institute injunctions against the enforcement of poll tax requirements; *Harper* v. *Virginia Board of Elections,* 393 U.S. 663 (1966), declared the poll tax unconstitutional.

41. The figures presented are derived from a table in William J. Keefe, *Parties, Politics and Public Policy in America,* (Holt, Rinehart and Winston, Inc., Inc. 1972), p. 88. The actual number of Negroes registered in the South are estimated to be 2 million. James Q. Wilson, "The Negro in Politics," in Sondra Silverman (ed.) *The Black Revolt and Democratic Politics,* (D. C. Heath and Co., Mass., 1970) p. 28. A higher estimate is given by Chuck Stone, "Measuring Black Political Power," in Lenneal M. Henderson Jr. (ed.) *Black Political Life in the U.S.,* (Chandler Publishing Co., 1972) p. 251. He approximates 2,700,000 for 1966—a far cry from 85,000 in 1940.

42. *Phoenix* v. *Ralodziejski,* 399 U.S. 204 (1970).

43. *Shapiro* v. *Thompson,* 394 U.S. 618 (1969).

44. Gerrymandering is deliberate arrangement of political districts to achieve partisan and other illegal political results.

45. *Lochner* v. *New York*, 198 U.S. 45 (1905); *Adkins* v. *Children's Hospital*, 261 U.S. 525 (1923).

46. U.S. Constitution, Article 1, sec. 9; *Pollock* v. *Farmers' Loan and Trust Company*, 158 U.S. 601 (1895); *Evans* v. *Gore*, 253 U.S. 245 (1920); *O'Malley* v. *Woodbrough*, 307 U.S. 277 (1939). Court debate never questioned the clear constitutional assertion that direct taxes should be apportioned. Debate centered on the question of which taxes should be classified as direct.

47. The following cases may be viewed as ones in which congressional taxing power posed a threat to liberty and expanded the use of taxes for purposes other than revenue: *Veazie* v. *Ferro*, 8 Wall 533 (1896); *McCray* v. *United States*, 195 U.S. 27 (1924).

48. *Brown* v. *Topeka Board of Education*, 349 U.S. 294 (1955).

49. *Cooper* v. *Aaron*, 358 U.S. 28 (1958), rejected postponement of desegregation; *Griffin* v. *School Board of Prince Edward County*, 377 U.S. 218 (1964), empowered federal district courts to order taxing authorities to open and maintain public schools; *Rogers* v. *Paul*, 382 U.S. 198 (1965), ordered immediate admission of blacks to previously white Arkansas schools; *Green* v. *County School Board of Kent County, Virginia*, 39 U.S. 430 (1968), rejected a "freedom of choice" plan for school integration; *Alexander et al.* v. *Holmes County Board*, 396 U.S. 976 (1969), rejected an "all deliberate speed" formula and set forth provisions for desegregation "at once"; *Carter* v. *School Board*, 396 U.S. 290 (1970), augmented *Alexander et al.* v. *Holmes County Board*.

50. *Swann* v. *Charlotte-Mecklenburg Board of Education*, 403 U.S. 912 (1971), empowered federal district courts to eliminate all vestiges of state-imposed school segregation, including alteration of attendance zones, busing, faculty and student ratios based on race, and minority transefer plans.

51. U.S. Constitution, Article 1, sec. 8.

52. Interstate Commerce Act, sec. 216(d), pt. 2, 49 U.S.C., sec. 1: "It shall be unlawful for any common carrier in interstate or foreign commerce to make, give, or cause any undue and unreasonable preference or disadvantage to any particular person . . . or to subject any particular person to any unjust discrimination or any unjust or unreasonable prejudice or disadvantage in any respect whatsoever."

53. *Morgan* v. *Virginia*, 328 U.S. 623 (1946), struck down segregation in buses; *Henderson* v. *United States*, 339 U.S. 816 (1950), struck down segregated dining; *Heart of Atlanta Motel* v. *United States*, 379 U.S. 294 (1964), struck down segregated public accommodations.

54. On February 1, 1971, the U.S. Court of Appeals for the fifth circuit held that the town of Shaw, Mississippi, must provide equal street, sewer, and other municipal services to its black ghetto area. The case had been brought by the NAACP under the equal protection clause (*Andrew Hawkins* v. *Town of Shaw, Mississippi*, 432 Fed. 2nd 1286 [1971]). See Jack Rosenthal, "Appeals Court Bids Town Give Races Equal Services," *New York Times*, February 2, 1971, p. 1.

55. Three Supreme Court justices voiced an eloquent dissent, reported in the *New York Times*, April 27, 1971, p. 1, against a majority decision (in a housing case) holding that the equal protection clause of the Fourteenth Amendment applied only to racial discrimination, not to the "poor."

56. *Griggs* v. *Duke Power Company*, 401 U.S. 424 (1971).

57. Ibid.

58. Some of the cases concerning the rights of disadvantaged groups have already been cited in connection with racial and religious discrimination. Here are some cases dealing with other groups:

Welfare rights: *Goldberg* v. *Kelley,* 397 U.S. 254 (1970), held that a welfare recipient must be granted a hearing before assistance can be curtailed; *Graham* v. *Richards,* 403 U.S. 365 (1971), held that the equal protection clause invalidated an Arizona statute denying welfare benefits to aliens.

Women's rights: *Phillips* v. *Martin Marietta Corporation,* 400 U.S. 452 (1971), required a single hiring policy for males and females in the absence of bona fide sex qualifications.

The poor: *Tate* v. *Short,* 401 U.S. 395 (1971), held that the equal protection clause bars a state from automatically converting a fine to imprisonment for those willing but unable to pay; *Boddie* v. *Connecticut,* 401 U.S. 371 (1971), held that the due process clause of the Fourteenth Amendment bars a state from denying access to a divorce court solely because of inability to pay court costs and fees.

There have also been some setbacks: *Carter* v. *Greene County Jury Committee,* 396 U.S. 329 (1970), held that absence of Negroes from a jury selection committee in a predominantly Negro county does not constitute prima facie evidence of discrimination, nor does the Fourteenth Amendment bar jury selection on the basis of reputation and community "esteem."

59. *Albertson* v. *Subversive Activities Control Board,* 382 U.S. 70 (1965), held that compulsory registration of members of the Communist party is unconstitutional; *NAACP* v. *Alabama,* 357 U.S. 449 (1958), upheld the NAACP in protecting its membership list from state scrutiny.

60. *Report of the National Advisory Commission on Civil Disorders* (Washington, D.C.: U.S. Government Printing Office, 1968), p. 5.

---

1. U.S. Constitution, Article 5.

2. U.S. Constitution, Article 2, sec. 2.

3. Ibid.

4. *Marbury* v. *Madison,* 1 Cranch 137 (1803).

5. *United States* v. *Butler,* 297 U.S. 1 (1936).

6. The following cases are among those establishing certain exclusive areas of power for the national government: *Cooley* v. *Board of Wardens,* 12 Howard 299 (1851); *Missouri* v. *Holland,* 252 U.S. 416 (1920); *United States* v. *Darby,* 312 U.S. 100 (1941).

7. The following cases are among those delineating areas of concurrent powers: *In re Rahrer,* 140 U.S. 545 (1891); *Whitfield* v. *Ohio,* 297 U.S. 431 (1936).

8. *Youngstown Sheet and Tube Company* v. *Sawyer,* 343 U.S. 579 (1952).

9. *Wisconsin* v. *Constantineau,* 400 U.S. 433 (1971). Justice Burger's dissent reads in part: "The reason for my dissent is that it seems to me a very odd business to strike down a state statute . . . without any opportunity for the state courts to dispose of the problem either under the Wisconsin Constitution or the U.S. Constitution. . . . It is the negation of sound judicial administration and an unwarranted use of limited judicial resources to impose this kind of case on a three-judge federal district court and then, by direct appeal, on this Court. Indeed, in my view, a three-judge district court would be

**CHAPTER 4**

well advised in cases such as these, involving no urgency or question of large import, to decline to act."

10. *Ohio* v. *Wyandotte Chemical Corp*, 401 U.S. 493(1971).

11. *Wade* v. *Wilson*, 396 U.S. 282 (1970).

12. *Everson* v. *Board of Education of Township of Ewing*, 330 U.S. 1 (1947).

13. *Walz* v. *N.Y. City Tax Commission*, 397 U.S.664(1970).

14. *School District of Abington Township, Pennsylvania*, v. *Schempp*, 374 U.S. 203 (1963); *Murray* v. *Curlett*, 374 U.S. 203 (1963).

15. Gabriel Almond and Sidney Verba, *The Civic Culture* (Boston: Little, Brown, 1965).

**CHAPTER 5**

1. Alexis de Toqueville, *Democracy in America* (New York: Vintage Books, 1957), 1:290.

2. "When we have examined in detail the organization of the Supreme Court and the entire prerogatives that it exercises, we shall readily admit that a more imposing judicial power was never constituted by any people" (ibid., p. 152; see also pp. 155–57).

3. *Marbury* v. *Madison*, 1 Cranch 137 (1803).

4. John R. Schmidhauser, "The Justices of the Supreme Court: A Collective Portrait," *Midwest Journal of Political Science*, 3 (1959): 1–57. There is a good bibliographical article on this subject: Glendon Schubert, "Behavioral Research in Public Law," *American Political Science Review*, 47 (June 1963):433–45.

5. *Champion* v. *Ames*, 188 U.S. 321 (1903), a lottery case, established that the word "regulate" can also mean "prohibit."

6. *Caminetti* v. *United States*, 242 U.S. 470 (1917), prohibited transportation of women in interstate commerce for purposes of "debauchery."

7. *National Labor Relations Board* v. *Jones and Laughlin Steel Corporation*, 301 U.S. 1 (1937), upheld the Wagner Labor Relations Act forbidding unfair labor practices in manufacturing enterprises impinging on interstate commerce.

8. *Coppage* v. *Kansas*, 236 U.S. 1 (1915), held unconstitutional a Kansas law attempting to force employers to permit workers to join unions; *Adkins* v. *Children's Hospital*, 261 U.S. 525 (1923), held unconstitutional a District of Columbia minimum-wage act.

9. *West Coast Hotel* v. *Parrish*, 300 U.S. 379 (1937), upheld a Washington State law setting a minimum wage for women, thus overruling *Adkins; United States* v. *Darby*, 312 U.S. 100 (1941), upheld a minimum-wage and maximum-hour law.

10. *Nebbia* v. *New York*, 291 U.S. 502 (1934), upheld a New York State milk price control law.

11. *United States* v. *Butler*, 297 U.S. 1 (1936).

12. *Schecter* v. *United States*, 295 U.S. 495 (1935).

13. *McCullough* v. *Maryland*, 4 Wheaton 316 (1819).

14. *Collector* v. *Day*, 11 Wallace 113 (1871); *Graves* v. *New York ex rel. O'Keefe*, 306 U.S. 466 (1939).

15. For a general discussion of the boundaries between national and state jurisdictions, one might well begin with *Coyle* v. *Smith*, 221 U.S. 559 (1911).

16. *Pacific States Telephone and Telegraph Company* v. *Oregon*, 223 U.S. 118 (1906).

17. *Martin* v. *Mott*, 12 Wheaton 19 (1827).

18. *Forster and Elam* v. *Neilson*, 2 Peters 253 (1829).

19. *Coleman* v. *Miller*, 307 U.S. 433 (1939).

20. *Kentucky* v. *Dennison*, 24 Howard 66 (1861).

21. *Colegrove* v. *Green*, 328 U.S. 549 (1946).

22. *Baker* v. *Carr*, 369 U.S. 186 (1962).

23. *Massachusetts* v. *Laird*, no. 42 orig., October 1970, pp. 18–24.

24. Glendon Schubert, ed., *Judicial Behavior* (Chicago: Rand McNally, 1964).

25. *Patton* v. *State of Mississippi*, 332 U.S. 463 (1948).

26. *New York Times*, July 10, 1970, p. 1.

27. In April 1969 President Nixon appointed a five-member advisory council under the chairmanship of Roy L. Ash, president of Litton Industries, to study the six major independent regulatory agencies of the federal government. Its report was submitted in August 1970. This is only the most recent in a long line of similar reports on these and other so-called independent agencies.

28. Alexander M. Bickel, "The Courts: Need for Change," *New York Times*, October 22, 1970, p. 47.

29. Andrew Schaffer, "A Report to the Mayor's Criminal Coordinating Council: The Problem of Overcrowding in the Detention Institutions of New York City," mimeographed (New York: Vera Foundation, 1969), p. 68.

30. Ibid.

---

**CHAPTER 6**

1. Kenneth Arrow, *Social Choice and Individual Values* (New York: Wiley, 1963), p. 3.

2. Donald Matthews, *U.S. Senators and Their World* (New York: Vintage Books, 1960).

3. Alexis de Tocqueville, *Democracy in America* (New York: Knopf, 1945), 1:204.

4. Ibid.

5. *New York Times*, October 18, 1970, p. 1.

6. Joseph Harris, *Congress and the Legislative Process* (New York: McGraw-Hill, 1972), p. 16.

7. Matthews, *U.S. Senators and Their World*.

8. G. William Dumhoff, *Who Rules America?* (Englewood Cliffs, N.J.: Prentice-Hall, 1967), p. 112.

9. Stephen K. Bailey, *The New Congress* (New York: St. Martin's Press, 1966).

10. See, for example, Nelson W. Polsby, "Strengthening Congress in National Policymaking," in *Congressional Behavior*, ed. N. W. Polsby (New York: Random House, 1971), pp. 3–13.

11. Logrolling is an informal legislative bargaining process in which Congressman A supports a project of Congressman B, although he has little interest in it, in exchange for Congressman B's support for his own favorite project.

12. Larry King, "The Road to Power in Congress," *Harper's Magazine*, June 1971, p. 39.

13. Ibid., p. 63.

14. Ibid.

15. See Alan Rosenthal, *Toward Majority Rule in the U.S. Senate*, Eagleton Institute Case Studies in Practical Politics, no. 25 (Rutgers Univ. Press: New Jersey, 1962). This excellent case study describes in detail the losing fight of Senator Joseph Clark of Pennsylvania to bring some semblance of majority rule to the Senate.

16. Raymond E. Wolfinger, "Filibusters: Majority Rule, Presidential Leadership, and Senate Norms," in *Congressional Behavior*, ed. Polsby, pp. 111–25.

17. William S. White, *Citadel* (New York: Harper & Row, 1957).

18. Polsby, "Goodbye to the Inner Club," in *Congressional Behavior,* ed. Polsby, pp. 105–110.

19. Samuel P. Huntington, "Congressional Response to the Twentieth Century," in *The American Political System: Notes and Readings,* ed. Bernard B. Brown and John C. Wahlke (Homewood, Ill.: Dorsey Press, 1971), p. 587.

20. Ibid., p. 588.

21. Clinton Rossiter, *The American Presidency* (New York: Harcourt, Brace & World, 1960), pp. 257–62.

22. Lawrence Chamberlain, "The President, Congress, and Legislation," in *The President: Roles and Power,* ed. D. Haight and L. Johnson (Chicago: Rand McNally, 1965), pp. 297–313.

23. Ronald Moe and Steven C. Teel, "Congress as Policy Maker," *Political Science Quarterly,* 85 (September 1970): 443–70.

24. Ibid., p. 446.

25. Tom Wicker, "The Presidency Under Scrutiny," *Harper's Magazine,* October 1969.

26. For an excellent discussion of congressional investigations, see Telford Taylor, *Grand Inquest* (New York: Simon & Schuster, 1955).

27. J. Leiper Freeman, *The Political Process: Executive Bureau–Legislative Committee Relations* (New York: Random House, 1965).

28. Aaron Wildavsky, *The Politics of the Budgetary Process* (Boston: Little, Brown, 1964).

29. Francis E. Rourke, *Bureaucracy, Politics, and Public Policy* (Boston: Little, Brown, 1969).

30. Norton E. Long, "Conflict of Interest: A Political Scientist's View" (paper delivered at annual meeting of American Political Science Association, Washington, D.C., September 1962), p. 2. See also Robert S. Getz, *Congressional Ethics* (Princeton, N.J.: Van Nostrand, 1966).

31. John Owens, *Money and Politics in California: Democratic Senatorial Primary,* study no. 11, Citizen Research Foundation (Princeton, N.J., 1964).

**CHAPTER 7**

1. See Robert S. Hirschfield, ed., *The Power of the Presidency* (New York: Atherton Press, 1968), pp. 238–55, for a good review of theories on the strength and weakness of the presidency.

2. Richard E. Neustadt, *Presidential Power* (New York: Wiley, 1964), p. 22.

3. James MacGregor Burns, *Presidential Government* (Boston: Houghton Mifflin, 1965), pp. 124–54.

4. Hirshfield, *Power of the Presidency.*

5. Tom Wicker, "The Presidency Under Scrutiny," *Harper's Magazine,* October 1969, p. 93.

6. Irving Kristol and Paul Weaver, "A Bad Idea Whose Time Has Come," *New York Times,* November 23, 1969, Sect. VI, p. 43.

7. Stokely Carmichael and Charles V. Hamilton, *Black Power* (New York: Vintage Books, 1967), pp. 88–97.

8. Joe McGinniss, *The Selling of the President 1968* (New York: Pocket Books, 1970).

9. Douglas Cater, "The Power of the President," *Center Magazine* (1970), p. 9.

**CHAPTER 8**

1. C. Northcote Parkinson, *Parkinson's Law* (Boston: Houghton Mifflin, 1957).

2. The latest critiques of the independent agencies can be found in the so-called Nader Reports; e.g., James S. Turner, *The Chemical Feast* (New York: Grossman, 1971), and Robert Fellmuth, *The Interstate Commerce Commission* (New York: Grossman, 1970).

3. U.S. Senate, Committee on Government Operations, 83rd Cong., 2nd sess., *Audit Reports of Government Corporations* (Washington, D.C.: U.S. Government Printing Office, 1954); Commission on Organization of the Executive Branch of Government (Hoover Commission), *Business Enterprises: A Report to Congress* (Washington, D.C.: U.S. Government Printing Office, 1955).

4. *United States Government Organization Manual*, obtainable from the U.S. Government Printing Office, Washington, D.C. 20401, describes the whole structure in detail.

5. W. Lloyd Warner et al., *The American Federal Executive* (New Haven, Conn.: Yale University Press, 1963). For a review of federal political executives, see David Stanley et al., *Men Who Govern* (Washington, D.C.: Brookings Institution, 1967).

6. James W. Fesler, ed., *The Fifty States and Their Local Governments* (New York: Knopf, 1967), p. 9.

7. For a full description of this term, see William H. Whyte, Jr., *The Organization Man* (New York: Simon & Schuster, 1956), pp. 3–14.

8. Woodrow Wilson, "The Study of Administration," *Political Science Quarterly*, June 1887, reprinted in ibid., 56 (December 1941):481–506.

9. See Turner, *Chemical Feast*, and Fellmuth, *Interstate Commerce Commission*.

10. Peter Blau, *Bureaucracy in Modern Society* (New York: Random House, 1956), p. 14.

11. Note the manner in which Anthony Downs treats the subject in *Inside Bureaucracy* (Boston: Little, Brown, 1967).

12. Max Weber, "Essay on Bureaucracy," in *From Max Weber: Essays in Sociology*, trans. H. H. Gerth and C. W. Mills (New York: Oxford University Press, 1946).

13. Chris Argyris, *Integrating the Individual and the Organization* (New York: Wiley, 1964); Warren Bennis, *Changing Organizations* (New York: McGraw-Hill, 1966).

14. Erich Fromm, *Escape from Freedom* (New York: Holt, 1941).

**CHAPTER 9**

1. Theodore Lowi, "The Public Philosophy: Interest-Group Liberalism," *American Political Science Review*, 61, no. 1 (March 1967):5–24.

2. Hadley Cantril, ed., *Public Opinion, 1935–46* (Princeton: Princeton University Press, 1951).

3. *New York Times*, August 23, 1971, p. 19.

4. *New York Times*, June 24, 1970, p. 46.

5. *New York Times*, October 4, 1970, p. 72.

6. V. O. Key, *The Responsible Electorate* (New York: Random House, 1967), pp. 7–8.

7. Angus Campbell et al., *The American Voter* (New York: Wiley, 1960), p. 58.

8. Blanche D. Blank, "The Meaning of Your Vote," *The Nation*, November 3, 1962.

9. William Riordon, *Plunkitt of Tammany Hall* (New York: Knopf, 1948).

10. Lloyd Free and Hadley Cantril, *The Political Beliefs of*

*America: A Study of Public Opinion* (New Brunswick, N.J.: Rutgers University Press, 1967), p. 180.

11. Ibid.

12. E. E. Schattschneider, *Party Government* (New York: Holt, Rinehart & Winston, 1942).

**CHAPTER 10**

1. Morton Grodzins, "The Federal System," in President's Committee on National Goals, *Goals for Americans* (Englewood Cliffs, N.J.: Prentice-Hall, 1960).

2. U.S. Bureau of the Census, *Census of Local Governments* (Washington, D.C.: U.S. Government Printing Office, 1969).

3. Joseph F. Zimmerman, ed., *Subnational Politics* (New York: Holt, Rinehart & Winston, 1970), pp. 11–12.

4. Robert Dahl, *Modern Political Analysis*, 2nd ed. (Englewood Cliffs, N.J.: Prentice-Hall, 1970), chap. 4.

5. See Norton Long, "Aristotle and the Study of Local Governments," *Social Research*, 24 (Autumn 1957):287–310; see especially p. 291.

6. C. Wright Mills, *The Power Elite* (New York: Oxford University Press, 1956).

7. Robert Dahl, *Who Governs?* (New Haven: Yale University Press, 1961).

8. Robert E. Agger, Daniel Goldrich, and Bert E. Swanson, *The Rulers and the Ruled* (New York: Wiley, 1964). See also Swanson, *The Concern for Community in Urban America* (New York: Odyssey Press, 1970), p. 134.

9. Lewis Mumford, *The City in History* (New York: Harcourt, Brace & World, 1961).

10. E.g., William M. Dobriner, *Class in Suburbia* (Englewood Cliffs, N.J.: Prentice-Hall, 1963).

11. G. Theodore Mitau, *State and Local Government* (New York: Scribner, 1966), p. 577.

12. Alvin Toffler, *Future Shock* (N.Y.: Random House, 1970).

13. U.S. Department of Commerce, *Pocket Data Book* (Washington, D.C.: U.S. Government Printing Office, 1971), p. 51.

14. Alexis de Tocqueville, *Democracy in America* (New York: Vintage, 1954), 1:61.

**CHAPTER 11**

1. Ernest Barker, ed., *The Politics of Aristotle* (New York: Oxford University Press, 1946); Kenneth Dolbeare and Murray Edelman, *America Politics: Policies, Power, and Change* (Lexington, Mass.: Heath, 1971); William C. Mitchell, *Public Choice in America* (Chicago: Markham, 1971).

2. Recent volumes on PPBS include Fremont J. Lyden and Ernest J. Miller, eds., *Planning-Programming-Budgeting: A Systems Approach to Management* (Chicago: Markham, 1968).

3. See Aaron Wildavsky, "The Political Economy of Efficiency" *Public Administration Review* Vol. XXVI, No. 4 (December, 1966), pp. 292–310; Charles Lindblom, "The Science of Muddling Through," *Public Administration Review*, Vol. XIX, No. 2 (Spring 1959) pp. 79–88; William A. Niskanen Jr., *Bureaucracy and Representative Government* (Chicago: Aldine-Atherton, 1971).

4. James Fallows, *The Water Lords* (New York: Grossman, 1971); Robert Fellmuth, *The Interstate Commerce Commission* (New York: Grossman, 1970).

5. Murray Weidenbaum, "Where Do All the Billions Go?," *Transaction*, January–February 1966.

6. Bruce Russett, "Who Pays for Defense?," *American Political Science Review,* June 1969, pp. 412–26.

7. Robert S. Ross and William C. Mitchell, eds., *Introductory Readings in American Government: A Public Choice Perspective* (Chicago: Markham, 1971); W. Lee Hansen and Burton A. Weisbrod, *Benefits, Costs, and Finance of Public Higher Education* (Chicago: Markham, 1969), pp. 49–65.

8. James Reston, "Dear Mr. Tax Collector," *New York Times,* April 11, 1969, p. 44.

9. James A. Davis, Jr., and Kenneth M. Dolbeare, "The Impact of Conscription," in *Introductory Readings in American Government,* ed. R. Ross and W. Mitchell, pp. 83–99.

10. Ira Sharkansky, *Spending in the American States* (Chicago: Rand McNally, 1968).

11. *Report of the President's Council on Economic Advisers* (Washington, D.C.: U.S. Government Printing Office, 1964).

12. U.S. Bureau of the Census, *Consumer Income,* pamphlet no. 77 (Washington, D.C.: U.S. Government Printing Office, 1971), p. 60.

13. *Report of the National Advisory Commission on Civil Disorders* (New York: New York Times Co., 1968), chap. 6.

14. John Galbraith, Edwin Kuh, and Lester Thurow, "The Galbraith Plan to Promote Minorities," *New York Times Magazine,* August 22, 1971, p. 9.

15. U.S. Bureau of the Census, *Social and Economic Condition of Negroes in the United States* (Washington, D.C.: U.S. Government Printing Office, 1967).

16. *Report of the National Advisory Commission on Civil Disorders,* p. 115.

17. Ramsey Clark, *Crime in America,* 3rd ed. (New York: Pocket Books, 1971), pp. 40–51.

18. Esther Penchef, ed., *Four Horsemen* (San Francisco: Canfield Press, 1971), pp. 155–64. Reprinted from *U.S. News and World Report,* "Where the Real Poverty Is: Plight of American Indians," April 25, 1966.

19. Alan Josephy, Jr., *The Indian Heritage of America* (New York: Knopf, 1968), p. 359.

20. Galbraith et al., "Galbraith Plan."

21. Bella Abzug, "Power to the Majority," *New York Times,* August 26, 1971, p. 37.

22. *New York Times,* May 28, 1971, p. 32.

23. Ben Seligman, "The Number of the Poor," in *Four Horsemen,* ed. E. Penchef, pp. 92–105.

24. Anthony Downs, *Who Are the Poor?* (Washington, D.C.: Committee for Economic Development, 1968).

25. Lloyd Free and Hadley Cantril, *The Political Beliefs of Americans* (New York: Simon & Schuster, 1968), p. 96.

26. Richard Parker, "The Myth of Middle America," in *Toward a New Public Policy,* ed. Harold Quinley (Center for Study of Democratic Institutes, Palo Alto, California: James Freel & Assoc., 1971), pp. 92–195.

27. An excellent article on this matter is Michael Harrington, "The Other America Revisited," in ibid., pp. 174–86.

28. U.S. Bureau of the Census, *Consumer Income.*

29. Drummond Ayres, Jr., "Meet the Henry Creuses: Average Americans," *New York Times,* August 2, 1971, p. 25.

30. U.S. Bureau of the Census, *Consumer Income.*

31. Downs, *Who Are the Poor?*

32. Davis and Dolbeare, "Impact of Conscription"; see also Davis and Dolbeare, "Selective Service and Military Manpower: Induction and Deferment Policies in the 1960's," in *Political Science and Public Policy*, ed. Austin Ranney (Chicago: Markham, 1968), pp. 83–121.

---

**CHAPTER 12**

1. Ralph K. Huitt, "Political Feasibility," in *Political Science and Public Policy*, ed. Austin Ranney (Chicago: Markham, 1968), pp. 263–75.

2. Ibid., p. 266.

3. E.g., Alan Block, "Determination of a Consensus," mimeographed (New York Univ.; October 1971). Publications such as *Common Cause* (November 10, 1970) frequently report consensus votes.

4. Poll concerning American anxiety, reported by Albert Cantril and Charles W. Rolls in the *New York Times*, June 27, 1971, p. 1 (to be included in Potomac Associates, *Hopes and Fears of the American People* [New York: Universe Books, forthcoming]).

5. Ibid.

6. James Reston, "Advice From Peking," *New York Times*, August 8, 1970, p. 51.

7. Daniel P. Moynihan, "The Silent Majority," *New York Times*, November 6, 1970, p. 41.

8. Reston, "ABM—Administration's Biggest Mistake," *New York Times*, March 12, 1969, p. 46.

9. Richard D. Lyons, "Nixon Reorganizing Vast Federal Science Complex," *New York Times*, November 1, 1970, p. 81.

10. Among the famous voting studies are Angus Campbell et al., *The American Voter* (New York: Wiley, 1964); Paul Lazarsfeld et al., *The People's Choice* (N.Y.: Duell, Sloan & Pearce, 1944).

11. Arthur S. Goldberg, "Social Determinism and Rationality as Bases of Party Loyalty," *American Political Science Review*, 63, no. 1:5–25.

12. Michael Shapiro, "Rational Political Man: A Synthesis of Economic and Psychological Perspectives," *American Political Science Review*, 63, no. 4:1107–1119.

13. Philip Converse et al., "Continuity and Change in American Politics," *American Political Science Review*, 63, no. 4:1083–1105.

14. V. O. Key, *The Responsible Electorate* (Cambridge: Harvard University Press, 1966).

15. Department of Health, Education, and Welfare, "Influence of Voter Turnout on School Bond and Tax Elections," mimeographed (Washington, D.C., 1961).

16. John Mueller, "Voting on the Propositions: Ballot Patterns and Historical Trends in California," *American Political Science Review*, 63, no. 4:1197–1212.

17. Raymond Wolfinger and Fred Greenstein, "The Repeal of Fair Housing in California: An Analysis of Referendum Voting," *American Political Science Review*, 62, no. 3:753–68.

18. I would offer similar arguments against the conclusion in Howard Hamilton, "Direct Legislation: Some Implications of Open Housing Referenda," *American Political Science Review*, 64, no. 1:124–37.

19. Report of American Business Committee on National Priorities, mimeographed (Washington, D.C., August 22, 1971).

# SELECTED READINGS

For a historical analysis of American liberalism, see Louis Hartz, *The Liberal Tradition in America* (Harcourt Brace & World, 1955) and Walter Lippmann, *The Public Philosophy* (Little Brown, 1955). A general overview of the topic can be found in Max Lerner's *America as a Civilization* (Simon & Schuster, 1957) and also in Joseph P. Lyford, *The Talk in Vandalia* (Center for Study of Democratic Institution, 1962). On the topic of liberty, one might also read Felix Oppenheim, *Dimensions of Freedom* (St. Martin's Press, 1961); Abe Fortas, *Concerning Dissent and Civil Disobedience* (New American Library, 1968); Robert Paul Wolff, Barrington Moore, Jr., and Herbert Marcuse, *A Critique of Pure Tolerance* (Beacon Press, 1965); Michel Walzer, "On the Nature of Freedom," *Dissent* XIII (1966); and Sidney Hook, *The Paradoxes of Freedom* (Univ. of California Press, 1964). On majority rule, see Henry Steele Commanger, *Majority Rule and Minority Rights* (Oxford Univ. Press, 1943); Alexis De Tocqueville, *Democracy in America I*, Chapters 15–16 (any edition); James Madison, *The Federalist Papers* No. 10 (any edition); J. G. Hunberg, "Theories of Majority Rule," *American Political Science Review*, XXVI (1932).

On the principle of equality, one might read Isaiah Berlin, "Equality as an Ideal" in *Justice and Social Policy*, ed. by Frederick Olafson (Prentice Hall, 1961); Richard Wallheim, "Equality and Equal Rights," in *Justice and Social Policy*, ed. Frederick Olafson (Prentice Hall, 1961); John Kenneth Galbraith, *The Affluent Society* (Houghton Mifflin Co., 1958) or his more recent *The Liberal Hour*, 1960. There is a judicious selection of essays that treat individualism in the small volume put together by David Riesman, *Individualism Reconsidered* (Doubleday, Anchor, 1955). Or consult his classical study, *The Lonely Crowd* (with N. Glazer and R. Denney; Yale Univ. Press, 1969).

On the value Americans attach to localism, states rights, and decentralization, see Onwar Syed, *The Political Theory of American Local Government* (Random House, 1966); A. C.

AMERICAN VALUES

Spectorsky, *The Exurbanites* (J. B. Lippincott, 1955); Joseph Bensman and Arthur Vidich, *Small Town in Mass Society* (Anchor Books, 1958). A view of the problem in terms of specific case studies can be found in Jewell Bellush and Stephan David, *Race and Politics in New York City* (Praeger, 1971).

**COURTS**    For a general work on the judicial system, see Herbert Jacobs, *Justice in America* (Little, Brown and Co., 1972). Two good philosophical works on the peculiar nature of constitutional law are Benjamin Cardozo, *The Nature of the Judicial Process* (Yale Univ. Press, 1921); and Edwin Corwin, *The Higher Law Background of American Constitutional Law* (Cornell Press, 1955; originally written in 1938). A good theoretical work on the topic of judicial review is Howard Dean, *Judicial Review and Democracy* (Random House, 1966). The "con law" textbook of cases most commonly used in law school is Gerald Gunther and Noel Dowling, *Constitutional Law, Cases and Materials* (The Foundation Press, 1970).

For an understanding of courts in the political process, I suggest Richard C. Richardson and Kenneth N. Vines, *The Politics of Federal Courts* (Little, Brown and Co., 1970); and Kenneth M. Dolbeare, *Trial Court in Urban Politics* (Wiley, 1967). The relationship of courts to judicial background and attitudes and to public opinion is pursued in the articles in Walter F. Murphy and Joseph Tanenhaus, *Frontiers of Judicial Research* (Wiley, 1969).

The other important books on the court are Alexander Bickel, *The Least Dangerous Branch* (Bobbs-Merrill, 1962); Paul Freund, *The Supreme Court of the United States: Its Business, Purposes and Performance* (Meridian Books, 1961); and Herbert Wechsler, *Principles, Politics and Fundamental Law* (Howard Univ. Press, 1961). My favorite case study remains Anthony Lewis, *Gideon's Trumpet* (Random House, 1964).

For a favorable review of the Warren Court, see Archibald Cox, *The Warren Court* (Harvard Univ. Press, 1968). For more critical reviews of Warren, see Alexander Bickel, *The Supreme Court and the Idea of Progress* (Harper & Row, 1970) and Philip Kurland, *Politics, the Constitution and the Warren Court* (Univ. of Chicago Press, 1970).

**CONGRESS**    Some general readings on Congress and the role of representatives can be found in Lewis Froman, *Congressmen and their Constituencies* (Rand McNally, 1963); Donald Matthews, *U.S.*

*Senators and Their World* (Univ. of North Carolina Press, 1960); Daniel Berman, *In Congress Assembled: The Legislative Process in the National Government* (Macmillan, 1964); Richard Bolling, *House Out of Order* (E. P. Dutton & Co., 1965); Charles Clapp, *The Congressman: His Work as He Sees It* (The Brookings Institution, 1963); and Stephen Bailey, *Congress in the Seventies* (St. Martin's Press, 1970). There is also an excellent collection of articles in Nelson W. Polsby's *Congressional Behavior* (Random House, 1971).

For case studies see Robert Peabody and Nelson Polsby, eds., *New Perspectives on the House of Representatives* (Rand McNally, 1963); John Bibby and Roger Davidson, *On Capitol Hill: Studies in the Legislative Process* (Holt, Reinhart & Winston, 1967); Richard Fenno, *The Power of the Purse: Appropriations Politics in Congress* (Little, Brown and Co., 1966); Daniel Berman, *A Bill Becomes A Law: Congress Enacts Civil Rights Legislation,* 2nd ed. (Macmillan, 1966); Robert Peabody, Jeffrey M. Berry, William Frasure, and Jerry Goldman, *To Enact a Law: Congress and Campaign Financing* (Praeger, 1972).

A number of special problems are handled in depth in the following works: Robert S. Getz, *Congressional Ethics: The Conflict of Interest Issue* (D. Van Nostrand Co., 1966); Alexander Heard, *The Costs of Democracy* (Univ. of North Carolina Press, 1960); Kenneth Kofmehl, *Professional Staffs of Congress* (Purdue Univ., 1962); David R. Mayhew, *Party Loyalty Among Congressmen* (Harvard Univ., 1966); Randall B. Ripley, *Party Leaders in the House of Representatives* (Brookings Institute, 1967); and Andrew Scott and Margaret A. Hunt, *Congress and Lobbies: Image and Reality* (Univ. of North Carolina Press, 1966).

On congressional relations with the bureaucracy, see J. Leiper Freeman, *The Political Process: Executive Bureau-Legislative Committee Relations,* rev. ed. (Random House, 1965); Aaron Wildavsky, *The Politics of the Budgetary Process* (Little, Brown and Co., 1964); and Nelson W. Polsby, *Congress and the Presidency* (Prentice Hall, 1964). And finally, be sure to consult the *Congressional Quarterly,* Weekly Reports and Special Reports (Congressional Quarterly Inc., Washington, D. C.).

---

Some general works on the nature and history of the office are Louis Koening, *The Chief Executive* (Harcourt, Brace & World, 1964); Clinton Rossiter, *The American Presidency* (rev. ed., Harvest, 1960); Harold Laski, *The American Presidency* (Harper, 1940). **THE PRESIDENCY**

Two good texts on the topic of presidential leadership are Richard Neustadt, *Presidential Power* (John Wiley & Sons, 1960) and Theodore Sorensen, *Decision-making in the White House* (Columbia, 1963).

A thoughtful review of current problems of the office is found in George E. Reedy, *The Twilight of the Presidency* (World Publishing Co., 1970), and another way of assessing the magnitude of presidential problems is to look at "The Presidency and Policy Foundation: The Task Force Device," in *Public Administration Review,* 29, Sept./Oct. 1969.

The works on individual presidents are numerous. See Arthur Schlessinger, Jr., *The Age of Jackson* (Little Brown, 1945); *The Age of Roosevelt,* 3 vols. (Houghton Mifflin, 1957–60); *A Thousand Days* (Houghton Mifflin, 1965). See also Theodore Sorensen, *Kennedy* (Harper, 1965); Robert J. Donovan, *Eisenhower, The Inside Story* (Harper, 1956); Eric Goldman, *The Tragedy of Lyndon Johnson: The Exercise of Power* (The New American Library, 1968).

For works on presidential campaigns, see Irwin Ross, *The Loneliest Campaign: The Truman Victory of 1948* (The New American Library, 1968); and Theodore White, *The Making of the President, 1960* (Atheneum, 1961); *The Making of the President, 1964* (Atheneum, 1965) and *The Making of the President, 1968* (Atheneum, 1969). The intricacies of the presidential election process can be found in Wallace S. Sayre and Judith H. Parris, *Voting for President* (Brookings Institute, 1970).

**LOCAL CHIEF EXECUTIVES**

For a good book of case studies on a strong mayor (Daley) see, Edward Banfield, *Political Influence* (Free Press, 1961). For material on Lindsay administration, see John Lindsay, *The City* (Norton, 1969), and Nat Hentoff, *A Political Life, The Education of John V. Lindsay* (Alfred Knopf, 1969).

For general commentaries on problems of American mayors see Roger Starr, "Power and Powerlessness in Regional City" and J. Q. Wilson, "The Mayors vs The Cities" in *Public Interest,* No. 16, Summer 1969.

**BUREAUC-RACY**

For anyone interested in an historical perspective on American administration, there is a well-written trilogy by Leonard D. White: *The Federalists* (1949); *The Jeffersonians* (1951); and *The Jacksonians* (1953; all by The Free Press). Another way to develop this perspective and to flesh out the procedural details of the American "fourth branch of government" is to consult certain landmark presidential task force reports:

*The Report on Administrative Procedures* by the President's Committee on Administrative Management (1946); *The Reports of the President's Commission on Organization of the Executive Branch of Government* (1949, 1955). The last two are popularly known as The Hoover Commission Reports and they, in turn, are backed by a large number of special task force volumes. For a briefer review of the national administrative apparatus, you might use Peter Woll's *American Bureaucracy* (1963, W. W. Norton & Co. Inc.) or Harold Seidman's *Politics, Position and Power* (Oxford Univ. Press, 1970). In all events, a very useful and inexpensive guide to the Washington bureaucracy is the *United States Government Organization Manual* (most recent issue).

To understand who's who in the appointive civil service of America, and how they are recruited and viewed, I recommend: John Carson and Paul Shale, *Men Near the Top* (John Hopkins, 1966); David Stanley et al., *The Image of the Federal Service* (The Brookings Institution, 1968); David Stanley, Dean Mann and Jameson Doig, *Men Who Govern* (The Brookings Institution, 1967). A power elitist point of view can be gleaned from William Dumhof, *Who Rules America?* (Prentice Hall, 1967); and a highly readable personal account from one of the many "men who manage," Charles Frankel, *High on Foggy Bottom* (Harper & Row, 1969). An excellent overview of the civil service at all levels is provided in Norman Powell's *Personnel Administration in Government* (Prentice Hall, 1956), and a further fleshing out of the municipal scene is in Theodore Lowi's *At the Pleasure of the Mayor* (The Free Press, 1964).

Those students who are interested in bureaucracy from a more theoretical perspective might find the following works on organization theory rewarding: L. Gulick and L. Urwick, *Papers on the Science of Administration* (Institute of Public Administration, 1937); Max Weber, *Essays in Sociology,* translated by Gerth and Wills (Oxford Press, 1946); Herbert Simon, *Administrative Behavior* (MacMillan, 1945); Philip Selznick, *Leadership in Organizations* (Harper & Row, 1957); F. J. Roethlisberger, *Management and Morale* (Harvard, 1944); James Thompson, *Organization in Action* (McGraw Hill, 1967); Robert Presthus, *Organizational Society* (Knopf, 1962); Alvin Gouldner, *Patterns of Industrial Bureaucracy* (The Free Press, 1954); Peter Blau, *Bureaucracy in Modern Society* (Random House, 1956); Anthony Downs, *Inside Bureaucracy* (Little, Brown and Co., 1967); and Joseph Uveges, *Dimensions of Public Administration* (Holbrook Press, 1971).

The ethics and pathologies involved in administration are amusingly covered in C. N. Parkinson, *Parkinson's Law*

(Houghton Mifflin, 1957), more seriously in Emette Redford's *Democracy in the Administrative State* (Oxford Univ. Press, 1969); Robert Golembiewski's *Men, Management and Morality* (McGraw-Hill, 1965); and Warren Bennis, *Changing Organizations* (McGraw-Hill, 1966). Or for a broader brush that paints the foibles of administration on the world scene, see James Burnham, *The Managerial Revolution*, 4th ed. (Univ. of Indiana Press, 1966), and Ludwig Von Mises, *Bureaucracy* (Yale Univ. Press, 1944).

Finally, I would recommend a number of quite recent works that try to tie the bureaucracy into a policy perspective; here any of the so-called "Nader Reports" are a case in point. They are all published by Grossman Publishers, New York, e.g., Robert Fellmuth, *The Interstate Commerce Commission* (1971). There are also many other similar studies: James Donovan, *The Politics of Poverty* (Pegasus, 1967); Lee Fritschler, *Smoking and Politics* (Appleton-Century-Crofts, 1969); Aaron Wildavsky, *The Politics of the Budgetary Process* (Little, Brown and Co., 1964); J. Lieper Freeman, *The Political Process* (Random House, 1965) Francis Rourke, *Bureaucracy, Politics and Public Policy* (Little, Brown and Co., 1969) and Ira Sharkansky, Ed., *Policy Analysis in Political Science* (Markham Publishing Co., 1970).

---

**CITIZEN PARTICIPATION**

For material on public opinion and voting, see Bernard Berelson et al., *Voting: A Study of Public Opinion Formation in a Presidential Campaign* (Univ. of Chicago Press, 1954); Angus Campbell et al., *The American Voter* (Wiley, 1960); V. O. Key, *The Responsible Electorate* (Harvard Univ. Press, 1966); Robert Lane and David Sears, *Public Opinion* (Prentice Hall, 1964); Lester Milbrath, *Political Participation* (Rand McNally, 1965); Philip Converse et al., "Continuity and Change in American Politics: Parties and Issues in the 1968 Election," *American Political Science Review* 63: 1083–1105; William Flanigan, *Political Behavior and the American Electorate* (Free Press, 1968); Joe McGinniss, *The Selling of the President 1968* (Simon and Schuster, 1969); David Leuthold, *Electioneering in a Democracy* (Wiley, 1968).

On parties and pressure groups, consult Maurice Duverger, *Political Parties* (Wiley, 1963); Robert Michels, *Political Parties* (Free Press, 1962); V. O. Key, *Politics, Parties and Pressure Groups* (Crowell, 1964); E. E. Schattschneider, *Party Government* (Holt, Rinehart & Winston, 1942); David Truman, *The Governmental Process* (Knopf, 1951); H. R. Mahood, *Pressure Groups in American Politics* (Scribner, 1967); Theodore Lowi, "The Public Philosophy and Interest Group Liberalism,"*American Political Science Review,* Vol. LXI (March 1967); Staughton Lynd, "The New Left," *Annals of the American Academy of Political and Social Science,* Vol. 382 (March 1969); Walter D. Burnham, "The End of American Party Politics," *Transaction* (Dec. 1969); Cornelius P. Cotter and Bernard C. Hennessy, *Politics Without Power: The National Party Committees* (Atherton, 1964); Donald Matthews, *Negroes and The New Southern Politics* (Harcourt, Brace Jovonovich, 1966); Hugh Bone, *American Politics and the Party System* (McGraw Hill, 1971); William T. Keefe, *Parties, Politics and Public Policy in America* (Holt, Rinehart and Winston, 1972).

**N-O**

**P**

**Q-R**

**S**